The Interrogation of Joan of Arc

Medieval Cultures

Series Editors
Rita Copeland
Barbara A. Hanawalt
David Wallace

Sponsored by the Center for Medieval Studies at the University of Minnesota

Volumes in the series study the diversity of medieval cultural histories and practices, including such interrelated issues as gender, class, and social hierarchies; race and ethnicity; geographical relations; definitions of political space; discourses of authority and dissent; educational institutions; canonical and noncanonical literatures; and technologies of textual and visual literacies.

The Interrogation of Joan of Arc

Karen Sullivan

Medieval Cultures
Volume 20

University of Minnesota Press
Minneapolis
London

An earlier version of chapter 2 appears as " 'I Do Not Name to You the Voice of
Saint Michael': The Identification of Joan of Arc's Voices" in Bonnie Wheeler
and Charles T. Wood, eds., *Fresh Verdicts on Joan of Arc,* Garland Publishing Co.,
1996; reprinted by permission of Garland Publishing Co.

Published by the University of Minnesota Press
111 Third Avenue South, Suite 290
Minneapolis, MN 55401-2520
http://www.upress.umn.edu

Library of Congress Cataloging-in-Publication Data

Sullivan, Karen, 1964–
    The interrogation of Joan of Arc / Karen Sullivan.
        p.   cm. — (Medieval cultures ; v. 20)
    Includes bibliographical references and index.
    ISBN 0-8166-3267-7 (hc) — ISBN 0-8166-3268-5 (pb)
        1. Joan, of Arc, Saint, 1412–1431—Trials, litigation, etc.
    2. Questioning — France — History — Sources.   3. Christian women
saints — France — Biography.   I. Title.   II. Series.
DC104.S85   1999
944'.026'092 — dc21
    [B]   99-043004

Printed in the United States of America on acid-free paper

The University of Minnesota is an equal-opportunity educator and employer.

11 10 09 08 07 06 05 04 03 02 01 00 99   10 9 8 7 6 5 4 3 2 1

For my parents,
Elaine Sullivan and Desmond Sullivan

Contents

Medieval Cultures

Acknowledgments

This book has benefited from the preliminary responses of many readers. I am grateful, first and foremost, to R. Howard Bloch, who has assisted this project from its inception and whose own work on the progression from inquest to Inquisition provided so much of the original inspiration for it. Deirdre d'Albertis and Mark Lambert read and commented on the entire manuscript, challenging me to rethink or recontextualize several aspects of my argument. Jody Enders, Nadia Margolis, Helen Solterer, and Jane H. M. Taylor have also shared thoughts and suggestions about the book, for which I am extremely grateful, as have Laurent Mayali, Joseph J. Duggan, and Timothy Hampton. Leon Botstein has encouraged the project's ambitions in a way not usually to be expected from a college president. I would like to thank, finally, my colleagues at Bard College and my students in the Joan of Arc and Medieval Heresy seminars for their valuable responses to this work at various stages.

Introduction

What does it mean to question? The Latin term *quaestio*, from which our word "question" derives, indicates an act of seeking and, by extension, an act of seeking truth. It suggests, through its linking of seeking and truth, that truth is something that must be sought and, hence, something that is not already present or not already evident among us. Because the process of questioning assumes that truth lies not in the self who seeks it but, rather, in an other outside that self, it is inherently modest and unassuming in its approach and inherently sensitive to the dangers of proclaiming too quickly or too confidently that truth has been found. From Socrates to Heidegger, a tradition of Western philosophy has identified the wisest of men, paradoxically, with those who allege that they themselves possess no wisdom, that wisdom is to be found in the other to whom they appeal, and that wisdom is to be elicited from this other only through such an act of questioning. Yet if inquiries are distinguished by their location of the truth they seek in an other, why is it that they are so often suspected of planting in their words the seeds of the truth they later profess to find? If inquiries are marked by their respect for the object that they address, why is it, then, that the *quaestio* signifies not only the verbal utterance that the interrogator performs but also the physical torture that has so often accompanied that utterance? Why is it that the word "interrogation" still to this day suggests the extortion of a confession from an unwilling respondent and the application of a pressure, sometimes mental, sometimes physical, to facilitate that avowal? What does it mean, finally, that all such concerns about questioning are themselves necessarily articulated in the interrogative and, therefore, always already subject to this mode's inner structure?

It is fitting that a study of the figure known today as Joan of Arc begin with a consideration of the meaning of interrogation, for it was interrogation that both began and ended her public career. In early March 1429, when Joan arrived at Chinon to inform the dauphin Charles de Valois that she had been sent by God to champion his cause in the Hundred Years' War against that of the English invaders and their Burgundian allies, she found herself questioned briefly by half a dozen or so high ecclesiastics suspicious of her claims. Not long thereafter, she traveled with the court to Poitiers, then the judicial capital of the Armagnac party, and submitted impatiently to another three weeks of examination at the hands of a larger assembly of theologians. Only after these clerics had completed their interrogations of Joan was she allowed to continue on to Orléans to relieve the city from an English siege and thus begin the chain of military and political victories that would culminate in the coronation of the dauphin as Charles VII at Reims that July. After a year of intermittent battle, Joan was captured by the Burgundians outside Compiègne, sold to the English, and transported to Rouen, where she was tried for heresy and interrogated anew. Over the course of twelve days spread between mid-February and mid-March 1431, she responded to questions from the two judges, Pierre Cauchon, the bishop of Beauvais, and Jean Le Maître, the vicar to Jean Graverent, the inquisitor of France, and their hundred or so clerical assistants. Only after these clerics had completed their interrogations was she condemned and burned at the stake in the Vieux Marché of this Norman capital. Though the clerics of Poitiers and those of Rouen were on opposing sides in the war and though they held opposing views on the Maid of Orléans, both sets of ecclesiastics interrogated her, and both sets of interrogations proved decisive in determining her fate.

As the act of interrogation shaped Joan's career during her lifetime, the minutes of her interrogation, especially those from Rouen, which have survived to this day, shaped opinion about her after her death. When the trial had concluded, the Rouennais notary Guillaume Manchon and the Parisian master Thomas de Courcelles, both of whom had taken part in the proceedings, translated the original French minutes of the interrogation into

Latin and collated them with other documents, including the correspondence, the various sets of accusations, and the several sentences, to create
the official transcripts of the trial.[1] Manchon prepared at least three manuscripts of the text, one for the bishop, one for the inquisitor, and one for
the king of England, and an unknown scribe produced two additional manuscripts, all of which were signed and sealed by the judges and notaries.[2]
The extensiveness of these transcripts is extraordinary, as becomes evident
when they are compared with the records of similar late-medieval French
trials. Whereas Joan was given a dossier of over one or two hundred fo-
lios, depending upon the size of the manuscript pages, Marguerite Porete,
the author and alleged practitioner of the Heresy of the Free Spirit, Jeanne
Daubenton, the leader of the Turlepin group in Paris, and Pierronne of
Brittany, a follower of Joan and fellow visionary, all received files of only
a few leaves in length, if that.[3] In 1430, a lawyer by the name of Jean Ségueut
was convicted of heresy in Rouen, yet though his trial was attended by
the same notaries who would shortly thereafter compose the minutes of
Joan's interrogation, he was accorded a few scant pages of notice.[4] In 1440,
Gilles de Rais, a great nobleman from Nantes and a former companion-at-
arms of Joan at Orléans, was condemned for notorious crimes, yet though
he was a lord of the realm, he too warranted a record less than half as long
as that of his onetime comrade.[5] If the clerics compiled a document this
thorough, it was presumably because they were Burgundians under pressure from the English, who were then occupying Rouen and subsidizing
the costs of the trial, to produce transcripts that would justify Joan's condemnation for heresy and, in doing so, defame the party to which she had
been attached. In letters appended to the last pages of the transcripts, rep-
resentatives of the University of Paris and the English monarchy wrote to
the temporal and ecclesiastical leaders of France and other lands publi-
cizing the trial's findings and urging them to support sermons that might
disabuse populaces long deceived by the Maid. From the Bourgeois of Paris,
we know that the inquisitor Graverent himself delivered one such sermon
on July 4, 1431, little more than a month after Joan's death, at Saint-Martin-
des-Champs in Paris and that he cited numerous details from the transcripts to bolster his diatribe against her. As history would have it, before
a quarter-century had passed, the Armagnacs would reconcile themselves
with the Burgundians and succeed in expelling the English from almost
all of France, and the clerics associated with this newly victorious party
would return to Joan's case, interviewing a series of witnesses who had
known her at various stages of her life, reconsidering the documents that
had led to her death, and ultimately annulling her condemnation in pro-

ceedings normally referred to as her "rehabilitation."[6] Though the record of Joan's answers to questions at Rouen was now read as depicting Joan positively, in contrast to the spirit in which it appears to have originally been written, it continued to be valued as the text in which Joan spoke at the greatest length and depth about the issues most central to her legend.

Whatever the political purposes to which the minutes of Joan's interrogations were put, clerics participating in her trial made clear that they were intended to be read as a pure representation of what Joan said and, by extension, as a pure representation of what she believed. In his letter appointing Manchon and Guillaume Boisguillaume as notaries, Bishop Cauchon ordered these men "to render themselves near the said Joan and elsewhere where, when, and each time it will be necessary, to interrogate her or hear her be interrogated, . . . to collect . . . the words and confessions of this Joan, to report them back to us orally or in writing, to set the entire trial in due form, and to edit it in writing" (20). From the testimony given at the rehabilitation, we know that Manchon and Boisguillaume attended the sessions of the interrogations and took notes on what was being said, while a third notary associated with the inquisitor, Nicolas Taquel, merely listened to the exchanges. After their meal, the three notaries reconvened, shared their recollections of the dialogue, and composed a draft of the minutes. When they were unsure as to Joan's response to a particular question, they would write *nota* in the margin of the page so that they could verify her answer the next day. At the end of all the sessions, the entire minutes were read aloud to Joan and she was recorded as confirming their accuracy. Even at the rehabilitation, when the clerics who had participated in this trial were encouraged by examiners of Armagnac bias to decry the defectiveness of these records, virtually all concurred that the notaries represented fairly what was said during the trial and that Joan herself seemed to trust what they wrote.[7] If Cauchon and the notaries took such pains to produce an accurate transcription of Joan's words, it was because these words would later be weighed so heavily in the trial. The judges had sent emissaries to Joan's native country and other lands she had frequented during her military campaigns in order to learn from outside sources what she was held to believe, yet they never included the results of this report in the transcripts, as would have been customary, so that Joan's responses alone provided the grounds for their ultimate deliberation about her. When the *promotor*, or prosecutor, Jean d'Estivet, and his assistants composed the *libelle d'Estivet*, the seventy articles that constituted the first set of charges brought against Joan, they cited extensive passages from her responses during the interrogations to buttress their accusations.[8] The authors of the subsequent sets of charges, though they did not quote the minutes so openly, relied upon Joan's responses no less. By questioning Joan in order to verify their suspicions that she held heterodox views and by judging her on the basis of her responses to these questions, the clerics showed their expectation that through their interrogations, they were gaining access not just to Joan's words but to her actual convictions. They showed their assumption that when they judged and condemned Joan, they were judging and condemning not just what she said during her interrogations but what she believed. If the minutes provide a pure means of access to the words Joan spoke and the words a pure means of access to the beliefs she held, as the transcripts' handling of them suggests that they do, the clerics themselves cannot be held to taint this evidence through their involvement.

Modern readers of the minutes of Joan's interrogations, including Jules Michelet and Jules-Etienne-Joseph Quicherat, the historians who revived her cult in the midnineteenth century, Anatole France and Andrew Lang, the biographers who composed the greatest lives of the Maid in the early twentieth century, and indeed most of these authors' successors in so-called Johannic studies in more recent decades, have tended to follow the clerics' lead in reading this text as a largely transparent representation of Joan's words and beliefs, through which we encounter the heroine herself.[9] Pierre Champion, for example, announces, "In the trial, we hear Jeanne's words truly. . . . How clearly Jeanne speaks, a language fresh as brook water! Here we have her words, we have Jeanne herself. . . . It is in the course of the trial that Jeanne, living, appears before us."[10] Marina Warner likewise declares, "In this document, Joan's turn of phrase brings her voice leaping from the page with dramatic, painful authenticity. Half a millennium later, her sincerity is unadulterated; her conviction rings like a bell."[11] In affirming that Joan's true voice can be heard and her true character apprehended in the transcripts, these authors affirm that the textual mediation of this document ceases to constitute a barrier to the historical reality it depicts. Popular collections like those of Willard Trask or Régine Pernoud, which present the responses attributed to Joan in the minutes as furnishing a portrait of Joan "in her own words" or "by herself," also intimate that the minutes give us direct access to Joan, so that the very means of this access seem to disappear from critical attention.[12] Insofar as these critics assume that the record of Joan's words reflects what Joan said and what she believed, they assume that there exists a direct line from the notaries' textual transcription of Joan's expression back to her actual, historical expression and a direct line from this actual, historical expression back to her actual, historical experience. They hold that the notaries transcribed

X because Joan said *X*, and that Joan said *X* because she underwent *X*. In their understanding both of the notaries' written transcription of Joan's words and of Joan's oral articulation of her beliefs, these readers conceive of language, whether expressed in writing or in speech, as a supplement to historical reality, a supplement that can make historical reality more accessible than it would be otherwise but without substantially altering or affecting it. These readers expect that through the text they can transcend the text and gain access to an extratextual historical reality, or in other words, that through the representation they can transcend the representation and gain access to what is represented.

Despite the consensus among readers of the minutes of interrogation, both medieval and modern, that this text represents the truth of what Joan said during these sessions, it is important to recognize the role of the clerics in composing what we read. Following the conventions of the genre within which they wrote, the notaries included in their document certain information about each of the sessions, namely, the date, the time, the location, and the names and affiliations of those persons in attendance, and they omitted certain other information.[13] They transcribed certain words, and they left out certain other ones. They organized what was said around the terms "*Interrogata*" and "*respondit*," editing and recasting what they heard so that it fit within these markers. Salomon Reinach has demonstrated that, far from transcribing all of the dialogues verbatim, the notaries seem to have occasionally left out certain questions or certain exchanges and thus to have followed the recommendation of the fourteenth-century inquisitor Bernard Gui to transcribe only those words that concern the substance of the matter and that seem best to express the truth.[14] The point is not that the clerics were or were not manipulative in composing the minutes but, rather, that as notaries they were required to make certain acts of discrimination. Even a modern interrogation, recorded with the most sophisticated audio and video equipment, requires that similar decisions about inclusion and exclusion of material be made. At what moment does one turn the equipment on or off? Where does one place the microphone? Upon whose face does one focus the camera? Even the recording that aims at the greatest possible completeness must frame what is recorded, determining its beginning and ending, distinguishing between primary voices and background noise, choosing or emphasizing one detail over another. Though in a historical sense Joan may have spoken and the notaries may have written down what she said, the production of the minutes reflects a collaboration between the speaker and her scribes.

Similarly, despite the agreement among readers of the minutes that Joan's responses under interrogation represented the truth of what she believed, it is important to acknowledge the role of the clerics in controlling the direction of the dialogues between them. It was the clerics who, by asking questions, introduced the topics that their respondent was to address. It was they who, by incorporating a certain vocabulary and syntax into their questions, provided the components out of which she was to construct her answers. Whether Joan welcomed the framework imposed upon her speech by the clerics' questions or resisted it, her words appeared in response to it and took on meaning within its context. Again, the point is not that the clerics were or were not "suggestive" in their questioning but, rather, that, as interrogators, it was they who opened up the space within which Joan was allowed to speak, and it was they who furnished the elements with which she was allowed to express herself. Even a modern interrogation, conducted with the most scrupulous concern for the rights of the accused, operates under similar linguistic constraints. How does one ask a prisoner about her experience without implying, through that very question, what that experience must have been? How does one extract information without contaminating the probe with which one extracts? Even the interrogator who tries to maintain the greatest possible integrity must, to some extent, affect the responses, prompting the respondent to address certain issues instead of others, from a certain perspective instead of another. The interrogation itself, even prior to its transcription, represented a collaboration between the respondent and her interrogators.

In recent years, scholars have begun to pay attention to the rhetorical aspects of historical writings, such as the relationship between the form and the content of minutes of interrogation. Dominick La Capra has undermined the traditional distinction between "documents," normally thought of as texts, like trial transcripts, that refer to an outside reality, and "works," normally thought of as texts, like novels or philosophical treatises, that do not do so.[15] He has argued, in particular, that a register of inquisition, far from being adequately treated as a "document," as a source of information about an external reality, "is itself a textual power structure with links to relations of power in the larger society. How it functions as a text is intimately and problematically related to its use for the reconstruction of life in the past."[16] Elsewhere, La Capra has insisted upon recognizing "what might ironically be called *la question préalable*—the need for a close, critical reading of documents such as inquisition records before they are used as quarries for facts and sources for inferential reconstructions of reality."[17] Several critics have already moved toward reading texts normally considered "documents" as "works." Hayden White's interpretation of the annals of Saint Gall constitutes perhaps the most beautiful example of a rhetorical approach to a supposedly historical document.[18] Arsenio Frugoni, Rita Copeland, and Steven Justice have already successfully evaluated the texts of selected medieval heresy trials in such a manner.[19] In recent years, a few critics from diverse fields have even begun to consider the textual aspects of Joan's own trial record. Jean-Pierre Barricelli, himself involved in the influential movement to bring together the study of law and literature, praises the transcripts of this trial as a work of "involuntary literature" and argues that if playwrights like George Bernard Shaw and Jean Anouilh have been able to exploit the dialogue from these minutes for their own dramatic purposes, it is because this dialogue already possesses in itself all the elements that characterize great literature.[20] Steven Weiskopf maintains that the historical Joan constructed herself as a text that destabilized her clerical readers, while Susan Schibanoff, in contrast, asserts that the historical Joan did not so much construct as find herself constructed by the clerics who composed these materials.[21] Susan Crane acknowledges both the historical reality of Joan and the textual mediation through which we apprehend her, so that she views the transcripts as a site of contention between the forces of immediacy and mediacy, history and literature, and representation and creation in their depiction of Joan.[22] Finally, the historian Barbara A. Hanawalt and the literary critic Susan Noakes describe the version of the French minutes from 1500 that they study as "a hybrid text that could not be adequately analyzed through historical study or literary criticism alone." They recommend that semiotics, with its recognition of a competition between different symbolic codes, can best account for the conflicting voices one finds in this work.[23] It is not only these scholars' recognition of the importance of the rhetorical level of Joan's trial transcripts but their recognition of the importance of the struggle between Joan and the clerics to define who she is, so evident on this level of the text, that I follow here.

Approaching the transcripts of Joan's trial from a rhetorical rather than historical perspective, one cannot help but perceive the resonance between the practical assumption made by these late medieval clerics that truth could be ascertained through interrogation and the similar philosophical assumption made by scholastics during this time period that truth could be ascertained through questioning. Throughout the early Middle Ages, when monks, instead of scholastics, filled the ranks of the learned, intellectual modes perceived as more concordant with the spiritual life of the monastery were dominant. Saint Benedict stressed the importance of reading in his monks' daily schedule, yet he placed it on the same level as prayer, meditation, and singing, all activities in which the monk aimed not at uncovering an as-yet unattained truth but at absorbing, on ever deeper levels, an already acquired truth. Speaking of the reading that accompanied the monks' meals, Benedict commanded explicitly, "No one should presume to ask a question [*requirere*] about the reading or about anything else." The context in which he made this remark suggests that such an act would involve a shift from the passive receptivity appropriate to a religious, who assumed that truth was already provided for him, to the active interrogation customary to a philosopher, who pridefully assumed that he might obtain truth through his own initiative.[24] For Saint Bernard of Clairvaux, whose writings represent in many ways the flower of monastic thought, scriptural exegesis resembled the sucking of honey from a rock or the chewing of bread in order to taste its full bounty: the honey is in the rock, the taste is in the bread, and it is the task of the exegete merely to draw out these desirable substances and to savor them.[25] It was in Bernard's own century, however, that the emphasis in intellectual life shifted from the *lectio* privileged by the monasteries to the *quaestio* privileged by the newer cathedral schools and universities. Far from treating texts as if truth were self-evident within them, Peter Abelard opened his *Sic et Non* by pointing out contradictions within the church fathers' writings and went on to consider and attempt to account for 158 such paradoxical passages. When Christ asked questions in the temple, Abelard maintained, he did so not in order to learn, for he already possessed full wisdom, but in order to provide a model of human comportment. "For consistent or frequent questioning [*interrogatio*] is defined as the first key to wisdom," he wrote.[26] Bernard was canonized and Abelard was condemned for heresy, but it was Abelard, in his use of questioning, who provided the model for intellectual activity in the next three centuries. Saint Thomas Aquinas, for example, organized the vast majority of his work around a series of *quaestiones* and did not even limit his inquiries to resolving actual contradictions within authoritative texts, as Abelard had. Asking questions as radical as "Does God exist?" and "Is the soul spiritual?" Aquinas showed his conviction that such interrogations lead to a greater appreciation of Christianity's verities by adding the support of rational understanding to faithful belief. As Marie-Dominique Chenu summarizes, "With the 'questions,' scholasticism reached the peak of its development. In them, it found the literary medium best answering its creative inspiration."[27] Even though scholasticism had crested in the thirteenth and early fourteenth centuries, both of Joan's judges and virtually all of their assistants were graduates of the University of Paris, mostly in theology and canon law, and all were immersed in an intellectual culture whose major scholarly texts continued to be structured around written *quaestiones* and whose major academic events continued to be organized around disputations highlighting these *quaestiones*. When the clerics interrogated Joan, the questions they asked recall those asked by scholastics, and the overall mode of their address recalled the mode most esteemed in these academic circles.

Questioning Joan as scholastics, the clerics also questioned her as jurists, who, at this time, also sought to obtain truth through inquiry. Throughout the early Middle Ages, when Germanic custom took the place of Roman law in most legal settings, magistrates relied upon judgments of God instead of inquiry to ascertain innocence and guilt in most cases.[28] They administered trials by oath, combat, or ordeal in which they depended not upon their own reason to infer the truth from the available information but upon God to reveal the truth to them by determining whether the accused could safely pronounce an oath over relics, could effectively defend himself in battle against his accuser, or could confidently expose himself to water or fire without fear of being repulsed by these pure substances. Just as Bernard of Clairvaux believed that God manifested truth through his exegesis, transforming the scriptural passage he studied into the spiritual food that would nourish his monkish brethren, the twelfth-century magistrate believed that God manifested truth through the trials he administered. Just as the exegete commented on, rather than questioned, the text he studied, assuming that truth lies imminent in these texts and that man's task is to open himself to this truth through hermeneutical techniques, the magistrate conducted a trial by God, rather than an inquest, assuming that truth lies imminent in the world and that it is man's job, through his observance of the rites that surround such a trial, to open himself to receive that truth. In the twelfth century, at the same time that Abelard was popularizing the use of philosophical questioning, jurists at the University of Bologna resurrected the use of Roman inquest. In the thirteenth century, at the same time that scholastic *quaestiones* were coming to dominate the university, judicial *inquisitiones* came to dominate the court.[29] At the Fourth Lateran Council of 1215, the church forbade priests from blessing the elements used in the trial by ordeal, censured trials by combat, and encouraged the use of inquest in their stead.[30] Saint Louis followed this ecclesiastical precedent in the 1250s, prohibiting trials by combat from being held on his lands, first in civil and then in criminal cases, and ordering inquests to be conducted in their place.[31] Like the scholastics, who were trained at the universities to question their masters and their opponents in debate, these new magistrates were also trained at the universities to ask questions of documents, of witnesses, and of suspects about cases in dispute.[32] Joan's judges and their assistants were all familiar with the procedures of judicial inquest, especially as the University of Paris had increasingly come to usurp the role of the Inquisition in prosecuting heresy in northern France and as those affiliated with the *alma mater,* like these clerics, had increasingly come to take part in such proceedings.[33] When the clerics interrogated Joan, the questions they asked recalled the questions of their fellow investigators in other inquests and the mode of their address recalled the mode now presiding in judicial circles.

The clerics questioned Joan not only as scholastics and as jurists but, finally, as confessors, who had also adopted inquiry as a tool for attaining truth in recent centuries. During the early Middle Ages, confession was a relatively rare act, usually undertaken only in the face of death or as the result of a spontaneous act of contrition. Because it was the individual rather than the church who initiated confession, it was the individual rather than the confessor who decided upon the extent of the avowals, while the priest merely encouraged the penitent's remorse and assigned a penance based upon the number and kind of misdeeds. In the twelfth century, however, at the same time that the use of *quaestiones* and *inquisitiones* was being revived, ecclesiastical authors increasingly recommended that confessors consider not simply external acts but the sinners' intentions in committing these acts as they determined their penances. As scholastics showed renewed interest in the ten Aristotelian "circumstances" thought to characterize any given substance and as inquisitors relied on those ten circumstances as they examined witnesses and interrogated suspects in order to obtain a full view of the crime committed, confessors too began to rely upon the same circumstances as they started questioning penitents in order to obtain a full view of their sin.[34] At the Fourth Lateran Council, the church instituted the requirement that all Christians confess their sins at least once a year and that their confessors be "discreet and cautious..., diligently inquiring [*inquirens*] into the circumstances of the sinner and the sin."[35] The *libri poenitentiales* of the early Middle Ages, which assisted confessors by listing sins and corresponding penances, were replaced by manuals for confessors and *summae confessorum,* which outlined the proper use of questions in dialogues with penitents.[36] As Thomas N. Tentler writes, "The most prominent feature of both manuals and summas bearing on the conduct of confession is usually the part devoted to the questions."[37] Joan's judges and their assistants were members of the church as well as scholastics and inquisitors, and thus were familiar with the investigative nature of such pastoral encounters. When they interrogated Joan, their questions recall not only the scholastic and the judicial spheres but this confessional context as well.

The clerics participating in Joan's trial were not alone in combining the scholastic, the judicial, and the confessional types of inquiry. The Inquisition, under whose aegis Joan's trial was conducted, is often thought to have been effective at eradicating heresy where other institutions had failed because the Dominican and Franciscan orders that staffed its office promoted education and indeed provided the home of virtually all the most important scholastics of the thirteenth and fourteenth centuries. The friars needed to be sufficiently knowledgeable in theology and canon law to detect heretical subtleties in a suspect's beliefs and to attempt to persuade such deviants of their errors and also experienced enough in university disputations to engage profitably in verbal conflicts with the accused. The Inquisition, whose very name derives from its reliance upon trials *per inquisitionem*, was distinguished not only by the training of its scholarly members but also by the progressiveness of its judicial procedures.[38] It was this office that popularized the return to inquest, with the accompanying recourse to interrogation and torture, and in doing so provided the model for both sacred and secular judicial practices through the ancien régime. The Inquisition was distinguished, finally, not only by the scholastic refinement of its members and by the judicial sophistication of its procedures but by the confessional rhetoric of its approach. The accused who admitted heresy and expressed repentance were assigned not "punishments," like those a secular magistrate might accord, but "penances," such as prayers, fasts, flagellations, and pilgrimages, like those a priest allots. The accused who proved impenitent, whether by defending their heterodox beliefs or by denying their heresy, were not burned at the stake by the inquisitors themselves but, rather, were "abandoned to the secular arm" by spiritual directors who sadly acknowledged their inability to convert those hardened to error.[39] Like the confessor, the inquisitor was seen as a "physician of souls" who carefully diagnosed the illness of the invalid he was examining and applied the remedy he saw as most fitting.[40] Though the reorientation of academic, judicial, and pastoral practices around questioning has generally been studied in the separate fields of theology, law, and religion, the same type of educated cleric brought about these developments in these different contexts, and the same conviction that truth would be acquired not by passively awaiting its revelation through God's grace but by actively seeking it through reason came to pervade the environments of the schools, the courts, and the parish churches.

The transcripts of Joan's trial show that the clerics interrogated Joan because they shared assumptions about the means of access to truth common to the scholastics, inquisitors, and confessors of the time, yet they also show that Joan resisted these interrogations because she did not share the assumptions of this clerical caste. Needless to say, Joan did not see herself as the mysterious feminine other possessing but hesitating to disclose a desirable truth, nor did she see the clerics as the earnest masculine selves seeking to overcome her hesitation and to extort that truth from her. The conflicts between Joan and the clerics, as we shall see, were less often cases in which the clerics sought information that Joan resisted revealing than cases in which the clerics demanded information that Joan believed she had already revealed. The conflicts concerned not so much differences between the clerics' and Joan's wills as differences between their perceptions. If Joan did not organize her experience according to the categories implicit in her interrogators' questions and, thus, did not succeed in responding easily to these queries, it was in large part because she did not possess the same academic, judicial, and pastoral training as the clerics, nor did she inhabit the same cultural milieus, permeated with the effects of this training, as they. Though the transcripts make clear that Joan struggled with the interrogations because she did not belong to the clerical culture, they do not make clear to what culture she did belong. In different places throughout the text, Joan cited a chivalric code, a children's saying, and a parish prayer, but she spoke no language that could consistently be identified with that of knights, children, or parishioners. Her speech, like her character, contained within it elements from various populations, both aristocratic and plebeian, both masculine and feminine, and both sacred and secular, but in its combination of all of these elements it remained anomalous to all of them. As we shall see, some scholars have understood Joan as a representative of a so-called popular culture of residual pagans, Romantic peasants, or women mystics, yet it is important to recognize that neither Joan nor the clerics identified her with these social groups or indeed with any social group at all. If Joan resisted the clerics' interrogations, as we shall see that she did, one cannot define that resistance positively by identifying it with one population, but, instead, one can only define it negatively, by construing it in reaction to the dominant clerical caste.

It is the series of clashes in the minutes between the clerics' questions, so reflective of the presuppositions of their clerical culture, and Joan's answers, so reflective of her own idiosyncratic resistance to these presuppositions, that I intend to examine in this study. In chapters 1, 2, and 3, I will show how the clerics' training as scholastics influenced their inquiries into Joan's childhood festivities, her audition of voices, and her departure for France. Because the clerics associated truth with the scholastic values of logic, precision, and analysis, they rejected Joan's answers to their questions about these matters for failing to respect those values. In chapters 4 and 5, I will demonstrate how the clerics' training as inquisitors shaped their inquiries into the sign with which Joan was said to have persuaded her king of her divine mission to save France and, indeed, how it shaped their inquiries in general. Because the clerics demanded objective evidence of Joan's claims to heavenly inspiration, they at once rejected her speech, insofar as it was an expression controlled by her and therefore potentially deceptive and judicially valueless, and attempted to transform this speech into an expression not controlled by her and therefore truthful and judicially valuable. As Joan failed to provide accounts of her experience that satisfied the clerics' scholastic criteria, so did she fail to provide proof of her experience that satisfied their judicial criteria. In chapters 6 and 7, finally, I will establish how the clerics' training as confessors affected their inquiries into Joan's attitude toward her imprisonment. Because the clerics looked upon themselves not as adversaries seeking to prove her criminality and to punish her for her crimes but as spiritual directors yearning to save her by leading her to confession and penance for her sins, they blamed her for insisting, almost until the very end of her trial, that it was her voices and not themselves who governed her conscience. If I will be arguing, on one level, that the minutes constitute not a representation but a production of the truth of Joan of Arc, I will be arguing, on another level, that they constitute a scene of confrontation between clerics, trained as scholastics, inquisitors, and confessors, who believe that truth can be attained through questioning, and Joan, who does not share the clerics' formation and does not conceive of truth as they do.

What, still, does it mean for a critic to raise these questions? On the one hand, insofar as I rely upon the minutes of interrogation from the trial as the source of a certain truth about Joan, I necessarily repeat the actions of the clerics who composed the text and judged her on its basis. Literate, and indeed, academically trained, I necessarily share the clerics' own valorization of logical analysis, rationality, and objectivity. Skeptical of claims to direct contact with a metaphysical realm of reality, I necessarily share their suspicions about Joan's claims to have heard voices from God. Institutionally authorized as a college professor, as they were themselves institutionally authorized as university masters, I necessarily partake in their desire to teach and advise those who might seem to benefit from this instruction. On the other hand, however, even if I cannot help but replay the role these clerics once enacted, I can attempt to keep in mind the cultural biases this role implies. Even if I cannot transcend the mentality of the educated, I can attempt to remain conscious of what is excluded by this mentality. Even if questioning is unavoidable, it remains nevertheless possible to interrogate the question.

1 | The Fairy Tree

In 1429, the year Joan of Arc appeared in the public realm, the Bourgeois of Paris expressed two views of the Maid of Orléans in his journal. He reported, first, that "things were said of her..., by those who loved the Armagnacs better than the Burgundians or the Regent of France, such as that, when she was very small and looked after the sheep, birds would come from the woods and fields when she called them and eat bread in her lap as if they were tame."[1] In his account of her alleged ability to attract birds, the Bourgeois attributed to Joan a superhuman power that was neither divinely miraculous nor diabolically monstrous and that tended, as such, to be identified with the marvelous. After recounting this anecdote, however, the Bourgeois added, "In truth, this is false [*In veritate appocrisium est*]."[2] It is not immediately clear why the Bourgeois rejected the tale of Joan's marvelous ability to call birds to her lap. The Bourgeois was a Burgundian and hence of political sensibilities opposed to Joan and to the Armagnacs who tell this tale about her. More importantly, he is also generally recognized to have been not a burgher, despite his traditional appellation, but a cleric. At the moment he shifted from communicating to judging the anecdote, he shifted from French to Latin, from the language of the vulgar to the language of the learned, from the language of the layperson to the language of the cleric. Aristocratic French literature, such as the romances and lays telling of "the matter of Britain," relies upon a tripartite conception of the supernatural, composed of the miraculous, the monstrous, and the marvelous. Clerical Latin literature, however, including the writings of monks and theologians, generally relies upon a bipartite conception of the supernatural, composed only of divine miracle and satanic magic.[3] The Bourgeois's transition to the learned, clerical language at the moment he rejected the Armagnacs' account of Joan's marvelous power suggests that his resistance to Joan was the result not just of political prejudice but of a clerical culture skeptical of a non-Christian supernatural.

The conflict evident in the Bourgeois's journal between a vernacular discourse that embraces the marvelous and a Latin discourse that rejects this category is also evident in the transcripts of Joan's trial for heresy. The clerics at the trial, having heard reports about Joan's childhood during their inquests in her native region, questioned Joan about a famous beech tree near her village and about the songs and dances she and her childhood companions were said to have performed in its vicinity.[4] As we shall see, though for the clerics these songs and dances clashed with the practice of the Christian faith, for Joan they did not do so. If the clerics and Joan differed in their interpretation of these rites, it was not, I will argue, because they differed in *what* they thought but, rather, because they differed in *how* they thought. Like the Bourgeois, the clerics were university trained and schooled in logic, while Joan was not formally educated. The clerics sought out and attempted to resolve contradictions, like that between the marvelous and Christianity, while Joan did not perceive, much less attempt to reconcile, these inconsistencies. A contrast between the ways in which the clerics of the University of Paris and the residents of Joan's native village thought in the first half of the fifteenth century will help us appreciate the opposition between the clerical and nonclerical mentalities so apparent in the transcript pages.

The University of Paris

At the time of Joan's trial, the University of Paris had long been in a period of decline. During the thirteenth and early fourteenth centuries, it had served as the home of virtually all the most-celebrated theologians in Europe, from Thomas Aquinas and Bonaventure to Duns Scotus and William of Ockham. In the late fourteenth and early fifteenth centuries, however, though scholars continued to defend the *via moderna* of the nominalists against the *via antiqua* of their realist predecessors, the quality of intellectual dialogue ceased to be what it once had been. Once, the Faculty of Theology had enjoyed a cosmopolitan student body to which it was empowered to grant the *ius ubique docendi,* or the right to teach anywhere. In recent years, however, the disturbances of the Hundred Years' War and the Cabochian revolts discouraged foreign students from attending the university, especially when the new universities of Prague, Heidelberg, and Vienna were opened and could be attended instead. When Paris fell to the Burgundians in 1418 and became dangerous for those not adhering to the duke's party, many masters and students fled south to found the University of Poitiers. As a result, the University of Paris, once international in its population, now became not only a national but a regional institution. Closing down intellectually, the university closed down socially as well.

Despite the increasing regionalism and sterility of the university, during the late Middle Ages, the masters who taught under its aegis demanded, and received, ever greater respect. It was during this period, as Jacques Le Goff has recounted, that the title *magister,* or master, became equivalent to *dominus,* or lord; that the master's biretta, squirrel hood, ermine collar, and long robe became official parts of his costume; and that the pulpit from which he spoke was raised on a dais.[5] It was also during this period that the masters, long organized along the lines of a corporation or guild, came to function as a class desirous of preserving its prerogatives. According to Jacques Verger, they vacillated between championing the Burgundians and the Armagnacs, depending upon which party seemed likely to bring an end to the Hundred Years' War, but their pacifism was based only on the belief that peace would best serve their own purposes. They mistook their personal interests for common interests, they cloaked their own ambitions in appeals to the glory of the university, and they thus succumbed, as Verger puts it, to a "collective selfishness and narrow-mindedness."[6] Though the university's reputation was based in accomplishments over a century old at this time, its masters continued to invoke that reputation and continued to seek to benefit from their association with it.

The clerics who were involved in Joan's trial were, first and foremost, graduates of the university, and they exhibited much of the self-importance associated with its faculty and alumni at this time. All of the clerics participating in the trial possessed masters of arts degrees or the equivalent from a mendicant *studium,* and a considerable majority among them is believed to have attained diplomas in the advanced fields of theology and canon law as well.[7] The bishop Pierre Cauchon was a licentiate in decretals, and he had been a student in the Faculty of Theology for six years. The inquisitor Jean Graverent was a master in theology, and his vicar, Jean

Le Maître, was a bachelor in this subject. If one considers not just the judges but the fifteen assistants whom Charles de Beaurepaire calculates as having been the most assiduous in the trial, thirteen are recorded as having pursued theology and two, canon law.[8] In the minutes, the notaries listed the clerics present at individual sessions in order of the prestige of their degrees and of the faculty from which they received them, naming first the masters, then the licentiates, then the bachelors, and, within those categories, first the theologians, then the canonists, then the artists, and then, when necessary, the physicians. The notaries characterized the clerics as "venerable lords and masters" (184 et passim) or as "reverend fathers, lords, and masters" (185 et passim), thus stressing the respect due persons possessing such distinctions. The clerics were trained at what was still arguably the most esteemed university of Europe, and they prided themselves on an academic status that they felt elevated them above those who did not possess it.

Attached to the university during the years of their academic preparation, these clerics often remained attached to the *alma mater* during their maturity and played important roles in its operations. Six of the theologians taking part in the trial, Jean Beaupère, Thomas de Courcelles, Gérard Feuillet, Pierre Maurice, Nicolas Midi, and Jacques de Touraine, are known to have been professors at the university during these years, and the first two to have enjoyed special repute.[9] At this time, the rector, or effective head of the university, was elected by the masters of the Faculty of the Arts every three months. Beaupère was chosen for this post in 1412 and 1413, Courcelles in 1430 and 1431, and Maurice in 1428; these repeated elections suggest the centrality of these individuals to university life. Though Cauchon was bishop of Beauvais and a member of Henry VI's council, he too served as rector in 1397 and 1403 and as protector of the university's privileges at the time of Joan's trial. It is thought that Cauchon would have been familiar with many of the clerics in these proceedings from his involvement with the university and that he would have selected them as his assistants on the basis of that familiarity.[10] Pierre Champion observes that in writing his notices about these clerics "I had the very clear impression that the trial had been led by a very small number of university men, of classmates," while Heinrich Denifle and Emile Châtelain estimate that two-thirds of the clerics participating in the trial were direct instruments of the university.[11] Their affiliation with the university and with the academic learning with which the university was associated provided the foundation of the clerics' identification with each other and of the authority with which they saw themselves invested.

The masters of the university advanced the rights of their caste perhaps most vehemently at the Council of Basel, which opened immediately after the conclusion of the trial.[12] Though university men made up approximately 28 percent of the clerics in attendance at the council in April 1433, their influence on the proceedings was disproportionate to their numbers because they used the skills acquired during their educations and, especially, the mystique associated with these skills to dominate the drafting of the meeting's positions.[13] The council affirmed, in general, that clerics gathered together in legitimate assembly possessed greater authority than the pope himself. Privileging "reason" over "dignity" and the rights of learned clerics over those of mighty prelates, the archbishop of Arles championed the council's decision to allow even parish priests to vote, maintaining that "a bishop, sometimes ignorant and without knowledge, must not become indignant . . . if the vote of a priest who is poor but intelligent is preferred to his."[14] During the years of the Great Schism, between 1378 and 1415, the authority of the pope had waned as two and even three claimants contested the right to the papal mantle, and the authority of the church councils had grown, as they attempted and ultimately succeeded in resolving this crisis. Now, in the aftermath of this affair, the conciliar movement and the learned clerics who supported it were only more vehement in their assertion of power.

Several masters of the university who played important roles at the Council of Basel, promoting the prerogatives of learned clerics in the church, had recently played important roles at Joan's trial in Rouen, where they had articulated similar positions. Jean Beaupère, a principal interrogator at the trial, argued that the church is composed of two bodies, a political body, which was to be identified with the pope, and a mystical body, which is to be identified with the council, and that this mystical body, duly formed, was prevented by a special divine grace from erring.[15] Thomas de Courcelles, one of the authors of the final version of the transcripts of Joan's trial, similarly maintained that the church was composed of two bodies, one of which included both clerics and laypersons and one of which included only clerics. He affirmed, "It is to the second that it pertains to enlighten, to direct, to correct the first. It cannot err. . . . It is to it that has been given the exercise of power over all the faithful and over the pope himself."[16] Courcelles cited Matt. 18:17, in which Christ says to his followers, about a wayward member of the church, "If he does not listen to the church, let him be to you as a pagan and a publican," and he glosses this passage by explaining, "It is as if he said, 'if someone does not listen to the Council.'"[17] In the course of one confrontation with Joan, a cleric, identified in one manuscript as Nicolas Midi, a professor of theology at the University of Paris and a conciliarist at Basel, is reported as having also quoted Matt. 18:17 and as having also explained that "the church" in this passage was to be interpreted as the group of learned clerics participating in the trial (332). The clerics at Basel identified themselves with "the church" and condemned Pope Eugene IV as a heretic in large part because he refused them the recognition that they felt was their due, just as the clerics at Rouen had identified themselves with "the church" and condemned Joan as a heretic largely for refusing them that same recognition. The masters of the university strengthened themselves not only by bonding together as a closed and elite caste and by identifying that caste with the mystical church but by condemning any one who seemed to deny that identification, whether a pope or an accused heretic.

Priding themselves on their educations, the clerics prided themselves on a way of thinking inculcated by that education. The Faculty of Arts, which served as a gateway to the more advanced faculties, ensured that all of the students who passed through its doors were familiar with the processes of dialectical reasoning. The students were schooled, for example, in the *principium contradictionis*, which holds that "it is impossible for something to be at the same time and in the same meaning A and not A."[18] With this maxim in mind, students were encouraged to define the relations between different entities, be they theological doctrines or canonical rules, to uncover apparent contradictions between these entities, and to resolve these contradictions through the scholastic processes of division, distinction, and definition. Anders Piltz has suggested that the preparation medieval university students received in such dialectical processes made them think in distinctive ways. He writes, "Training in logic results in awareness of contradictions and obscurities in both speech and thought.... Such discoveries will lead to intellectual discontent and a strong desire to find out whether the contradictions are irreconcilable or whether they can be ironed out in some way or another."[19] Medieval scholastics, like those who participated in Joan's trial, when faced with loose sequences of items, were accustomed to reconfigure those items so that they stood in definite, meaningful relation to each other. They were prepared to think, if one can employ a syntactical term in a conceptual context, "hypotactically" rather than "paratactically." It is this logical manner of thought, which resists all vagueness, all randomness, and all unexplained juxtaposition, that distinguished the clerics from those social groups that had not enjoyed university schooling.

One can apprehend the effects of this logical training upon the clerics' evaluation of Joan in the *libelle d'Estivet*. The clerics wrote of Joan's native land, "Near the said village of Domrémy is a great, big, and antique tree, commonly called *l'arbre charmine faee de Bourlemont*, and near this tree is a spring. Around them are said to gather evil spirits called fairies, in French, *faees*" (197). The clerics referred to the tree in the vernacular as "the enchanting [*charmine*] Fairy Tree of Bourlémont," as it appears to have been called in Domrémy, where they sent emissaries to collect information about Joan. With this phrase, they acknowledged not only the connection between the tree and the Bourlémonts, an aristocratic family recently of this region on whose property the tree was located, but also the connection between the tree and "fairies," supernatural beings who were said to be neither angels nor devils but beings independent of the Christian angelology and, indeed, of the Christian religion altogether. Yet they also referred to this tree in Latin as "a great, big, and antique tree" near which are said to gather "evil spirits called fairies." With this last phrase, they rejected the possibility of supernatural beings who do not fit into the ordered structure of the universe suggested by scholastic Christianity. By equating *faees* with *maligni spiritus*, they equated a marvelous entity, foreign to a Christian worldview, with a diabolic entity that *is* encompassed within this worldview. The clerics went on to recount that

> Joan was accustomed to frequent the said tree and spring, most often at night, sometimes during the day, above all at the times when the divine office was being celebrated at the church, in order to be alone, and she turned around this spring and the tree in dance. Then she hung numerous garlands of different herbs and flowers on the branches of the same tree, made by her own hand, saying and singing, before and after, certain songs and incantations with certain invocations, spells, and other witchcraft. The following morning, these garlands could by no means be found in that place. (198)

In this passage, the clerics took certain actions imputed to Joan, namely, her visits to the tree and its nearby spring, her fashioning of garlands and placing them on the tree, her dancing and singing in this vicinity, and they connected these actions causally to the tree and the tree's fairy namesakes. Joan came to the tree, wove the garlands, danced and sang, the clerics suggested, because of the fairies associated with the tree. Her garlands were offerings, her dancing venerations, and her utterances incantations, invocations, and spells. In interpreting the fairy ladies as demons and Joan's practices as demon worship, the clerics showed their tendency to relate the various elements of an account to each other, to reconcile apparent discrepancies between them, and to provide causal explanations for the links between them.

The clerics not only relied upon dialectical reasoning in their approach to Joan's childhood rites but they expected Joan to rely upon that process as well. They conceded that the community in which Joan was raised was not conducive to the development of an exclusively orthodox spirituality. They acknowledged that "a great, big, and antique tree" and a spring were located near Domrémy, that evil spirits were said to gather by this tree and spring, and that "those who use spells are accustomed to dance at night, all around the said tree and spring" (197). With these words, they recognized that when Joan was a child, she lived within a certain environment that existed well before she did, both geographically, with its "great, big, and antique tree," and culturally, with its tradition of witchcraft "since antiquity." They further acknowledged of Domrémy and its neighboring towns, "Several inhabitants of these villages have been observed since antiquity to use witchcraft" (196), and of Joan's education in these environs,

> The said Joan in her youth was not entirely educated or instructed in the belief or the essential principles of the faith, but by some old women was accustomed to and steeped in the use of spells, divinations, and other superstitious works or magic arts.... And from several people and especially from her godmother, the said Joan says to have heard many things about visions and apparitions of fairies or spirits of fairies, in French *faees;* and by others she was educated and steeped in evil and pernicious errors about these spirits. (196)

The clerics thus recognized that, having been raised in a particular environment, Joan was led to share the religious beliefs and practices of that environment. By asserting that Joan "was not entirely educated or instructed [*non fuit edocta nec instructa*]" in Christianity but, on the contrary, "was accustomed to and steeped [*assuefacta et imbuta ... fuit*]" in various magical arts and "was educated and steeped [*erudita ... et imbuta fuit*]" in various errors, they described Joan's training in a passive voice that admitted her powerlessness, as a child, in having been deprived of a full Christian education and in having been exposed, instead, to diabolical practices. At the same time, however, they depicted Joan as so imbued with evil and pernicious misconceptions that "she confessed judicially... that... she did not know whether these fairies were evil spirits" (196). They shifted from depicting Joan's onetime education in error, passively and even innocently received, to depicting her current belief in error, actively and culpably expressed. During her interrogations, they appear to have inquired whether her godmother who claimed to have seen fairy ladies by the tree had actually done so, whether the feverish who went to drink from the spring in order to be cured actually did recuperate, and whether the fairy ladies were evil spirits. By asking her these questions, the clerics indicated that though Joan as a child might have been passive in hearing and absorbing the tales of her godmother and other old women, eventually she should have become active in examining and evaluating them. At a certain point, they suggest, she should have perceived the contradiction between fairy ladies and Christianity, should have realized that the reputedly benign *faees* were in fact evil spirits, and should have repudiated the "spells, divinations, and other superstitious works of magic arts" devoted to these beings. Joan should have made the transition from a childish acceptance of the views of one's immediate environment to a more adult skepticism toward that environment, they intimated.

By asking Joan to distance herself from her native community and to pass judgment upon its members, the clerics ask her to undergo a process that was identified with adolescence in the Middle Ages, as it continues to be identified today. In answer to those who might reject the concept of adolescence as anachronistic in the Middle Ages, Donald Weinstein and Rudolph M. Bell conclude, after examining the patterns of medieval saints' lives, that "not merely a transitional phase between childhood and adulthood, nor a period of sexual limbo between puberty and marriage, the years between eleven and seventeen came to be understood as a time for self-discovery and commitment, regularly described in the sources as a period characterized by both internal conflict and family contest."[20] The lives of several of the most popular saints of the later Middle Ages, from the early Christian martyrs to Francis of Assisi and Thomas Aquinas, reflect this pattern of "family contest" to which Weinstein and Bell allude. These saints defied social expectations, they broke, radically and disruptively, with their environments, and they incurred the wrath of those around them. Yet according to the clerics, though Joan should have made the transition from childish passivity to adolescent activity by exchanging the heterodox beliefs and practices of her community for their more orthodox counterparts, she in fact did the contrary. If she separated herself from her community, it was not in order to withdraw from the ceremonies at the tree and spring but in order to withdraw from the ceremonies at the church and, hence, not to become less superstitious but to become more so. Like a saint raised in a pious family who at adolescence might make an independent profession of Christianity, the Joan of the *libelle d'Estivet*, raised in a historically heterodox community, made an individual profession of diabolism. The clerics implied that Joan should have perceived the contradiction between a belief in the fairy ladies and a belief in Christianity and should have rejected her rites by the Fairy Tree in favor of Christian ceremonies, and in so doing they showed that she failed to perceive the contradiction between these beliefs and failed to reject these rites.

Domrémy

The village of Domrémy, which the clerics characterized so unfavorably in the *libelle d'Estivet*, remained relatively peaceful and prosperous during the first decades of the fifteenth century. Its southern region, overlooking the solidly Burgundian Lorraine across the Meuse River, belonged to the duchy of Bar, whose duke vacillated between the Burgundian and the Armagnac parties, while its northern region, which encompassed the house of Joan's parents, belonged to the castellany of Vaucouleurs, a direct possession of the French crown and, by the 1420s, the only fortified Armagnac city north of the Loire Valley aside from Mont-Saint-Michel. On occasion, the children of Domrémy who attended school across the river returned home bloodied from fights with their Burgundian classmates, and in July 1428, when Joan was sixteen, she and her neighbors had to take refuge in nearby Neufchâteau for two weeks in order to avoid Burgundian attack. The sufferings these villagers endured as a result of the war were, nevertheless, nowhere near the same level as those experienced by peasants in more central parts of the realm.[21] Here, in Joan's native land, the farmers continued to harvest their oats, wheat, rye, and hay and to graze their cattle and sheep on the hills surrounding the town. Here, Joan and other girls of her class continued to spin, sew, and occupy themselves with other household duties, hearing about the troubles of more central areas of the realm from travelers, yet only sporadically affected by these troubles themselves.

Politically and economically stable during the years of Joan's childhood, Domrémy was for the most part culturally conservative as well, and even, for some, too conservative. Though historians from Johan Huizinga to Richard Kiekhefer have remarked on the importance of meditations on the inevitability of death, the likelihood of eternal suffering, and the imminence of the apocalypse in late-medieval spirituality, neither Joan, in her responses to interrogations at her trial, nor the villagers, in their testimony at the rehabilitation, alluded to these recent spiritual tendencies.[22] As Francis Rapp has discussed, it was not images of *danses macabres*, processions of flagellants, or distributions of indulgences but, rather, church bells calling the peasants to kneel down to pray in the fields, like the figures of Jean-François Millet's *Angelus*, that distinguished Domrémy's religious life.[23] The names of the Virgin Mary and Jesus Christ, not of newly canonized saints such as Catherine or Bernardino of Siena, figured on a ring that Joan received from her parents and on the standard that she carried into battle. Despite this conventionality, Joan recalled during her interrogations that "when she came to her king, some people asked her if there was in her country a grove that was called, in French, *le bois chesnu*, because there were prophecies saying that from around this grove would come a maid who would accomplish marvels" (67). The people who associated Joan with this oak wood associated her with a species of tree connected, at least since the writings of Maximus Tyrius and Pliny, with the pre-Christian rites of the Gauls.[24] They associated her in particular with the prophecy in Geoffrey of Monmouth's *Historia regum Brittaniae* that "from an oak grove a maid will be sent to remedy certain ills through her curing art" and hence with Merlin — a sorcerer, druid, even a pagan god in some accounts — who was said to have uttered this prophecy.[25] To identify Joan with this maid from the oak grove is to identify her not with the current, dominant, Christian ethos but with an older, repressed, and marginalized culture. Joan dismissed the importance of this prophecy in her interrogations, yet the clerics continued to suspect she had links to a pagan past.

Joan did not attend the school across the Meuse, nor does she seem to have received any formal instruction from a priest or other literate person. During her interrogation, she claimed to have learned the Our Father, the Hail Mary, and the Creed from her mother, and testimony at the rehabilitation suggested that she had learned the Ten Commandments as well. When Joan replied to the clerics' inquiry as to whether she knew herself to be in a state of grace by averring, " 'If I am not, let God put me there, and if I am, let God keep me there' " (62), she echoed and thus revealed her knowledge of a parish prayer of similar phraseology.[26] In addition to these prayers, she no doubt absorbed the sermons delivered at the masses she frequently attended and the counsels given at the confessions she frequently made. No reading of texts appears to have enriched her knowledge — she told her examiners at Poitiers, " 'I know neither A nor B' " — nor does she seem to have acquired anything but the general, pastoral education available to most peasant girls.[27] Given Joan's lack of schooling, the clerics at her trial never ceased to juxtapose their learning with her ignorance in an effort to persuade her to heed their admonitions rather than her own conscience. Cauchon described the assistants as "very learned men experienced in divine and human law" (189), in contrast to Joan, who was "not...sufficiently learned and instructed in letters and such difficult matters" (189) and, later, as "lettered and knowledgeable men" (328), in contrast to "a woman unlettered and ignorant of Scripture" (328). Pierre Maurice portrayed the university to which the assistants belonged as "the light of all the sciences and the uprooter of errors" (381) because its doctors "know the law of God and Holy Scripture" (381), in contrast to Joan, who was marked by "[her] state and the simplicity of [her] knowledge" (381). According to the clerics, whereas they were "learned [*docti*]" and "very learned [*perdocti*]," Joan was "not sufficiently learned [*non...satis docta*]." Whereas they were "lettered [*licterati*]," Joan was "unlettered [*illicterata*]." Whereas they knew "the law of God and Holy Scripture [*legem Dei et sacram Scripturam noverunt*]," she was "ignorant of Scripture [*ignorans Scripturas*]." If the clerics had consolidated as a class defined by its university education and its skill at dialectical reasoning, Joan represented the untrained, unlettered, illogical populace against which they had consolidated themselves.

When Joan responded to the clerics' questions about the fairy tree, she revealed the difference between her thinking and that of her examiners. To begin with, Joan did not identify the fairy ladies with demons as the clerics did. She said, in response to their questions, "fairly near the village of Domrémy is a tree called the Ladies' Tree. Others call it the Fairies' Tree, in French, *faees*" (65). In referring to "the Ladies' Tree" and "the Fairies' Tree," Joan did not reject the customary names for this tree, as did the clerics when they spoke of "evil spirits called fairies, in French, *faees*," and thus did not correct the false, positive term *faees* with the true, negative term "evil spirits." She did not indicate clearly that though fairy ladies might seem to be beautiful and endearing beings beneficent to mankind, she recognized they were foul and repulsive demons striving to lead this race to damnation, or that though the fairy ladies might seem to be independent of the Christian angelology, and indeed of the Christian religion altogether, she knew such independence to be impossible. Instead, when the clerics later asked if the fairy ladies were evil spirits, she went so far as to reply that "she knows nothing about it" (169). Nor did Joan identify the festivities pursued in the vicinity of the tree with the fairy ladies and, hence, with demons, as the clerics did. She recounted,

Sometimes she went to take a walk with other girls, and she made near the tree crowns of flowers for the image of Our Lady of Domrémy.... She saw young girls put garlands on the branches of the tree, and she herself sometimes put them there with other girls.... And she does not know, after she had discernment, if she danced near this tree, but she could have danced there sometimes with children, and she sang there more than she danced. (65–66)

In this midst of this narrative, Joan stated, "Several times she heard from old people who were not of her family that the fairy ladies gathered there. And she heard from a woman named Jeanne, the wife of the mayor Aubéry, in French, *du maire Aubery,* of this village, who was godmother to she, Joan, who is speaking, that she had seen the fairy ladies there" (66). Joan asserted that she and other young girls undertook various festivities in the environs of the tree, that fairy ladies were said to assemble in its vicinity, and that her godmother claimed to have seen them there, but she made no connection between her festivities and the fairy ladies. Even though they were performed in the region associated with the fairy ladies, these walks, these weavings, these dances and songs were depicted not as acts of devotion to these spirits but, rather, as activities pleasurable in and of themselves. The garlands were not for the spirits of the tree but, rather, for Our Lady of Domrémy. The dances were not "around [*circa*]" the tree but, rather, "near [*iuxta*]" it, so that the tree was not the focus but, rather, the background of these dances. The tree and its spring were "enchanting [*charmine*]" in the secondary sense of the word: they were beautiful, delightful, and inspiring of happiness. The hypotaxis of the clerics' account, which connected the festivities and the fairy ladies and perceived the festivities as idolatrous because of this connection, is replaced by the parataxis of Joan's account, which juxtaposed the festivities and the fairy ladies but named no connection between them. Because Joan's thinking was paratactic, she accepted the coexistence of multiple elements without attempting to define their interrelations. She did not seek, and therefore did not find, a contradiction between them. The point is not that Joan did or did not revere demons but, rather, that the clerics, in submitting Joan's paratactic thinking to hypotaxis and in making connections where she did not, redefined her childhood activities as devil worship.

Joan represented herself as having distanced herself from the fairy ladies at adolescence, as the clerics felt she should have done, yet she did not do so for the reasons the clerics expected should have guided her. Even during the trial, when the clerics asked if the feverish truly recovered when they drank from the spring, if her godmother truly saw the fairy ladies by the tree, and if the fairy ladies were evil spirits, she replied that "she knows nothing about it" (65, 66, 169). With these claims to ignorance, she refused to step back from her fellow villagers and to pass judgment upon them. Though Joan did not depict herself as ever condemning the festivities around the tree, she did nonetheless depict herself as withdrawing from them and as developing the adolescent's sense of difference, separation, and even alienation from her community as a result of this withdrawal. She affirmed, as we recall, that she may have lessened her involvement in these activities "after she had discernment" (66) and that "after she knew that she must come to France, she took little part in the games and walks and the least she could" (66). In these passages, Joan showed that at a certain stage in her development, she had renounced the recreations in which she had once participated, not because she recognized the devilish nature of the fairy ladies but because she learned she "must come to France" or because she acquired "discernment." If Joan did cease to frequent this tree and to engage in the merriment surrounding it, as she claimed that she did, it was not the diabolic seriousness that the clerics perceived in these activities but the juvenile lack of seriousness that she perceived in them that repelled her. Weinstein and Bell argue in their study of medieval saints that the medieval people associated childhood with "a time of self-indulgence and relatively harmless frivolity," from which the saintly child retires early, and it was in this spirit that Joan retired early from the festivities by the Fairy Tree.[28]

Though Joan depicted herself as having separated herself from the fairy ladies, she did not indicate that she had relied upon the process of dialectical reasoning that the clerics expected should have assisted her. The shift identified with Joan's adolescence, if one can use that term, involved not a movement from error to truthfulness or from heterodoxy to orthodoxy but a movement from childish games to mature endeavors. It involved not a rejection of her childhood community but a progression beyond it. Given the nature of this shift, the manner in which Joan withdrew from the festivities around the fairy ladies' tree was not dramatic. When she stated that "she took little part in the games and walks and the least she could," she suggested that though she would have liked to retire entirely from these games and walks, she was able only to diminish her participation and to take "little part" in them. By contrasting that which she would have liked to have done and that which she was able to do, Joan contrasted an external, social pressure to participate in these games with an internal, private desire not to do so. She contrasted not only her community, which supported these activities, and her self, which resisted them, but her outer behavior, which continued to conform somewhat to the expectations of her community, and her inner desire, which had diverged from these expectations. Joan did not openly defy her environment but, instead, reduced, without eliminating, her participation in village rites. She depicted the alienation from one's native surroundings, the split between an external, social identity and an internal, private identity, and the creation of a solitary consciousness that we continue to identify with adolescence, yet without the ruptures and the violence often associated with this stage. Her behavior in general agreed with the tendency that Caroline Walker Bynum observes in medieval saintly girls to seek continuity rather than rupture in their progress toward holiness.[29] Joan's mediation of public expectation and private desire reflected not an oppositional manner of thinking, which, when faced with multiple elements, seeks out and resolves contradictions among them, but a sequential manner of thinking, which links one term to another without attempting to detect or reconcile differences.

The villagers who testified at the rehabilitation trial spoke of the fairy tree much as Joan did and, in doing so, reinforced the impression of the aggregative nature of her thought. To begin with, the villagers too identified the tree near where they live with the fairy ladies. Most of them stated simply, as Joan did, that "the tree is called the Fairies' Tree" or "the tree is called the Ladies' Tree," without any attempt to disassociate themselves from the heterodox implications of these names. Only Simonin Musnier, who acknowledged that he had heard that "those commonly called *fées*" collected under this tree, added that "he has never seen any sign of evil spirits," though it is not entirely clear that he himself equated these fairies with evil spirits.[30] Like Joan, the villagers treated the fairy ladies as a third category of supernatural beings, neither angelic nor demonic, neither inside nor outside Christianity, neither to be venerated, as one venerated God and his saints, nor to be abhorred, as one abhorred the devil and his minions, but to be accepted as one accepted the tree and the spring themselves, as part of the landscape. The villagers also stated that the young people of Domrémy took part in festivities in the vicinity of this tree. On the fourth Sunday of Lent, when "Laetare Jerusalem" was sung in the church, they reported, the girls and boys gathered by the tree to *faire leurs fontaines*.[31] Under the branches of this tree, they sang carols, danced rounds, collected flowers, and ate rolls their mothers had baked for them, and on their return from the tree, they stopped by the *fontaine aux Rains* and drank water from it. In addition to participating in this annual rite, the villagers related, the young people frequented this tree and the nearby stream in the spring and summer in order to entertain themselves. Yet, again like Joan, the villagers declined to connect the fairy ladies associated with the tree with the festivities around it, much less to depict the fairy ladies as the focus of these rites. Instead, Jean Morel, Jean Moen, and Isabelle d'Epinal suggested that the young people went there "in order to have a walk and to amuse themselves."[32] Dominique Jacob praised the great beauty of the tree and stated that its beauty "is the reason for which, as he believes, girls and boys willingly go under it to dance."[33] It was the chance for diversion and delight, not for witchcraft and demon worship, that drew the young people to this site. Like Joan, the villagers revealed paratactic rather than hypotactic thinking that allowed for the simple coexistence of both a Fairy Tree and a Christian God and of both festivities in the vicinity of this tree and ceremonies in a church instead of insisting upon defining a relation between these two sets of entities and reconciling any contradictions between them.

The villagers shared and thus reinforced the character of Joan's thought about the fairy ladies, yet they also helped situate this thought within a particular cultural context. Unlike Joan, who used the present tense in describing the fairy ladies' visits to the tree and who cited her own godmother's claims to have seen these creatures, her former neighbors invariably employed the past tense in speaking of these visitations and invariably denied that they knew anyone who had seen these beings. Hauviette, the wife of Gérard de Syonne, reported of the Ladies' Tree, for example, that "it was said formerly that ladies called *fées* went to this tree. All the same, she never heard that anyone ever saw them."[34] Jean Waterin related, similarly, that "he heard that formerly women, ordinarily called *fées,* went under this tree. All the same, he never heard said that anyone saw them under this tree."[35] Beatrice Estellin provided an explanation for the fairy ladies' disappearance when she testified that "she heard that earlier the fairies, in French, the *fées,* went under this tree, but, because of their sins, . . . they do not now go there any more."[36] This connection between the fairy ladies' departure and "sins," presumably the sins of the human beings whom they once used to visit, recalls a pattern in French fairy tales, romances, and lays where fairies unite with mortal men on the condition that their mates respect a particular rule, where the men cannot help but break this rule despite the benefits they enjoy as a result of these unions, and where the fairies then depart, as they had threatened.[37] In all of these accounts, fairies constitute beautiful but elusive beings who withdraw from us because of our failings.

The villagers helped situate Joan's thoughts within particular social and literary, as well as cultural, contexts. Numerous witnesses testified that before the Bourlémonts died off in 1412 and before their castle on an island in the Meuse fell into disrepair, the lords and ladies of the household would visit this site in the company of their servants and some of the young girls from the village. Jeannette, the widow of Thiesselin de Vittel, added that "the tree in question is called 'the Ladies' Tree' because it is said that, formerly, a lord named Pierre Gravier, knight, lord of Bourlémont, and a certain lady who was called *Fée* visited each other under the tree and spoke together there. And she said that she heard this read in a romance."[38] In Jeannette's anecdote, the "ladies" of the Ladies' Tree were no longer supernatural beings but noblewomen, their elevated status no longer mythical but social, and the word "fairy" no longer a generic term for certain ethereal creatures but the proper name for one such person. Here, the enchantment associated with the tree reflected not so much the charm associated with fairies as the courtly love associated with aristocrats. The nostalgia with which fairy ladies were recalled resonated with the nostalgia with which courtly love was remembered, as far back as the period when it was thought to have been invented. Even in the twelfth century, for example, the heroine of Marie de France's lay "Yonec" describes courtly love as a past phenomenon that no longer occurs. She states, "I have often heard tell that in this country one used to encounter adventures which relieved those afflicted by care: knights discovered maidens to their liking, noble and fair, and ladies found handsome and courtly lovers, worthy and valiant men."[39] Even at that time, when Arthurian literature was first being transcribed, the fine days of Camelot and its courtly customs were already being portrayed as something long past and sorely missed. If both Joan and the villagers perceived recognition of fairy ladies and of the Christian faith as compatible, Jeannette's tracing of the fairy legends to a romance helps locate this pattern of thought within a specific genre.

Joan's and her neighbors' utterances recall romance not only thematically but structurally as well. The literary works that fall into this category portray a world where enchanted woods and fairy ladies coexist with chapels and hermits, where knights employ magical weapons and hear mass in the morning, and where the line between the human and the superhuman is not always fixed. They depict a universe dominated by mythology rather than theology, where elements from disparate codes, which would clash irreconcilably in a Latinate, logically developed system, appear together in harmony. Though Joan's paratactic manner of

thinking can be identified wholly no more with the system of thought inherent in romance than with any one system of thought, the "matter of
Britain" does suggest one context outside the university where her manner of reasoning does prevail.

Any evaluation of Joan's relationship to an alleged residual stratum of
pagan religiosity in her village society must take into consideration the
two sides that fifteenth-century sources take on this issue. On the one
hand, Joan did confess to having participated in festivities near the Fairy
Tree and did quickly become connected with folkloric beliefs through the
legends that soon circulated about her. On the night of Epiphany 1412,
the cocks of her village were said to have crowed for two hours to announce her birth and the neighbors to have run to each other for an explanation of the inexplicable joy they felt at that time.⁴⁰ There was an oak
wood not far from her father's house, so that she could legitimately be
said to have come from such a mythologically potent site. Joan was said
to be capable not only of calling birds to her lap but also of causing but-
terflies to swirl around her standard, finding lost silver cups, and unmask-
ing concubinary priests. Not least among her apparently marvelous tal-
ents was her ability, though a maid, to comport herself admirably as a
captain-at-arms and even to bring about a reversal of the fortunes of the
Armagnac party. On the other hand, despite village rites linked to fairy
ladies in which she acknowledged having joined and despite accounts of
her life presenting her as somewhat of a fairy lady herself, Joan consistently
situated herself within a Christian register. As we have seen, she dismissed
the relevance of the prophecy about the maid from the oak wood. She
claimed to hear voices not from fairy ladies or other mythological beings
but from God and, later, from saints and angels recognized by the church.
She differed sharply from Catherine de La Rochelle, a married woman who
attached herself to the Armagnac entourage and who alleged she had experienced nocturnal visions of a fairylike "white lady" (104), in her own
insistence upon an exclusively Christian counsel. Though Joan denied
knowing whether fairy ladies were evil spirits, she made clear that there
were certain folk beliefs that she associated with witchcraft and that she
repudiated for that reason. When the clerics inquired about those who
travel with fairies, in French, who go "*en l'erre avec les fees*," for example,
Joan declared that "that is nothing but witchcraft" (178). When they
asked if her godmother was reputed to be a wisewoman, Joan retorted
that she was a worthy woman and not "a soothsayer or a witch" (168). In
addition to these Catholic responses, Joan further demonstrated her ortho-

doxy in her requests to hear mass on the first day of the trial at Rouen, to receive Easter communion later that spring, and finally, to receive last rites on her sickbed. She may have sung and danced near the Fairy Tree, yet her attachment to Christian figures proved ultimately far more influential in her later career than that to these folkloric beings.

Critics have responded to the mixture of fairy ladies and angels, of oak trees and Christian sacraments in the pages of the transcripts of Joan's trial in different ways, yet I would argue that they have always accepted the clerics' assumption of an opposition between these categories. In 1921, the British Egyptologist Margaret Alice Murray affirmed that Joan was a practitioner of the "old religion" of Europe, which she maintained still survived during the fifteenth century and was about to become the focus of the witch persecutions of the early modern age; she even went so far as to declare that Joan was the "incarnate God" of this Dianic cult.[41] Norman Cohn has argued, against Murray's claim of the persistence of an "old religion" at such a late date, that the fantastic elements that appear so regularly in the confessions of accused witches prove that these avowals reflect less the actual religious rites of these persons than the projected fantasies of their interrogators. Jeffrey Burton Russell has stressed, in opposition to Murray's identification of Joan with ancient practices, that though Joan was initially accused of crimes related to witchcraft, such as devil worship and sorcery, these charges were abandoned as the trial progressed, so that she was burned exclusively as a heretic.[42] More recently, Carlo Ginzburg has defended what he sees as a "kernel of truth" in Murray's argument, though he has not extended his reaffirmation of a pagan substratum of belief in early modern Europe to the documents of Joan's case.[43] Though Murray and her refuters have tended to take extreme positions, arguing that a pre-Christian religion did or did not persist into the early modern era and that Joan did or did not belong to it, other authors have taken more nuanced views. Rapp has stressed the testimony from the rehabilitation trial that on the eve of Ascension, the priest would carry the cross to the Fairy Tree and sing the Gospel underneath its branches. He interprets this ritual as an act of exorcism, ultimately successful in banishing these alleged demons from the minds of the local populace. Madeleine Jeay, in contrast, reads this priest as attempting less to expel the fairy ladies than to co-opt their popular appeal by incorporating the tree with which they are linked into a Christian ceremony.[44] Whereas Rapp views the fairy ladies of Domrémy as increasingly overshadowed by the Virgin Mary, increasingly marginalized, and increasingly forgotten during the years between Joan's original trial and the rehabilitation, Jeay sees these supernatural beings, in their connection to the traditional cycles of the seasons and the human body, as ultimately holding sway over the more abstract concepts of Christianity. For Murray and Russell, the question of the fairy ladies is whether Joan was or was not a witch; for Rapp and Jeay, it is the more subtle question of to what extent Domrémy was dominated by popular myth and to what extent by Christian doctrine. Here, I have attempted to reframe this discussion by suggesting that to accept this polarization of the fairy ladies and the Christian God, as do Murray and Russell, or even the opposition of these two sets of supernatural beings, as do Rapp and Jeay, is to accept implicitly the clerics' view that these two sets are irreconcilable.

A close reading of the trial transcripts reveals that though Joan may have shown herself to be less willing to condemn the fairy ladies as demons than were the clerics, what she really believed was neither a purely folkloric legend nor a purely Christian doctrine but a creed that did not recognize these structures as antagonistic. For Joan, as for her former neighbors who testified at her rehabilitation, there were legends about fairy ladies and there were Christian doctrines about Jesus Christ and the Virgin Mary. The two beliefs did not contradict each other. For the clerics, the coexistence of fairy ladies and God as autonomous supernatural beings was a logical impossibility for a Christian who recognized, as Joan should have recognized, that all supernatural beings are subordinated to the one, true God. When the clerics censured Joan for her failure to perceive fairy ladies as evil spirits, what they were really censuring her for was her failure to compare a belief in fairy ladies with a belief in Christianity, her failure to perceive the discrepancies between these two beliefs, and her failure to reinterpret fairy ladies as evil spirits on account of those discrepancies. Though nominally condemning her for superstition, sorcery, and devil worship, what they were really condemning her for was her lack of university training.

2 | The Voices from God

During the late Middle Ages, when Joan claimed to hear voices speak to her, women visionaries were increasingly prominent in religious life.[1] Between the twelfth and the thirteenth centuries, the rate of women among those canonized doubled from 11.8 to 22.6 percent and, during the fourteenth and fifteenth centuries, stabilized at 25 and 23 percent, only to decline in subsequent years.[2] This shift in figures can be attributed primarily to a shift in the identification of sanctity from those who exhibited holiness in ruling an outer kingdom, bishopric, or monastery, who were normally upper-class and male, to those who exhibited holiness in ruling an inner self, who could be middle- or even lower-class and female. As inner experience became an ever more important determinant of saintliness, supernatural states of mind, including the hearing of voices and the seeing of visions, came to be ever more valued, and women showed themselves particularly blessed with these gifts. In their statistical survey of saints from 1000 to 1700, Weinstein and Bell find extraordinary powers to be twice as common among female saints as among their male counterparts. Some women visionaries, such as Clare of Assisi, Angela of Foligno, and Catherine of Siena, were affiliates of the new Franciscan and Dominican orders, responding to the same appeal of the mendicant life that men were also finding so powerful at this time. Others, such as Marie d'Oignies, Hade-wijch of Brabant, and Mechthild of Magdeburg, were beguines, or women who pursued a religious life without taking formal vows.[3] Several visionaries, however, were simply *beatas,* or holy women, sometimes laywomen who wandered about in the world, like Bridget of Sweden or Margery Kempe, and sometimes anchoresses who enclosed themselves within church or cathedral walls, like Julian of Norwich or Dorothy of Montau. In France, during the course of the Great Schism, as André Vauchez has demonstrated, a few visionaries of this latter, eremetical variety claimed the ability to prophesy and sought out the king in order to inform him of that which they knew, thus foreshadowing Joan's own actions a few years later.[4] Jeanne-Marie de Maillé, a recluse living on the grounds of a Franciscan convent in Tours, announced the election of a Franciscan pope who would end the Schism and traveled to Charles VI to advise him of this and other matters. Marie Robine, otherwise known as Marie the Gascon, a hermit residing in a cemetery in Avignon, also experienced visions about the Schism and also journeyed to the French court to offer her counsel. At Joan's rehabilitation, it was said that Marie had once had a vision in which she beheld a mass of weapons and, fearful lest she was intended to assume them, to have heard a voice reassuring her that they were meant for another maid.[5] With spiritual life increasingly centered around inner experience and the charismatic gifts that developed out of that experience, women, whether tertiaries, beguines, or ordinary laywomen, increasingly appeared to exemplify the current models of sanctity.

These women visionaries aroused admiration and even veneration among the people, but they also sparked suspicion in the church. Though the cleries at times served as advisers of their spiritual lives, transcribers of their visions, and promoters of their canonizations, they at times remained wary of an authority grounded in revelation rather than reason. Caroline Walker Bynum writes of the development of a distinctly feminine, mystical spirituality in the late Middle Ages: "Women's religious role ... had come to seem utterly different from man's religious role as priest, preacher, and leader by virtue of clerical office. And because it was so different, it titillated — and was both encouraged and feared."[6] Supernatural powers like those exhibited by these visionaries were inherently and dangerously ambivalent. The divine possession of which the mystic boasted, the clerics reasoned, might actually be diabolic. Her prophecies might be satanically inspired and her miracles the result of sorcery. Her levitations might be a form of night flying and her stigmata the marks of incubi. Though her remarkable abilities might be attributed to divine favor, they might also be attributed to witchcraft.[7] Even if the visionary were judged not to be possessed by the devil, she might still be deluded in her perceptions, whether because of illness, madness, or frenzy, or she still might be lying about these visions in order to gain fame, esteem, and influence. Anxious about the many possible origins of such claims to revelations, clerics penned treatises on the methods of distinguishing true from false visions and submitted mystics to investigations based upon these treatises to establish the truth of their claims. As a result, the beguines, already ridiculed by vernacular authors as hypocrites, were accused of adhering to the Heresy of the Free Spirit and of engaging in the antinominian rites associated with that creed. Though never officially suppressed, they were condemned by the Council of Vienne in 1311 and soon lost their original independence and vitality. Both Catherine of Siena and Bridget of Sweden, before ultimately being approved by the church, were subjected to extensive inquiries and even opposition during their lifetimes and afterward.[8] If Joan asserted that she heard voices and if she found herself subjected to clerical investigation because of this assertion, her experience mirrored that of other women mystics at this time, however much, as we shall see, what she heard differed from what her contemporaries beheld.[9]

In interrogating Joan about her voices, the clerics appeared merely to seek the truth about these voices and, in particular, about whether they were divine, diabolic, or delusory, yet their quest was not always innocent in its outcome. In order to ascertain who these voices were, the clerics repeatedly asked Joan to identify them and then to explain how she made that identification. In doing so, however, they made an assumption that truth can be attained only by those who are precise, analytical, and objective, an assumption that derived from their university training and that remained foreign to Joan's nonacademic heritage. As we saw in chapter 1 how the clerics' scholastic background influenced their reading of Joan's participation in village rites, we shall see in this chapter how that same background influenced their reading of her encounter with the voices. Far from merely eliciting a representation of Joan's visionary perceptions, the clerics relied upon their learned presuppositions about what such experience must be to help construct what they were willing to recognize as the truth of her perceptions.

Saints and Angels

Since the birth of modern Johannic scholarship in the midnineteenth century, it has generally been agreed that Joan identified the voices that inspired her with Saint Catherine of Alexandria, Saint Margaret of Antioch, and Saint Michael the Archangel, and to a far more minor extent, with Saint Gabriel the Archangel, yet the overwhelming majority of the witnesses who testified at Joan's rehabilitation and the authors who recounted her feats in their chronicles depicted Joan as claiming to be guided not by individual saints but by God himself.[10] The knight Raoul de Gaucourt, who was present when Joan first appeared before the court, recalled her telling the king, " 'I have come and am sent on the part of God to bring help to you and to the kingdom.' "[11] Jean, the duke of Alençon and one of Joan's closest comrades-in-arms, remembered being informed while he was out hunting that a maid had arrived at court "declaring herself sent on the part of God to put the English to flight and to lift the siege set by them before the city of Orléans."[12] Most speakers said that Joan had referred to God as "God," but some also suggested that she had referred to him, along the lines of a feudal seigneur, as "my Lord," "the king of heaven," and "*messire*." If we put together these various allusions to the deity, approximately four out of five medieval depictions of Joan's celestial contact outside the transcripts of her trial state, in some combination of words, that she was sent by God to help France and thus stress not so much her inner experience of the deity as the outer effects of this experience upon the kingdom.

A few sources do employ the more subjective vocabulary of "voice" or "voices" and "counsel" or "counselors" that has come to be most associated with her heavenly communications. Seguin de Seguin, a cleric who examined Joan at Poitiers, recalled her speaking of "a voice" that came to her when she was guarding animals and taught her that God felt great pity for the people of France and that he wanted her to go to its aid.[13] Jean, the count of Dunois, the bastard son of the late duke of Orléans and another of Joan's closest companions, averred that when Joan was discouraged, she would withdraw and pray to God and that when her prayer was finished, "she would hear a voice saying to her, 'Daughter of God, go, go, go. I will be there to help you. Go.' "[14] When she heard this voice, Dunois continued, "she rejoiced greatly and wanted always to stay in this same state and, what is even more striking, in reciting the words of her voices, she became exulted in an amazing manner, lifting her eyes to heaven."[15] Jean d'Aulon, Joan's squire, quoted his former leader as speaking of "three counselors," the first of whom always resided with her, the second of whom came and went, and the third of whom deliberated with the other two.[16] Some depictions of Joan's celestial contact show her not being sent by God to France but hearing voices and receiving their counsel and, in doing so, emphasize not the external public domain of the kingdom's political situation but the internal, private domain of her spirituality, but it is a minority among them that do this.

Of the abundance of sources we possess about Joan, only a handful identify the "voices" or "counselors" who spoke with her with particular individuals, let alone with the Saints Catherine, Margaret, and Michael with whom they later become so linked, yet all who do so either were or might have been influenced by the content of the transcripts of Joan's trial. Among the witnesses who testified at the rehabilitation, only four associated her voices these figures. The mason Pierre Cusquel stated that one of the clerics at her trial pretended to be Saint Catherine in order to elicit confessions from Joan, as if she were in the habit of speaking to this saint. The priest Pierre Bouchier, the physician Guillaume de La Chambre, and the usher Jean Massieu all affirmed that Joan had invoked Saint Michael when confronted with the stake, as if she were in the habit of appealing to this angel. Yet all of these deponents spoke of Joan on the basis of contact they had with her during or after her trial. Among the chroniclers who recounted her deeds, only four, the anonymous dean of the collegiate church of Saint-Thibaut de Metz, the anonymous author of the *Miroir des femmes vertueuses,* and the Burgundian counselors Jean Le Fèvre de Saint-Remi and Georges Chastellain, associated the voices with Saint Catherine or Saint Michael, though they often confused the issue by joining them with other holy figures, such as David, the Virgin Mary, and Saint Agnes. Yet all of these chroniclers wrote more than a decade after Joan's death. Indeed, only one fifteenth-century text identified Joan's voices with Saint Catherine, Saint Margaret, and Saint Michael, exactly as the transcripts of the trial did, and did so at a relatively early date, yet here, too, the circumstances under which it was composed are telling. When the Bourgeois of Paris referred to Joan the first four times, in 1429 and 1430, he made no allusion to her contact with saints and angels. Only when he referred to her the fifth time, in 1431, did he write, "The glorious archangel Saint Michael, Saint Catherine, and Saint Margaret, and several other saints appeared to her often." In this final entry, however, the Bourgeois made clear that he had recently heard the inquisitor Jean Graverent's sermon about Joan at Saint-Martin-des-Champs and hence that he had had indirect contact with the trial manuscripts through this speech.[17] Though it is a commonplace in scholarship to speak of Joan as having heard the voices of Saint Catherine, Saint Margaret, and Saint Michael, no witness who knew Joan prior to the trial and no chronicler who wrote without probable access to information from this trial did so.

In the minutes of the first few days of Joan's interrogations during her trial at Rouen, Joan, under the influence of the clerics' questioning, moved from speaking of God to speaking of a voice, yet she still refrained from referring to individual heavenly figures. During these initial days of the proceedings, she continued to claim that she had been sent by God, as the vast majority of outside sources depicted her as doing. On January 24, the third day of the public trial, for example, she affirmed that "she came on the part of God and does not have any business here, asking that she be sent back to God from whom she had come" (57). She warned her judges to take care what they did because, as she put it, " 'I am sent on the part of God and you put yourself in great danger, in French, *en grant dangier*' " (59). With these declarations, Joan echoed the assertions attributed to her by witnesses at the rehabilitation and in the chronicles by stating that she had come or been sent "on the part of God," but now she held back from mentioning the relief of the siege of Orléans or the expulsion of the English for which she had come or been sent. Now Joan spoke of her contact with God without stressing the political purpose of that contact, perhaps because now she was speaking to Burgundians who would be opposed to that purpose. This shift from the political purpose of the mystical experience to the mystical experience in and of itself is reflected by the gradual shift from references to God to references to the voices. For whereas four out of five allusions to Joan's divine communications in the documents outside the trial are to God, in the minutes of the first three days of this process, only one out of twelve of such allusions is to him and, with the exception of a few lone references to Joan's "counsel," all the rest are to her voices. On February 22, the second day of the public trial and the first day of her interrogations, Joan related that "when she was thirteen years old, she had a voice coming from God to help her govern herself" (47) and that this voice came to her, accompanied by a light, at noon in her father's garden from the direction of the church. The focus moves from the besieged cities of France to a paternal garden and from the government of a kingdom to the government of a soul, though the voice who assists in this self-regulation still remains unnamed.

As part of this shift from God to the voices, from the public to the private, from the external to the internal, the clerics asked Joan repeatedly for further identification of her voice. Already on February 22, the second day of the public trial, Joan stated in response to an unrecorded question that "her interrogator would not have from her, at this time, in what appearance this voice appeared to her" (48). On February 24, the third day of the public trial, the minutes report that Joan was "interrogated, of the voice which she said appears to her, if it is an angel or if it is from God unmediated or if it is the voice of a saint" (60). On February 27, the fourth day of the public trial, the minutes relate that Joan was again "interrogated if it was the voice of an angel which spoke to her or if it was the voice of a saint or of God without intermediary" (71). For three days, therefore, the clerics appear to have pressed Joan for the appearance of her voice, for the form under which the voice appeared to her, or for the angelic, saintly, or divine nature of that form. They presupposed that a voice from God, like that which Joan claimed to hear, would assume a particular form and that Joan would be able to perceive, recall, and communicate that form to them. They presupposed that someone who names a vague entity, such as a "voice," must be able to detect, remember, and express the precise saintly, angelic, or divine nature of that entity. They presupposed, in other words, that reality exists with a high degree of definition and that anyone is capable of grasping and representing that definition. Indeed, if one considers the experiences of other medieval visionaries, from Hildegard of Bingen to Catherine of Siena, it is true that most identify the beings that appear to them as angels, saints, or God, so that their precedent might seem to justify the clerics' questions. Pierre Duparc has hypothesized that Joan's judges "pressured" Joan to identify her voices as saints or angels because they "probably found themselves disconcerted in front of a mysticism, inspired by God, without a handle on it. The intervention of angels or saints would permit them to operate in a more familiar world."[18] In making such demands, the clerics presupposed that their questions would merely push Joan to share with them information that she already possessed and that if she did not answer, it was because she was obstinately refusing to do so. If the clerics asked Joan to clarify the identity of her voices as angels, saints, or God himself, their demands, with their various presuppositions, may appear entirely warranted.

At first, Joan refused to identify her voices, and then she did so only reluctantly. On February 22, as we have seen, Joan refused to specify "under what form the voice appeared to her." On February 24, when asked whether the voice was an angel, a saint, or God himself, she replied, "The voice comes on the part of God, and I believe that I do not tell you entirely that which I know, and I have greater fear of failing them by saying something which displeases these voices than I have of responding to you. And, as for this question, I ask for a delay" (60). Only on February 27, after she had twice deferred answering the clerics' questions about the angelic, saintly, or divine nature of the voice, did she identify the voice, yet even then she did so with a series of self-contradictory statements. She began by stating that "the voice was that of Saint Catherine and Saint Margaret, and their faces are crowned with fair crowns, very opulent and very precious." The minutes continue,

> Interrogated which of them appeared to her first, she responded, "I did not recognize them so quickly, and I knew well once, but have forgotten, and if I had permission I would say willingly, and it was set down in the register at Poitiers." Item she also said that she had had comfort from Saint Michael. (71)

In this passage, Joan initially claimed that she did not recognize her voices soon enough to be able to know which came to her first but then stated that she did once know but had now forgotten. She conveyed that she had forgotten which voice came first, but then she asserted that she would provide the clerics with this information if she had permission to do so, as if it were still within her memory. She implied that she did not have permission to reveal this information, but then she stated that she had revealed it to the clerics who had questioned her earlier at Poitiers, as if she at least once had been at liberty to disclose it. Finally, after protesting that she could not tell the clerics which voice came to her first because she never knew, because she had once known but has now forgotten, because she now knew but did not have permission to tell them, and because she had previously told their Armagnac predecessors, presumably with permission, Joan uttered the name of Saint Michael and thus seemed to provide the information she had resisted giving all along. Even so, however, though appearing to relent to the clerics' demand, she insisted upon altering its terms, saying not that Saint Michael had appeared to her first but, rather, that "she had had comfort from Saint Michael." She thus left it unclear whether Saint Michael ever did appear to her at all or whether he had merely sent her his comfort. Through deferrals, self-contradictory protests, or ambiguous replies, Joan resisted providing the answer the clerics sought.

As the interrogation proceeded, Joan frustrated her questioners not just by what she said but by what she did not say. When the clerics asked again about the first voice to speak to her, she responded satisfactorily, affirming that Saint Michael had come to her first. Yet when they moved on to a new question, she retracted what she had just said and stated, " 'I do not name to you the voice of Saint Michael, but I speak of a great comfort' " (73). Though the clerics demanded that she inform them of the objective identity of the being who had appeared to her, she withdrew her objective identification of the voice immediately after having made it and stressed, instead, her subjective sensation of "comfort" at the moment of contact. When the clerics asked her yet a third time which voice first appeared to her, the minutes relate, "she responded that it was Saint Michael whom she saw before her eyes, and he was not alone, but was well accompanied by angels from heaven. She said also that she did not come to France except by the command of God" (73). Earlier in this dialogue, Joan had refused to limit her answer to merely identifying the voice with certain saints but, rather, had added that these saints "are crowned with fair crowns, very opulent and very precious," as if she were dissatisfied with the mere neutral naming of these beings and felt it necessary to stress their worthiness. Now she refused to limit her answer to merely affirming that Saint Michael was the first voice to have appeared to her and added, instead, that he was accompanied by angels and, even more irrelevantly, that it was only on God's orders that she came to France. When Joan did not respond to the clerics' questions with too little information, she responded with too much; whether by restraint or by excess, she refused to tailor her responses to the clerics' questions.

Though one might hold, with the clerics, that Joan resisted identifying her voices clearly and satisfactorily because she did not want to share this information with her interrogators, one might also hold that she resisted because she could not share it with them. Joan finally identified her voices as Saint Catherine, Saint Margaret, and Saint Michael only after having been requested to do so several times, only after having deferred granting these requests several times, and only after having explained, in numerous and contradictory ways, why she could not fulfill them. By finally providing the clerics with the answers they sought, she gained relief from a further repetition of the demands, but only by ceasing to depict her voices as she had depicted them in the early days of the trial and as they are represented in the documents outside these minutes. She volunteered the information that the voice came on the part of God, that the faces of the voices were crowned with opulent and precious crowns, and that she had had comfort from Saint Michael, however, not only without any delay or protest but even without having been asked for it. By interjecting such remarks into the interrogations, Joan rebelled against the strictures of the interrogation, which dictated that she speak only in response to questions, and against the strictures of the assumptions embedded within the clerics' questions, which dictated that she express her experience only in terms of these assumptions. By interjecting such remarks, she failed to satisfy the clerics' demand for answers or to gain relief from their repeated interrogations, yet she expressed herself in terms consonant with

her utterances earlier in the trial and in other documents. This juxtaposition of the two modalities of Joan's speech in the minutes of her interrogations, the one seemingly forced, the other seemingly spontaneous, indicates that Joan's ultimate naming of her voices as these three saints may
have resulted more from the clerics' suggestive questioning than from her
own understanding of the voices, particularly since no document written
prior to the transcripts of the trial shows Joan to identify her voices in
this manner. This juxtaposition may also indicate that Joan's depiction of
her voices as anonymous beings who brought her comfort when she was
distressed, who reassured her of their help when she was discouraged, and
who brought her a joy that she wanted to retain forever resulted, in contrast, from her own free avowal. We might conclude that Joan experienced her voices not as Saint Catherine, Saint Margaret, and Saint Michael
but, instead, as a comfort, and that she was forced by her interrogators'
demands to identify them with these saints.[19] Yet, even if a close reading
of the text supports this second interpretation more than the first, it too
ultimately provides only a partial explanation of the dynamic between the
interrogators and their respondent.

One cannot dismiss Joan's identification of her voices with Saint Catherine and Saint Margaret, despite the pressure the clerics imposed upon her
to do so, because though it was the clerics who insisted that Joan identify
her voice, it was Joan who decided to shift from speaking of "a voice" to
"voices" and to associate these voices with two virgin martyrs. It is important to emphasize that in the minutes of interrogation Joan never refers
to the particular legends of these saints, so it is impossible to know not
only what versions of their legends she had encountered and what aspects
of these legends appealed to her but also whether she conceived of these
figures as anything more than holy ladies. The fifteenth-century statue of
Saint Margaret that may have been in Joan's church in Domrémy when
she worshipped there represents a generic woman, undistinguished by any
iconographic markings. Nevertheless, connections between the legends of
these particular figures and Joan's own life have often been pointed out.
Saint Catherine of Alexandria and Saint Margaret of Antioch resemble
Joan in that they were virgins who emerged in public life out of obedience to the Christian God and who, despite their youth, their gender, and
their lack of familial or social support, became powerful in their societies.[20]
When fifty philosophers attempted to convert Saint Catherine to paganism, she defeated them with arguments so convincing that she converted
them all to Christianity and became, for this display of theological elo-
quence, the patron saint of the University of Paris. The clerics and spec-

tators at the inquiry at Poitiers, hearing how wisely Joan responded to her interrogators, compared her to this holy predecessor. While Saint Catherine exemplified verbal force, Saint Margaret exemplified another, more physical, form of power. When the devil appeared to her in the form of a dragon, she crushed him under her foot. These saints achieved such victories over pagan philosophers and devils at least in part because they were virgins, that is, because their physical intactness mirrored a spiritual intactness that enabled its possessor to deflect the demons' attempts at penetration. It was in order to ascertain whether Joan could boast a similar immunity that she was on more than one occasion physically examined to verify her claims to maidenhood. These two saints resemble Joan in their patience under suffering as well. Though the discomfort of which Joan complained in prison cannot be compared to the multiple tortures to which these virgin saints were submitted, when Joan recalled the voices telling her that she must accept her *martyre* willingly and that she would ultimately come to the kingdom of heaven, it was to this model of heroic forbearance that she alluded. The clerics compelled her to identify her voices with specific beings, but the saints whom Joan chose reflected her own particular situation as a virgin martyr.

One cannot dismiss Joan's identification of her voices with Saint Michael, likewise, because it was Joan who selected this angel and Joan who can be seen, again, to share some characteristics with him. While Saint Catherine and Saint Margaret resemble Joan in their virginity, their forcefulness, and their resilience, Saint Michael resembles her in his angelic status and in his association, in the fifteenth century, with the royal family of France. Like an angel, Joan appeared to bypass the corporeal distinction of masculinity and femininity, dressing in men's clothes and performing men's deeds though never denying that she was, in fact, a woman.[21] Like an angel, Joan mediated between God and humans, conveying to her countrymen God's position in the Hundred Years' War and undertaking military feats on his behalf. Like Saint Michael, in particular, whose stronghold on Mont-Saint-Michel remained throughout the war an island of French soil in English-occupied territory, Joan was continually faithful to the Valois dynasty.[22] It was to an angel that many of her contemporaries compared her, as the clerics admitted when they cited them as proclaiming her "to be a messenger of God and an angel rather than a woman" (261), and it was to an angel, as we shall see, that Joan compared herself at one point during the trial. As an androgynous intermediary between God and man and as a partisan to the French cause, Michael, like Catherine and Margaret, reflects the particularities of Joan's position.

In addition, however hesitantly Joan first identified her voices with Saint Catherine, Saint Margaret, and Saint Michael on February 27, as the trial proceded, this reluctance disappeared and was replaced by an apparent eagerness and spontaneity. Four days later, on March 3, the minutes cite her as saying of these saints, " 'I saw them with my eyes and I believe that they are they as firmly as God exists' " (92). Though on February 22, Joan had stated merely that a "voice" had come to her when she was thirteen and had taught her to govern herself and to frequent the church, by March 15, three weeks later, she confidently maintained that it was Saint Michael who had instructed her. On March 28, a week and a half after the conclusion of the interrogations, when Joan was responding to the charges of the *libelle d'Estivet,* "she said that she believed, as firmly as she believes that Our Lord Jesus Christ suffered death for us in redeeming us from the torments of hell, that these are Saint Michael, Saint Gabriel, Saint Catherine, and Saint Margaret, whom our Lord sent to her to comfort and counsel her" (248). It is as if once Joan was obliged to identify her voices as Saint Michael, Saint Catherine, and Saint Margaret, the voices began to reveal themselves, and she began to perceive them, as Saint Michael, Saint Catherine, and Saint Margaret. In this way Joan collaborated with the clerics in the construction of the truth of her voices.

Discretio Spirituum

Just as the clerics stood out from their contemporaries in their demand that Joan identify her voices with saints, angels, or God himself, they also stood out from them in their demand that she justify this identification with an account of her inner experience of these figures. Very few of the witnesses at the rehabilitation or the chroniclers of her accomplishments showed an interest in this inner experience, and virtually none of them relied upon it as an indication of the legitimacy of her voices. At the rehabilitation, Jean de Nouillompont, who helped escort Joan from Vaucouleurs to Chinon, reported that he believed Joan's claims to a divine mission because of her holy behavior in hearing mass willingly, in crossing herself when she took an oath, and in refraining from swearing. In his chronicle, Perceval de Cagny affirmed that he believed her claims because of her miraculous success in subjugating numerous castles and cities in four months, in leading her king to his coronation, and in motivating the soldiers to continue to fight despite their low pay. In her *Ditié de Jehanne d'Arc,* Christine de Pizan wrote that she put faith in Joan's assertions not only because of the virtue she displayed and the miracles she performed but because of the existence of prophecies that foresaw her advent. When the clerics at Rouen evaluated Joan's allegations of divine communications, they too sought evidence of the saintly comportment and miraculous signs, and yet they did not limit themselves to these criteria cited by these various commentators.

In contrast to their lay contemporaries, the clerics attempted to determine the truth about Joan's voices by relying most heavily upon an ecclesiastical practice known as "the discernment of spirits" (*discretio spirituum*) well-established in clerical circles by the fifteenth century. In his first letter to the Corinthians, Saint Paul named *discretio spirituum* as one of the graces of the Holy Spirit, alongside speaking in tongues and faith healing.[23] Over the course of subsequent centuries, church fathers, including Augustine of Hippo, Gregory the Great, Bernard of Clairvaux, and Hugh and Richard of Saint-Victor, elaborated upon this capacity to distinguish true revelations from false ones, yet they treated it, in general, as a mystical, ineffable intuition granted from above.[24] It was only at the beginning of the fifteenth century that Jean Gerson, the chancellor of the University of Paris, composed a series of treatises, "De distinctione verarum visionum a falsis" in 1400–1401, "De probatione spirituum" in 1415, and "De examination doctrinarum" in 1423, that depicted *discretio spirituum* as a rational, articulable process and developed guidelines to train clerics in exercising it.[25] In 1429, the last year of his life, Gerson was living in his brother's monastery in Lyons and teaching catechism to the neighborhood children, having been exiled from the capital and the *alma mater* of which he remained titular head since the Burgundian conquest of the city, when he heard report of the maid who claimed to have been sent by God to save the kingdom and drafted one or possibly two short works in her favor.[26] Dorothy G. Wayman argues that Gerson wrote "De quadam puella" in the days before Joan had been given leadership over French troops in order to defend her, either in person or by proxy, before the clerics then examining her at Poitiers, and H. G. Francq asserts that he drafted another treatise, "De mirabili victoria," possibly in addition to "De quadam puella," a week after Joan's relief of the siege of Orléans.[27] It is not surprising that the clerics at Joan's trial in Rouen did not cite Gerson's treatises on Joan, given his Armagnac stance and the positive view of the Maid that resulted from it. At the same time, however, it is also not surprising that these clerics, many of them former colleagues of the chancellor's at the university familiar with his writings and all of them fellow academics aware of his considerable prestige, would follow Gerson's criteria for judging visions in their approach to Joan's voices.[28] As the clerics revealed their scholastic training in their insistence that Joan be precise in identifying her voices, so did they reveal their scholastic training, inherited most directly from Gerson, in their insistence that she be skeptical, analytical, and objective in determining those identities.

Though his three treatises on *discretio spirituum* were directed to advising fellow clerics how to evaluate the experiences of alleged visionaries, Gerson did suggest implicitly that the visionary herself should respond to the spirit who appears to her in a certain manner and, in particular, that she should not take what it says at face value. When the Virgin Mary heard the Archangel Gabriel address her as favored one, Gerson pointed out, "she kept in mind all these words, pondering them in her heart."[29] Similarly, when Saint Martin of Tours heard a spirit introduce himself as Christ and claim to have descended to earth so as to be adored by him, he noted, "for a while, like the Virgin Mary, this holy man remained wrapped in thought, pondering what kind of greeting this could be."[30] The Virgin Mary did not immediately accept that God had favored her, nor did Saint Martin immediately accept that Christ had chosen to appear to him personally. Like these saints, the visionary should not assume too quickly that God has chosen to honor her by allowing her such a celestial visitation. Like them, she should, instead, recall that the devil often appears in the guise of a good angel to taunt those who, out of pride in their own virtues, believe themselves worthy of such a grace or who, out of curiosity for esoteric knowledge or the hope for a reputation for holiness, desire to experience such apparitions. She should bear in mind that she lives in a world where things are not what they seem and where she must be ever-vigilant, lest she be deceived.

Attentive to possible discrepancies between superficial analysis and deeper truth, Gerson continued, the visionary should rely upon analysis as the means through which she might rip the veil off what the spirit seems to be and expose what it is. He suggested that a careful study of the spirit's speech can reveal whether the apparition is divine or diabolic in its origin. Whereas the teachings of good spirits are in accord with Christian doctrine and morals, those of evil spirits are in opposition to them. Whereas the utterances of good spirits are directed toward holy purposes, such as the furtherance of the Christian faith, those of evil spirits are absurd and foolish in their aims. Gerson wrote, "Whenever we attempt a scientific testing of spirits ... it is necessary to gather evidence [*signa*] from their works."[31] In order to obtain such evidence, he recommended that the visionary select certain aspects of the spirit's identity, such as its teachings and its purpose in coming to her, that she isolate these aspects from its overall self, and that she subject them to individual scrutiny. If, with the assistance of her spiritual adviser, she finds harmony between the spirit's characteristics and those of the Catholic faith, she may be allowed, tentatively, to accept the spirit as authentic, but if she finds discord between these sets of categories, she should reject it as false. Only through such analysis can she pierce through the possible deceptions of appearance and attain the security of truth.

Through this analytical process, Gerson maintained, the visionary can translate her personal, solitary perception of the spirit into impersonal and universally readable information. The visionary who insists upon her subjective impressions of a spirit, impressions that are by definition inaccessible to others, cannot convince others of what she perceives as its identity, nor can she be convinced by a more expert third party, such as a theologian, that she is mistaken. She remains alone, unjudged and unjudgeable, in her inner perceptions. The visionary who is willing and able to transform her subjective impressions into objective data and to share this data with others, however, can either persuade her listeners of her conclusions or stand liable to correction by a greater authority. The visionary who follows Gerson's prescriptions — that is, who suspects a possible discrepancy between the appearance and the truth of the phenomenon she perceives, who analyzes the phenomenon in order to transcend appearance and attain truth, and who translates her personal impressions of the phenomenon into impersonal information — functions like a cleric and, in doing so, becomes subject to a cleric's supervision.

Joan did hesitate before giving credence to her voices, yet it was not skepticism about the truthfulness of their appearance that held her back. The first time she spoke of her voices in the minutes of the interrogation she stated that "when she was thirteen years old, she had a voice coming from God to help her govern herself. And the first time she had great fear. . . . She said also that . . . , after she heard the voice three times, she recognized that it was the voice of an angel" (47–48). Later, she reported of this first encounter that "the first time she had great uncertainty if it was Saint Michael who came to her, and this first time she had great fear, and she saw him many a time before she recognized that it was Saint Michael" (162). Fearful and uncertain, Joan may seem to differ greatly from the overeager visionary Gerson warned against who succumbs to pride, in her willingness to accept that God has honored her with such visions, and ambition, in her willingness to encounter heavenly beings. In her hesitation to believe that the spirit who appears to her is an angel, she may seem to resemble the Virgin Mary and Saint Martin as Gerson depicted them. The source of this praiseworthy cautiousness, however, seems to have been not fear that the voice might be a devil but simply youth. Contrasting the first time she saw Saint Michael, when "she had great fear," with later times she saw him, when "she recognized that it was Saint Michael," Joan suggested that, the first time, she was afraid because Saint Michael was unfamiliar to her and because children are often afraid of those unfamiliar to them and that, later, she recognized him because he was no longer so strange and no longer such a stranger. She suggested that she came to recognize Saint Michael not because he corresponded to any external conventions of angelic appearance or behavior but because he corresponded to himself in his previous apparitions. The voice, heard once, is unfamiliar and frightening in its unfamiliarity. The voice, heard a number of times, is no longer unfamiliar, no longer frightening, but something that she has become used to. Joan attained confidence that the first voice to appear to her was Saint Michael not because she stepped back and reflected upon evidence of its purported angelic identity, as the Virgin Mary is described as "pondering" the angel's words to her and Saint Martin as "pondering" the spirit's greeting to him, but because Saint Michael had gradually revealed himself to her through various manifestations. She attained confidence that the subsequent voices to appear to her were Saint Catherine and Saint Margaret in a similar way. When the clerics asked how she could tell these two saints apart, she answered that she could do so because they greeted her and because they named themselves to her. When the clerics inquired whether she had had a sign that these saints were good spirits, she replied that "Saint Michael certified it to her, before the voices came" (162), explaining that he had advised her that she should believe in what they told her and should act according to their counsel. She claimed to have known who these spirits were because they identified themselves and each other. While the clerics aimed at uncovering not only who the voices told Joan they were but who they actually were, Joan showed no suspicion that their alleged identities might not be the same as their actual identities. She showed no suspicion that the voices might be deceiving her. She was not skeptical because she did not entertain the possibility that there might have been a discrepancy between the appearance of the voices and the truth about them.

Joan's inability to distinguish between what the voices seemed to be and what they were struck the clerics as objectionable because it made her vulnerable not only to the deceits of Satan but to the deceits of an empiricism unrestrained by logic. According to medieval theologians, in particular, Thomas Aquinas, the *doctor angelicus* who most codified

Catholic doctrine on separated substances, angels are purely intellectual beings who do not possess bodies. Even though angels may on occasion seem to possess bodies when they appear to human beings, these bodies are not "natural" to them, that is, intrinsic to their nature, but, rather, are "accidental," that is, assumed when and where they please. It follows that these bodies are not "created," as subsisting things are said to be created, but, rather, are "concreated," as nonsubsisting things are said to be. Interrogating Joan about the relationship between the angels and their illusory bodies, the clerics gave her the opportunity to distinguish between the superficial appearance of the voices, perceived through sensory impressions, and the deeper truth of what lay behind this appearance, perceived through intellectual understanding. When they asked her "whether she saw Saint Michael and the angels corporally and really" (74), they echoed Aquinas's question "whether an angel is altogether incorporeal" and, thus, gave her a chance to clarify that though she saw Saint Michael and the other angels, she did not see them with real bodies.[32] When they asked her "whether she believes that Saint Michael and Saint Gabriel have natural heads" (92), they evoked Aquinas's question "whether the angels have bodies naturally united to them" and, thus, gave her the opportunity to clarify that though she saw these two angels with heads, she knew that these bodily parts were not "natural" to them.[33] Finally, when they asked her "whether she believes that God formed them in the manner and form in which she sees them" and "whether she believes that, in the beginning, God created them in this manner and form" (92), they recalled Aquinas's question "whether to be created belongs to composite and subsisting things" and, thus, allowed her to maintain that though she saw these angels in a corporeal manner and form, God did not create them, from the beginning, in this way.[34] Such responses would have kept Joan within the boundaries of orthodoxy, yet those were not the answers she provided. Asked if she saw Saint Michael and the other angels "corporally and really," she replied, " 'I saw them with the eyes of my body, as well as I see you' " (74). Asked whether Saint Michael and Saint Gabriel have "natural" heads, she responded, again, " 'I saw them with my eyes and I believe that they are they as firmly as God is' " (92). Finally, asked if she believed that God formed them in the manner and form that she saw and that God created them thus in the beginning, she stated, " 'yes' " (92). With these answers Joan gave no indication that she distinguished between the corporeal appearance and the incorporeal truth of the angels and, hence, between a sensory and an intellectual appreciation of the angels. She thus showed that she understood not the two levels of appearance and truth imagined by theologians but one level of reality, in which such a distinction between appearance and truth could not be made.

Failing to perceive reality as divided between appearance and truth, Joan also failed to analyze her voices in order to ascertain that truth. When the clerics separated the various parts of the voices' bodies and interrogated her about them individually, she resisted this dissolution of a whole into its parts.[35] When they inquired, for example, if Saint Michael were naked when he appeared to her, Joan responded flippantly, " 'Do you think that God has not the wherewithal with which to clothe him?' " When the clerics then asked if he had hair, she answered, " 'Why would it have been cut off him?' " After these attempts to deflect the clerics' questions, Joan stated, without apparent provocation, that "she has a great joy when she sees him and it seems to her that, when she sees him, she is not in a state of mortal sin" (87). Questioned about Saint Michael's physical characteristics, Joan did not answer directly but, instead, insisted upon the happiness and the blessedness that she felt when he was there. At yet another time, when the clerics requested to know the "form, size, appearance, and clothes" in which Saint Michael appeared to her, Joan stated, "he was in the form of a very true worthy man, [*unius verissimi probi hominis* or *un tres vray preudomme*]" (165) and, as for the clothes and the other things, she would not say anything more.[36] Time and again, Joan rejected questions that encouraged her to speak of the angels in terms of corporality and, hence, encouraged her to speak of the angels factually, neutrally, scientifically. Time and again, Joan insisted upon speaking of the angels in terms of her own inner sensations, such as her joy when she was near them or her sorrow when they had departed. Whereas the clerics treated the angels like anatomists' cadavers, dead objects to be dissected, broken into their parts, and analyzed with scientific dispassion, Joan insisted upon treating them as living beings, to be respected in their integrity and loved in their goodness. Though both the clerics and Joan rejected attributing corporality to the angels, for the clerics the corporality was dangerous insofar as it suggested an essential attribute that angels do not possess, while, for Joan, the corporality was dangerous insofar as it suggested an emotional neutrality that would strip the angels of their affective power.

Neither skeptical of the relationship between appearance and truth nor analytical as a result of that skepticism, Joan is also not objective in the evidence that she advances to prove the legitimacy of her voices. When the clerics asked how she knew that Saint Catherine and Saint Margaret are these two saints and how she recognized the one from the other, she responded, "she knows well that they are they and . . . she recognizes well the one from the other" (71–72). The minutes record Joan as later adding, seemingly unprovoked, that "she saw so well the said Saint Michael and the female saints that she knew them well to be saints in paradise" (91). When the clerics inquired how she would distinguish a good from an evil spirit if the devil were to assume the form of a good angel, she answered that "she would know well whether it were Saint Michael or something counterfeited in his manner" (162). Identifying Saint Michael and his companions as angels, she stated that "she believes firmly that they were angels" (162) and that Saint Michael taught her and showed her so much "that she believes firmly that it was he" (163). In all of these interrogations, the clerics asked Joan *how* she knew the voices' identity, and she responded that she knew the voices' identity "well" (*bene*) or "firmly" (*firmiter*). Asked why she was certain of her voices' identity, Joan responded by speaking of the strength of her certainty. Because she had not analyzed the voices' identities, because she could not, therefore, point to objective data to support her belief in their saintly and angelic identities, and because she was ultimately persuaded of their identities only through her subjective convictions, she insisted upon the strength of those convictions in order to persuade her hearers. Joan not only emphasized the quantity of her convictions to offset their lack of apparent quality, but worse, from a clerical point of view, she pointed to her desire to believe in the holiness of these voices' identities as an explanation for her belief. The minutes record, "Interrogated how she knew that they were angels, she responded that she knew it early enough, and she had this will to believe it" (162). She made clear that she was persuaded of the voices' holy identities not only because the voices revealed these identities to her but because she wanted to believe these identities. Though she may not have displayed the pride that, as Gerson saw it, makes visionaries want to interpret their visions positively, she did nonetheless display the desire to interpret them in that manner.

Given these exchanges between the clerics and Joan, it is not surprising that the clerics made clear throughout the trial their skepticism about her identification of the voices. During these interrogations they repeatedly asked her the same questions, as if dissatisfied with her responses to them. After she told them that she knew well that her voices were Saint Catherine and Saint Margaret, they demanded to know what sign she had to prove this, and they reiterated their original inquiry, how she knew that her voices were these saints, a few weeks later. Where the repetition of the clerics' questions does not indicate frustration with Joan's failure to provide satisfactory answers, their content reveals a frustration with the self-enclosed world of these replies. When Joan asserted, for instance, that she knew Saint Catherine and Saint Margaret to be good because Saint Michael certified it to her, the clerics inquired how she knew this spirit was Saint Michael. When she answered that she knew him to be Saint Michael "by his speech and by the language of angels" (162), they expressed wonder that she could understand, let alone recognize, this tongue, as angels were believed to communicate through the exchange of concepts instead of words. In the second part of the trial, when the clerics presented their charges against Joan, they made explicit their belief that Joan did not adequately identify her voices prior to putting her faith in them. In the *libelle d'Estivet*, they asserted that "the said Joan said herself to have believed and to believe the spirits appearing to her to be angels and archangels and saints of God, as firmly as she believes in the Christian faith and in articles of this faith, though she refers to having had no sign that would be sufficient to recognize them" (247). They charged that "the said Joan, basing herself on her fancy alone, venerated these spirits, kissing the earth on which she said them to have passed, embracing and kissing these same spirits on her knees, and making other reverences to them, thanking them with joined hands...even though she did not know whether they were good spirits" (249). Because Joan's identification of her voices ultimately derived not from a critical, objective reading of signs but from the voices' presentation of themselves and from her own subjective impulses, the clerics followed the advice of Gerson's treatise and dismissed her conclusions.

In all of these interrogations about Joan's voices from God, the clerics and Joan differed not only in their conceptions of the identity of such voices and of the manner in which such identities should be ascertained, but also in the presuppositions that underlay such conceptions. The clerics took for granted that such voices must ultimately be not "voices from God" but, rather, entities that could be further defined as angels, saints, or God himself, while Joan appears to have imagined the voices, at least at the opening of the trial, without such definition. The clerics believed that the apparent identity of these voices was not necessarily the same as their actual identity, but Joan did not show the same skepticism. The clerics thought that in order to ascertain the truth of who the voices were, it was necessary to break them into their constituent parts and analyze them with scientific detachment, yet Joan seemed to hold that such a critical distance would imply a denial of the voices' sanctity and hence a denial of the truth about them. The conflict between the clerics and Joan reflects, therefore, not so much a conflict between investigators who strive to verify certain claims and a respondent who resists that verification as a conflict between the learned, who are steeped in the assumptions of an academic discourse, and the unlearned, who do not share their assumptions, who do not partake in their discourse, and whose responses, thus, often go unheard.

3 | The Departure for France

When Joan donned a man's tunic and leggings, mounted a horse, and rode off to France to lead Armagnac forces into battle, she behaved in a manner that was, to medieval clerics, deeply troubling.[1] On the one hand, these clerics generally condemned women who wore men's clothes and performed men's deeds out of their own desire to do so. The Book of Deuteronomy had long ago warned that a woman who wears a man's clothes is an abomination to God, and medieval clerics never failed to cite this biblical prohibition to justify their opposition to the practice.[2] Among canonists, Gratian decreed, "If a woman, judging it useful according to her own decision, puts on male clothing, she is anathematized because this is imitating male dress."[3] Among theologians, Aquinas judged, "Of itself... the wearing of the clothes of the opposite sex is wrong, and especially because it can give rise to lasciviousness."[4] As clerics like Aquinas knew, temple prostitutes of antiquity had adopted contradictory garments in order to arouse lust in possible clients. Idolatrous in the religious rites they practiced, these prostitutes were also idolatrous in drawing viewers' attention to their gendered body through their clothes: they led the thoughts of the beholder not outward toward a spiritual and transcendent Creator but inward toward a material and immanent creature. Both canonists and theologians reviled a transvestitism that was prompted by desire and that led to a fixation on the corporeal self.[5]

Though these clerics repudiated women who adopted masculine habits in order to give rise to lecherous inclinations, they defended women who adopted these clothes in order to protect themselves from such lust. Gratian directed that the woman who dressed as a man "according to her own decision" be excommunicated, but he left open the possibility that the woman who wore men's clothing in response to a particular situation was not to be molested. Though Aquinas attacked the woman who cross-dressed "of itself," he championed the one who did so "in case of necessity, for instance, in order to hide from enemies, or because there are no other clothes, or for some such good reason."[6] In the early years of the church, a number of young Christian virgins were said to have bowed to such a necessity when they disguised themselves as men in order to flee forced marriages or seductions. Margaret, for example, was said to have escaped her husband on her wedding night by pretending to be a monk, and Anastasia was said to have escaped a lustful emperor and his jealous wife by living out her life as a male hermit. Other women who were said to have passed as men in order to enter monasteries, such as Marina and Theodora, were seen as acting appropriately despite the absence of a threat of sexual danger because their conduct was motivated not by the hope of indulging in pleasure but by the intention of renouncing it.[7] During the high Middle Ages, when more reliable historical records replaced these apocryphal hagiographies, women were still respected for dressing and acting as men in their pursuit of Christian virtue. Christina of Markyate assumed masculine apparel in her flight from an arranged marriage, and Dorothy of Montau and Margery Kempe wore men's clothes on pilgrimage in order to safeguard themselves from the perils of the road. Hildegund of Schönau, who dressed as a boy for a youthful journey to Jerusalem, continued to wear masculine clothing for the rest of her life, even after she entered religious orders.[8] Despite their qualms about the circumstances under which much cross-dressing was undertaken, clerics tolerated and even approved a transvestism that was derived from need and that enabled dedication to a spiritual other.

Secular as well as clerical authors demonstrated ambivalence toward cross-dressing during this period. When women adopted the attire and role of men without any external compulsion obliging them to do so, they did not earn praise for their actions. To take the example most relevant to Joan's case, in these years before the Bradamantes, Clorindas, and Britomarts of Renaissance romance epic, Amazons were normally portrayed as cruel, bloodthirsty, and unnatural in their warlike appetites.[9] It was commonly said that after a particularly devastating military defeat, these women killed the men who were left among them in order to form their all-female state; that after coupling with the men of neighboring areas, they slew any male children born from these unions; and that in order to facilitate military gestures, they removed one of their breasts, all actions that betoken a certain violence, whether toward men, children, or themselves. Though Amazons were acknowledged to have displayed heroic virtues on the battlefield, Deborah Fraoili writes that their "purposeless and empty quest for masculine prowess" earned them little approbation in the late Middle Ages.[10] Works such as Giovanni Boccaccio's *De mulieribus claris* and Christine de Pizan's *Le Livre de la cité des dames,* informed by Boccaccio's example, do express admiration for the Amazons' manly valor at war, yet they contrast the martial orientation of these pagan women with the holy orientation of their later Christian counterparts. Boccaccio juxtaposes pagan women who were "spurred by desire for . . . fleeting glory" with Christian women who were motivated by hope for "true and eternal glory."[11] Christine commends the Amazons for their valor and their high-mindedness and includes them as the first inhabitants of her idealized City of Ladies, yet she places these women warriors, as ladies exceptional in their accomplishment, on the lowest rung of her City, below women exceptional in their virtue and women exceptional in their faith.[12] Both Boccaccio and Christine qualify their praise of the Amazons because they acted out of personal desire rather than impersonal necessity and because human training rather than divine miracle empowered them. In contrast, when women in medieval literary narratives adopt the attire and role of men because extraordinary circumstances force them to do so, they are almost always commended for their actions.[13] Yde in *Yde et Olive,* Blancandrine in *Tristan de Nanteuil,* and the various cross-dressed women in Boccaccio's *Decameron* are portrayed as acceptable and even admirable in their transvestism because they assume masculine clothing and comportment in order to respond to exceptional circumstances, such as the imposition of an unwanted marriage or the disappearance of male protectors, and because they abandon these disguises as soon as they are no longer needed. For lay as well as for clerical authors, women's assumption of a masculine demeanor was excusable and even praiseworthy only under emergency conditions.

It was within the context of these two models of women's adoption of masculine clothes and occupations that Joan's contemporaries and even Joan herself evaluated her actions. On the one hand, Joan's opponents, including the clerics who participated in her trial at Rouen, depicted her as having donned a tunic and grasped a sword because she desired to do so, and they cite Aquinas's attack upon women who cross-dress out of desire to justify their criticisms of her. They compared her to mountebanks, sorceresses, and false prophets, who transgress social norms out of personal ambition for wealth, fame, and power, and to dissolute men, who act in such a manner out of a sinful longing for lewd pleasure. On the other hand, Joan and her supporters, including Christine de Pizan, who extolled her accomplishments in the *Ditié de Jehanne d'Arc,* the clerics who participated in the inquiry at Poitiers, and the clerics who reviewed her case at the rehabilitation, depicted Joan as having assumed this attire and these mores because she had been compelled to do so by God, and they cited Aquinas's defense of women who cross-dress out of necessity to defend this stance. They compared her to Esther, Judith, and Deborah, who transgressed social norms in order to rescue the Chosen People, and to Marina and Theodora, who comported themselves in such a way in order to cloister themselves from the world.[14] In the transcripts of the trial, as we shall see, the first model of female transgression led the clerics to depict Joan as a subject who initiated, realized, and bore responsibility for her acts, whereas the second model led Joan to depict herself as an object through whom God initiated his actions and realized his goals, for which he bore ultimate responsibility. It would be incorrect to postulate that the clerics understood the self, in general, as a humanistic subject, active and accountable for its own deeds, especially as they made clear elsewhere that they regarded the soldiers who captured Joan and even their colleagues who tried her for heresy as vehicles through whom God acted. It would also be incorrect to postulate that Joan understood the self, in general, as a theistic soul through whom God was active and for whose deeds he remained accountable, especially as she made clear elsewhere that she did not view all people nor all of her endeavors as guided by God. Yet these two models, the one humanistic, the other theistic, do distinguish different ways of thinking about this issue and thus contribute to the portrait of Joan that emerges from the transcripts.

A Captain-at-Arms

While the clerics attributed a disturbing subjectivity to Joan throughout their various sets of accusations against her, they first expressed their concern about her pursuit of her own will in their account of her departure for France in the *libelle d'Estivet.* In general Joan is said to have approached Vaucouleurs, the fortified city nearest Domrémy, first in May 1428, over the course of a visit to a certain Durand Laxart and his wife, in their house halfway between this city and her village. At that time, she urged Robert de Baudricourt, the captain of Vaucouleurs, to inform the king that he should not wage any pitched battles until mid-Lent because he would receive aid from God before then. She is said to have traveled to Vaucouleurs again in December 1428, now with the assistance of Laxart, while she was spending six weeks attending his wife in childbirth, and to have identified herself to de Baudricourt as the person who would bring their sovereign the promised help. Finally, she is said to have journeyed directly to Vaucouleurs in February 1429 and to have succeeded this time in persuading de Baudricourt to grant her an escort to the king's court in Chinon. In their own rendition of these events, the clerics established that Joan undertook this departure for France not because she was ordered to do so by the voices but because she wanted to do so. In the *libelle d'Estivet,* they cited Joan as claiming that "it was clearly revealed to her on the part of God that she would lift the siege of Orléans, have Charles, whom she calls her king, crowned, and expel all his adversaries from the kingdom of France" (201). They portrayed the voices not as giving Joan a command but as giving her a promise and, hence, as appealing to her vain ambition to accomplish great deeds rather than to her pious duty to obey God. Enticed rather than compelled by her voices, Joan left for France, they maintained, "of her own motivation" (201) and "spontaneously" (201, 294).

The clerics established not only that Joan acted voluntarily in quitting her village but that she disrupted familial structures by doing so. In the *libelle d'Estivet,* they related that in abandoning her village, Joan had acted "despite her father and mother and their opposition" (201), and, in the twelve articles composed for the University of Paris and the canons of Rouen, they confirmed that she had acted "against the will of her father and mother, who, when they knew of her departure, were almost insane over it" (294). When they made these charges, the clerics also recalled Joan's account of her father's dream that she would go off with soldiers and his assertion to her brothers that if he believed she would actually do this, he would either want them to drown her or else he would drown her himself. They recalled her allegation that her parents later kept her in great subjection and that when she did leave, they almost lost their minds. Though the clerics only restated Joan's acknowledgment of her parents' opposition when they suspected her plans to depart and their distress when they discovered her gone, they implicitly criticized her for having disregarded their judgment. In the twelve articles, they related that Joan had abandoned her paternal house to meet "a certain squire whom she had never seen before" (294) and then to join "a multitude of soldiers, living with them night and day, never or rarely having another woman with her" (291). They suggested that, having abandoned her familial circle, Joan recklessly exposed herself to sexual advances from the squire and soldiers, sexual advances from which her parents had sought to protect her. According to the traditional understanding of how a family should function, children should submit their wills to parental authority, as they should submit their youthful desire to attain glory to their elders' more mature concern that virtue and reputation be preserved. Yet Joan, tempted by the voices' diabolical application to her pride and indifferent to her parents' cautionary application to her filial piety, privileged the will of the self over the duty to the other, as she privileged ambition over honesty, and quit her village for France.

When Joan was staying in Vaucouleurs, the clerics maintained in the *libelle d'Estivet,* she continued to assert her will by assuming the outward appearance of a man. The clerics' description of Joan's choice of coiffeur and wardrobe supported their contention that she presented herself in such a way because she wanted to rather than because she had to. In the *libelle d'Estivet,* they wrote that she had her hair cut bowl-fashion "in the manner of fops [*ad modum mangonum*]" (205) and that she wore "sumptuous and magnificent clothes of precious cloth and gold cloth and also furs" (207), including short, cropped tunics and surcoats and robes slashed on both sides. They charged that "she used all of the styles and clothes which the most dissolute men [*homines dissolutissimi*] are accustomed to assume, having rejected all womanly modesty and being contrary, not only to womanly decency, but to that which is common to honorable men" (207). Adrien Harmand's research into Joan's coiffeur and wardrobe confirms the clerics' characterization of them as elegant, fashionable, and dramatic to an extent that ecclesiastics might find objectionable.[15] According to Harmand, Joan had her hair cut in a particularly contemporary style, trimmed in short bangs over the forehead and shaved above the ears and around the neck. Though she wore relatively simple clothes at her departure from Vaucouleurs, namely, a long hood, a dark pleated tunic with a belt at the hips, and high leather leggings with pointed toes and attached spurs, she assumed far richer garments at later stages of her career. At Orléans, she received from the magistrates a forest-green surcoat trimmed with marten, which she wore over a red velvet jacket, like Giovanni Arnolfini in Jan van Eyck's contemporaneous *Giovanni Arnolfini and His Bride,* and a vermillion tunic trimmed with beaver, which she wore with a belt and attached dagger. When she was captured at the skirmish outside Compiègne, she

was wearing over her plate armor a vermillion-and-gold brocaded surcoat decorated with fur or lace. Though Joan's adoption of a generic masculine haircut, such as that worn by peasants and soldiers, and a generic
masculine costume, such as the hood, tunic, and leggings that she wore
during her early adventures, might be understood to reflect a preference
for a toilette more convenient for the masculine tasks she had undertaken,
her liking for the styles of hair and attire preferred by fashionable young
men, such as the bowl-cut, the slashed robes, and the ornate surcoats that
she adopted during her later campaigns, indicated to the clerics that she
did not take a purely utilitarian approach to her appearance. Joan's tendency to adorn herself "in the manner of fops" and in the manner of "the
most dissolute men" suggests that she experienced her coiffeur, her wardrobe, and, by extension, her body not only as a means to an end but as an
end in themselves. Because the clerics perceived that Joan took pleasure
in her masculine trappings, they concluded that she chose them out of
the desire to experience such pleasure.

Concerned that Joan willfully assumed a dress and lifestyle customary
to men, the clerics were also concerned that she disrupted symbolic structures in doing so. They reproached her by asserting that she had left "nothing on her body that proves or indicates her female sex except those things
that Nature has attributed to this woman as distinction of her female sex"
(293). Their horror that only natural signs were left to notify the onlooker
of Joan's sex reveals their expectation that other, artificial signs would reflect that form as well. According to the traditional understanding of the
way symbolic structures should function, clothing should subordinate itself to the body as the sign should subordinate itself to the thing and as
the creature should subordinate itself to the Creator, out of a recognition
of the natural and fitting correspondence between these two sets of categories. The woman who allowed for the customary correspondence between her body and her clothes permitted an affinity between her sex and
her gender, between her femaleness and her femininity, and between her
natural identity and her cultural identity. The woman who refused that
correspondence, as Joan did, not only defied Deuteronomy's injunction
against cross-dressing but upset the relation between nature and art, ref-
erent and sign, thing and word, and in brief, the epistemological framework
upon which the clerics' conception of reality rested. As Susan Schibanoff
has remarked, if clothes normally function as a sign directing attention
from themselves toward the higher reality they signify, as an icon directs
attention from its own materiality toward the divine or saintly essence it
indicates, Joan's clothes functioned as a thing unto themselves, drawing

attention back to their paradoxical relation to the body they covered, as an idol draws attention back to its own autonomous being.[16] It was this traditional association of cross-dressing and idolatry that Pierre Maurice evoked when he informed Joan, "You are suspect of idolatry and of the consecration of your person and your clothes to the devil in imitation of the rite of the pagans" (377). Delighting in the idolatrous immanence of her cross-dressed body, Joan disregarded the importance of maintaining a traditional symbolic hierarchy and, thus, as the clerics protested, "approve[d] examples of total dissolution in the human race" (208).

When Joan arrived at Chinon in late February or early March, after about two weeks of travel from Vaucouleurs, in her hood, tunic, and leggings, the clerics maintained that she was still following her own will in seeking to gain spiritual power over the Armagnacs by persuading them of her ability to perform supernatural deeds. If Joan had discovered a sword buried near the altar of the church of Saint Catherine of Fierbois, they alleged, it was not because divine guidance had informed her of its location but because she had consulted with demons or, alternatively, because she had previously buried the weapon there herself so as later to claim, "maliciously, fraudulently, and artificially" (210), to have found it through divine revelation. If she found a lost cup and exposed a concubinary priest, they argued, it was, again, not through divine guidance but through "divinations ... so that a greater faith be granted to her words and deeds" (214). At times, the clerics depicted Joan as openly admitting her reliance upon her own abilities in order to do what normally could not be done. In the *libelle d'Estivet,* they related that when she gained admittance to the king in the great hall of the castle of Chinon, she promised him three things: "first, that she would lift the siege of Orléans; second, that she would have him crowned at Reims; and, third, that she would revenge him on his adversaries, English as well as Burgundian, by her art either killing them all or expelling them from the kingdom" (214). Though an ordinary devout Christian might have acknowledged God's involvement in allowing her to lift the siege, crown the king, and expel his enemies, nowhere in this summary of her promises to the king did Joan recognize divine participation in these events. On the contrary, she identified herself as the agent who would accomplish all of these feats, and who would do so alone, through the practice of her presumably magical "art." At other times, the clerics depicted Joan as disguising the fact that she relied upon her own abilities in performing surprising feats by pretending that she relied upon divine aid instead. In the twelve articles for the Parisian masters and the Rouennais canons, they portrayed Joan as informing the king "that she wanted to wage war against his adversaries, promising him that she would establish him in a great dominion, that she would vanquish his enemies, and that she was sent for this by God of heaven" (294). Here, as earlier, Joan insisted upon her own agency in accomplishing marvelous goals, yet now she linked this accomplishment to miraculous rather than magical assistance. In her apparently illuminated discoveries of buried swords, lost cups, and secret sins, the clerics complained, she resembled those who, "seducing princes, noblemen, clerics, and the people," strove to win the support of all ranks of society, and in her apparently inspired prophecies to the king of his conquests and his enemies' defeats, she resembled "false prophets who . . . are accustomed to pretend that they have divine revelation about matters that they understand to please temporal lords" (263). The clerics made clear that, overtly or covertly, Joan depended upon her own often occult powers in performing the deeds that gave her influence over the Armagnacs and that she performed these deeds in order to acquire that influence.

When Joan set off for Orléans and, even more, when she arrived in this city, the clerics maintained, she continued to follow her own will by assuming a position of leadership in the Armagnac armies. The Faculty of Decretals at the university protested that "having abandoned the dress [*habitu*] of women, she imitated the behavior [*habitum*] of men" (363).[17] The double meaning of the clerics' term *habitus,* as indicating both clothing and comportment, points to a connection between the habits of one's wardrobe and the habits of one's behavior. It suggests that what one wears will influence what one does, so that a woman who dresses like a man will start to act like a man as well. Indeed, the clerics complained in the *libelle d'Estivet* that, having ceased to wear women's clothes, Joan had also ceased "to do the other work appropriate to the female sex, comporting herself in all things like a man rather than like a woman" (212). Historical sources, whether Armagnac, Burgundian, or English, concur that Joan manifested all the boldness and prowess at arms usually seen as distinctive to men. At Orléans, she is said to have led the troops in driving the English back to their fortress of Les Tourelles, in setting these towers aflame, in obliging their inhabitants to flee, and ultimately in lifting the siege of the city. At Jargeau, a city downstream from Orléans, she is said to have led the attack by attempting to scale the external walls with a ladder and, when struck by an opponent's stone and thrown to the ground, to have quickly scrambled to her feet and rallied her men so that the city was soon taken. At Compiègne, she is said to have remained with the rear guard when the rest of her forces sought protection within the city. Georges

Chastellain, a Burgundian chronicler, wrote, "The Maid, surpassing the ture of woman, performed great feats and put much effort into saving her company from loss, remaining behind as the head and most valiant of her troop."[18] She was captured only when a rough archer, enraged that "a woman... should be the rebuttress of so many valiant men," as Chastellain put it, pulled her from her horse by her surcoat.[19] The clerics made clear that Joan not only had exceeded the nature of women in becoming a captain-at-arms, as Chastellain acknowledged in a more positive way, but had disrupted social structures in doing so. They wrote in the *libelle d'Estivet*,

> against the commands of God and the saints, Joan presumptuously and pridefully assumed dominion among and over men, constituting herself as head and leader of an army sometimes as numerous as sixteen thousand men, in which there were princes, barons, and many other noblemen whom she made serve under her as under a principal captain. (262)

Joan acted against the commands of God, who in Genesis made Eve only after having made Adam and only for his sake and later punished her for her role in the Fall by decreeing that she submit to her mate, and against the commands of Saint Paul, who in his letters observed that on account of Adam's temporal and causal priority to Eve, it is right for men to dominate women and for women to submit to men, covering their heads as a sign of this subservience. Instead of following these divine and saintly precepts, Joan dominated men, indeed, sixteen thousand men, and not only ordinary men but princes, barons, and other nobles. Instead of submitting to men, as women are supposed to do, she made them, however numerous and highly ranked, submit to her. Instead of covering her head, as an expression of her meekness and humility, she cut her hair, as a reflection of her presumption and pride. According to the clerics, Joan not only rejected God's and Saint Paul's commands in rejecting women's outer veiling and inner quietude but overturned her society's customs by making the man serve the woman, the nobleman serve the peasant, and the higher serve the lower.

The clerics attributed Joan's predilection for a masculine *habitus* to what they called *curiositas,* a word of complex meanings.[20] At times, they use this term to refer to Joan's predilection for masculine attire. In a set of admonitions on May 2, they described her as "wearing this deformed dress through curiosity [*pro curiositate*]" and as holding in contempt church prohibitions against transvestism "on account of curiosity [*propter curiositatem*] for indecent and dishonorable clothes" (339). In English at this time, "curiosity" could mean "care or attention carried to excess...

undue niceness or fastidiousness as to food, clothing, matters of taste and behavior," and though no Latin or French lexicons suggest similar definitions for *curiositas* or *curiosité* during these years, the clerics' language at Rouen could well have been contaminated by that of the English invaders, so that in their use, the term *curiositas* could well suggest an excessive interest in one's attire.[21] Pierre Tisset translates the *curiositas* with which Joan is characterized not as niceness or fastidiousness but as "désir pervers" or "goût pervers," however, and in doing so he correctly renders the term's connotation of unseemly and even unnatural erotic inclinations.[22] In comparing Joan's haircut to that of "fops" and her dress to that of "the most dissolute men," the clerics identified the desire expressed in her curiosity not with the sensuality of women, which would customarily show itself in a taste for jewelry, cosmetics, and feminine finery, but with the sensuality of men, and, indeed, of unnatural men who are made effeminate through their concern with personal attractiveness. Unable to accuse her of the sexual misdeeds of wanton women, such as temptresses and harlots, from whom she differed in her masculinity as well as in her virginity, they associated her, instead, with seducers and sodomites, even though she might seem to differ from them in her femaleness. As a woman delighting in doublets, surcoats, and banners rather than gowns and headdresses, Joan incarnated for the clerics a new and monstrous eroticism transgressive of traditional categories.

At times, the clerics used the term *curiositas* to denote Joan's penchant not for unsuitable dress but for inappropriate knowledge. In the *libelle d'Estivet*, they asserted that Joan's voices and visions, "rather than coming from God, have been made up by Joan at the instigation of the devil or have been shown to her by the demon himself in apparitions due to spells, in order to mock her curiosity [*sue curiositatis*] while she seeks things that are higher than her and that are above the faculties of her condition" (255). In their admonitions of May 2, they warned, "How grave also is the danger of curiously [*curiose*] probing into those things that are above oneself and wanting to believe new things, beyond the counsel of the Church and the prelates, or even inventing new and unaccustomed things" (340–41). Curiosity here appears to recall not so much the daintiness of coxcombs and profligates as the overzealousness of scholars. In contemporaneous works, such as Jean Gerson's *Contra curiositatem studentium*, Thomas à Kempis's *De Imitatione Christi*, and Nicholas of Cusa's *De docta ignorantia*, students are chastised for curiosity when they speculate about the hidden nature of God, about the time and manner in which the world began, and about other topics unfathomable by human reason or, even if fathomable, of no practical help in human life. One falls prey to this less fashionable and more intellectual variety of curiosity when one attempts to exceed limits not of what one can or should wear but of what one can or should know in general or what one can or should know given one's social position. Gerson, for example, asserted that curiosity ends in activities that are not beneficial to their perpetrators and then added that

> when one considers the end to which such an activity leads according to time, place, person, generation, station in life, profession and state, then this judgment of what is more and less beneficial changes in accordance with the different circumstances. Indeed, what is found harmful and improper for one is fitting and even commanded for another.[23]

If Joan fell prey to curiosity "while she seeks things that are higher than her and that are above the faculties of her condition" or while she consents to "probing into those things that are above oneself and wanting to believe new things," it was because she acted in a manner that may have been appropriate for high ecclesiastics but was inappropriate for laywomen. For the clerics, Joan was of a modest "condition," or social status, which corresponded to modest "faculties," or abilities at perception and understanding, and she should have recognized the lowliness of who she was and what she could know and should have acted in accordance with it. Yet Joan, far from acknowledging and respecting proper social and intellectual limitations, sought that which surpassed these boundaries and, hence, that which she would never be able to attain. As the clerics saw it, because of Joan's overweening desire to venture beyond what she was and what she could therefore know, she exposed herself to the temptations of the devil. As they suggested when they claimed Joan made up her apparitions or invented novelties, this demon might have goaded her to claim to have experienced what she had not experienced. Alternatively, as they suggested when they supposed Joan might have undergone actual apparitions, he might have appeared to her under the guise of an angel of light and thus induced her to take himself and his minions to be the saints and angels with whom she desires to confer. In either case, her desire for that which lay beyond her led her astray.

Through the double resonance of *curiositas*, the "curiosity" that led Joan to assume a man's clothes was linked to the "curiosity" that led her to assume a saint's revelations, and her transgression of sexual boundaries was linked to her transgression of human and social boundaries. Curious in the sense that she attempted to change who she was into who she wanted to be, Joan was perceived as a young peasant woman who tried to make herself into a debonair nobleman, a humble *vilaine* who tried to make herself into a proud captain-at-arms, and a devil-worshiping witch who tried to make herself into a popularly venerated holy woman. Throughout her various actions, the clerics intimated, Joan erred from the moment of her departure for France not only in pursuing her own will but in attempting to transform her natural identity through this pursuit of her will. If Joan was disturbing to these clerics, it was because she represented to them a self-fashioning subject, like the idolatrous temple prostitutes and the manly Amazons of ancient history, oblivious to the multiple levels of forces that had already fashioned and that continued still to fashion her.

A Simple Maid

Though the clerics depicted Joan as following her own will when she departed for France, Joan depicted herself as following the will of another at this time. In the minutes of interrogation, in telling how a voice first addressed her in her father's garden when she was thirteen years old, she stated that

> it ... told Joan it to be necessary that she, Joan, come to France. ... [T]he voice told her two or three times a week that it was necessary that she, Joan, leave and come to France. ... [T]he voice told her that she should come to France and that she could no longer stay where she was, and ... the voice told her that she should lift the siege set before Orléans. (48)

Three times in succession, Joan maintained that the voice conveyed an impersonal necessity that she leave her village. Three times in succession, she suggested that it was this impersonal necessity on the part of the voice and not any personal desire on her part that prompted her to leave. Though she did represent the voice as promising her that she would lift the siege of Orléans, she depicted herself as less enticed by this promise than compelled by the commands that preceded it. Just as the clerics highlighted Joan's will to leave for France by contrasting it with her parents' opposition to this project, Joan highlighted the voice's insistence that she go by contrasting it with her reluctance to depart. After the voice told her that it was necessary for her to go to the aid of France, she said, she protested that she was "a poor girl who knew neither how to ride a horse nor how to lead a war" (48). Far from expressing any ambition to perform the great deeds proposed by the voice, as the clerics represented her as doing, she recalled expressing concern that she was not capable of performing such great deeds. She went on to say that she incorporated the voice's vocabulary of impersonal necessity into her own explanations of her departure to those she encountered. When she appealed to Durand Laxart to take her to Vaucouleurs, she stated, "she . . . told her said uncle that it was necessary for her to go to the said fortified city of Vaucouleurs" (49). When she appealed to Robert de Baudricourt to grant her escort to Chinon, she reported similarly that "she . . . told Robert that it was necessary for her to come to France" (49). She portrayed herself as having presented to these men not an individual caprice, which they could or could not have chosen to indulge, but a general duty to which they, like she, had to submit. Though the clerics blamed Joan for having disrupted familial life by not respecting her parents' authority, Joan excused this failure by stressing the greater authority of him whose order she did heed. Asked if she believed that she had failed to honor her parents in leaving their home against their wishes, she replied, "when God commanded, it was necessary that it be done," adding, "as God commanded it, if she had had a hundred fathers and mothers and if she were the daughter of a king, nevertheless, she would have left" (124). It was not that Joan opposed her will to that of her parents but, rather, she affirmed, that God opposed his will to theirs. If it had merely been a question of her own will, she suggested that she would have readily submitted to her parents, but it was a question, instead, of God's will, to which she could not say no. The clerics depicted Joan as a subject rebelling against familial power, yet she depicted herself as a soul obeying a power even more demanding than that of her family.

While the clerics maintained that Joan wore men's clothes and carried men's arms because she wanted to do so, Joan insisted that she acted in this manner, again, because a higher force compelled her to do so. As she claimed that it had been necessary for her to leave for France, she averred, "It had been necessary for her to change her clothes into men's clothes" (51). When the clerics exhorted her to abandon this attire, she replied that "she could not change her clothes, nor was it in her to do so" and that "if it were in her, it would be quickly done" (182–83). Though the clerics repeatedly attempted to trace the source of this impersonal necessity that made her adopt men's attire, Joan repeatedly deflected these attempts by responding to their specific queries about her assumption of this costume with general answers about her deeds altogether. When the clerics inquired if the voices demanded that she wear men's apparel, for example, she replied ambiguously, "She did not take these clothes, nor do anything, but by the command of God and the angels" (75), and " 'All that I have done of worth, I have done by the command of my voices' " (128). When the clerics asked if the command to assume such apparel was legitimate, she answered, again ambiguously, " 'All that I have done is by the command of the Lord and, if he had commanded me to assume others, I would have assumed them' " (75). Even when the clerics asked if Joan believed she had acted well, "in this particular case, in taking men's clothes" (75), she replied, "there was nothing in the world that she did which was not done by the command of God" (75), still insisting upon subsuming the small issue of her vestments into the larger issue of her overall accomplishments. Throughout their discussions, Joan consistently refused to isolate the costume she wore from the feats she performed while wearing this costume. She stated that the clothes were "the least of things" (75), as if they had meaning not in and of themselves but only insofar as they were a part of her greater mission. At one point, she declared, "still now, if she were among those of the other party, in these clothes and acting as she had acted before her capture, it seems to her that it would be one of the great benefits for France" (128), as if her garments and the deeds she had performed in them were so closely connected that renouncing the one would mean renouncing the possibility of ever returning to the other. Though Joan refused to affirm that God or the voices directly commanded her to dress as she did, she did affirm that they indirectly commanded her to do so by ordering her to perform deeds for which such a costume would be necessary, and she insisted that she must obey this more subtle demand no less than its more obvious counterparts. Once again, it was an external force, separate from herself and even in opposition to herself, that compelled her to do what she did.

Whereas the clerics depicted Joan as having engineered the seemingly supernatural deeds she accomplished, whether through magic or through fraud, Joan attributed them to God's divine powers. The clerics, as we remember, represented Joan as having boasted to the king that she herself would restore his country to him. Joan, in contrast, stated that she had informed her sovereign "that our Lord would return to him his kingdom of France, would have him crowned at Reims, and would expel his adversaries," adding, "And of this she was a messenger from the part of God" (214). The clerics, as we also recall, portrayed Joan as having claimed that she would accomplish these deeds through the exercise of her magical art. Joan, in contrast, alleged she had repudiated all such sorcery. When the clerics, suspicious of the seemingly enchanted standard she bore in battle, asked if the victory she experienced when carrying it was due to the standard or to herself, she replied, "it was based in the Lord and not in another" (173). As it was not herself but "our Lord" who, she prophesied to her king, would bring about her feats in France, it was neither herself nor her standard but "our Lord" who, she recollected to the clerics, brought about these feats.

It is true that God's role in determining and executing Joan's actions does not appear to have been absolute, though it was no less important as a result. Joan declared, for example, that "she would like better to be torn apart by horses than to have come to France without the permission of God" (75). With this reference not to God's "command" but to his "permission," she indicated that God had not so much imposed his will upon her as allowed her to pursue her own will. Similarly, she stated that however much she would like to escape her captivity, God had not yet granted her "permission" to do so and that "without permission she would not leave" (156). Again, she indicated that it was not so much that God would someday compel her to escape as that he would someday tolerate her flight. Furthermore, even though Joan insisted that she must receive God's permission before acting, this requirement does not appear to have prevented her from responding positively to situations in which she found herself. Of her imprisonment in Rouen, she said, "If she saw the door open, she would leave. And she believes firmly, if she saw the door open and if the guards and the other Englishmen were unable to resist, she would understand that this was her permission and that God had sent her help" (156). With these words, Joan established that she was not obligated to receive a communication of God's "permission" before taking advantage of an opportunity to escape. Instead, she made clear, she might find that God's "permission" took the very form of just such an opportunity to flee. Finally, even as Joan insisted that she needed God's "permission," whether in the form of a communication or in the form of a chance to do what she wanted, before acting, this stipulation did not restrict her to waiting passively for such a chance. She stated, "But without permission she would not leave, unless it be that she made an undertaking, in French, *une entreprise*, to know whether God would be content." The minutes continue, "And she cited the proverb in French, '*Aide toy, Dieu te aidera*'" (156). Here, God's "permission" might take the form not merely of an opportunity to escape but of her own successful effort to gain her liberty. Instead of deferring her action until she received some mystical message permitting it, she indicated, she acted because the permission is implicit in a situation favorable to her action or even in a successful performance of this action. When Joan asserted that if she did not succeed in escaping her previous prisons at Beaulieu and Beaurevoir, despite her attempts to do so, it was because "it did not please God that she escape at that time" (156), she revealed that her perception of God's permission functioned less to curb her own will and consequent actions than to explain the otherwise inexplicable outcomes of these actions. Even though what God wanted Joan to do might manifest itself only in what she succeeded in doing, this perception of divine agency as determinative of her fate was nonetheless influential in her thinking.

Though the clerics portrayed Joan as transforming herself from a village maid into a captain-at-arms, Joan represented herself as essentially unaltered despite this change in social status. The clerics questioned Joan about a letter in which she was said to have referred to herself as a *caput guerre*, but she denied that she had ever used this expression. Later she clarified her statement, saying that "if she was a captain-at-war, it was in order to beat the English" (262). By presenting her identification as a captain as a hypothetical rather than an actual condition, Joan demonstrated her hesitation to identify herself as a professional military leader. By limiting this identification to her mission of routing the English, she showed that she became a captain only in order to accomplish a specific goal, which, being completed, would presumably leave her free to return to her earlier persona. Indeed, Joan indicated throughout the minutes of her interrogations that she regarded this shift from village maid to captain as affecting only what she did and not what she was. If Joan had been affected essentially rather than accidentally by this shift in her status, one might expect her to have associated her parents with her earlier self and to have distanced herself from them because of that association. One might expect her to resemble the Pucelle of Shakespeare's *Henry VI, Part One*, who rejects her father as a "Decrepit miser! Base ignoble wretch!," refuses to kneel before him and take his blessing, and disdains his rough, peasant idiom with her lofty, literary speech.[24] Yet when the clerics asked why when she was in battle she had looked fondly upon a ring that her parents had given her, Joan replied that she contemplated it "out of pleasure and for the honor of her father and mother" (176). Though she stated that her parents had threatened her with drowning if she went off with soldiers and that they had almost lost their minds after her departure for France, Joan nonetheless conveyed that she took comfort in recalling them when she was in a context so different from and even opposed to that in which she had once known them. If Joan had been transformed by this change in her condition, one might expect her to have connected her former tasks with her former self and to have spurned them for that reason. Yet when the clerics asked if she had acquired any trade in her youth, Joan replied that she had learned how to sew and spin and that "she did not fear any woman of Rouen in spinning and sewing" (46). Though she had long since exchanged the feminine, domestic skills of her childhood for the masculine, martial skills of her adult career, she continued to compare herself to other women and continued to pride herself in the abilities she had once cultivated in her village.

Far from regarding herself as having become a captain-at-arms, Joan indicated that she regarded her military position as a temporary one that she would abandon as soon as she could. She consistently maintained that the time would come when she would have completed her masculine deeds and, hence, would be able to discard the masculine clothes that had marked and facilitated her performance of them. She informed the clerics, " 'when it pleases God to command, these clothes will be put off' " (154), and " 'when I have done that for which I have been sent on the part of God, I will take women's clothes' " (344). In the *libelle d'Estivet*, Joan is depicted as praying to her voices, " 'I know well, as for the clothes, how I took them, but I know not in what manner I should leave them. For this, would that it pleased you to teach me' " (252). As Joan depicted her masculine costume and comportment as temporary in their duration, she depicted her virginity, which also masculinized her in medieval eyes, removing her from the female sphere of materiality and biological reproduction to the male sphere of spirituality and cultural production, as likewise impermanent. The "maid" or *pucelle*, with whom Joan identified herself and was identified by others, differs from the "virgin" or *vierge* in that her maidenhood was seen as a transitional period in her life, after which she might or might not marry, whereas virginity was a lifetime vocation. When asked whether she had been told that the voices would no longer come to her if she were married, Joan replied that "that was not revealed to her" (174). Still attached to her parents, still proud of her feminine skills, Joan did not exclude the possibility that someday, if not now, she would abandon her masculine attire and pursuits and would marry, bear children, and resume a conventional existence. For Joan, as she depicted herself in her responses at Rouen, this life of warfare, horses, and politics was a play in which she appeared. Like all actors, she did what was necessary to fulfill her part in the play, organizing battles, spurring on her troops, and leading them to victory. As masterfully as Joan appeared to act the role and as naturally as it appeared to come to her, it remained a role, something separate from what she perceived as her self.

Neither the subject who transforms others nor the object who is transformed, Joan did, at one point, define her position in regard to the actions with which she was associated. When the clerics asked why God chose her rather than another to perform the tasks she had undertaken, Joan replied that "it was pleasing to God to have the adversaries of the king repelled by a simple maid" (139). While God serves as the subject, arranging for the king's adversaries to be repelled, and the adversaries serve as the object, being driven away, Joan functions as the object of a preposition, the simple maid by whom the action was effected. Joan presented herself as the instrument of divine volition, and in doing so can be seen to resemble not the pagan women who wore men's clothes of their own will but the Christian women who wore such attire by God's will, and not the Amazons who fought out of their own desire for "fleeting glory" but the biblical Esther, Judith, and Deborah, who entered into public life to fulfill God's desire to save his people.

The vast majority of authors on Joan, whether they be neoclassicists or Romantics in the seventeenth and eighteenth centuries, nationalists or Catholics in the nineteenth century, or suffragettes or spiritualists in the twentieth century, have stressed either Joan's agency, as a captain-at-arms, or her mediation of an other's agency, as an envoy of God, in saving her country. On the basis of the transcripts of the trial, however, it becomes difficult to state either that Joan was a diabolical self-creator, defiant of all authorities and of all identities established by such authorities, or that she was a blessed medium of a transcendent will, obedient to the highest of all powers as well as to the lower familial or societal powers whose expectations mirrored that divine volition. One can argue with equal conviction that Joan was distinguished by an active, almost Blakean initiative in transforming herself into what she wanted to be and that she was marked by a more passive, almost Marian willingness to serve as the handmaid of the Lord. It is not clear that these two portraits of Joan are irreconcilable, that the woman who believed herself destined to go to the aid of her country might not also have taken pleasure in that for which she felt ordained, however much she was unable to articulate this pleasure, to defend it, or to integrate it into her self-image, yet both parties clearly perceived them as irreconcilable, the one as wicked in its selfishness, the other as virtuous in its altruism. In their failure to reconcile Joan's subjectivity and her objectivity, her transgressiveness and her submissiveness, her pleasure and her duty, the transcripts illustrate the difficulty, then as now, of perceiving these categories as not intrinsically opposed.

4 | The Sign for the King

Throughout the sessions of the trial in which the participants discussed Joan's festivities near the Fairy Tree, her audition of voices from God, and her departure for France, they also addressed the sign with which Joan allegedly proved the legitimacy of her mission to her king and with which she might again prove it to her interrogators. In the exchanges about the fairy ladies, the voices, and the departure, the clerics questioned Joan in the manner of scholastics. They sought to elicit her views as to whether a Christian should join in rites held near locales associated with supernatural beings, whether a Christian should trust voices claiming to be saints and angels, and whether a Christian should assume the costume and comportment of the opposite sex, and they decided whether these views adequately corresponded to their preconceptions, as theologians and canonists, of what she should believe. In the exchanges about the sign, however, as we shall see, the clerics questioned Joan in the manner of inquisitors. They sought to learn through what sign Joan had proved her claims to divine inspiration to the Armagnacs, and they determined whether this sign sufficiently matched their preconceptions, as judges and assistants, of what such evidence should be. As they shifted from

lastic to the judicial level of their inquiry, the clerics were con-
less with the content of Joan's doctrine than with the proof of her
ence.

During the late Middle Ages, both peasant visionaries and clerical examiners appear to have expected those who alleged supernatural encounters to furnish signs of these encounters before they would be believed.
The Spanish and Catalan seers studied by William A. Christian counted
upon those around them, lay as well as clerical, to reject their tales unless
they were given proof. Some of these visionaries were so anxious about
the likelihood of a skeptical response to their claims that they discussed
this eventuality with the spirits who appeared to them. When the Virgin
Mary ordered one man to inform his neighbors that they must resume
religious services at a local chapel in her honor, he objected, " 'Señora,
they will not believe me,' " to which the Virgin replied, " 'Go, and if they
do not believe you, let them be.' "[1] Some visionaries suffered such trepidation at the thought of a hostile reaction that they shrank from disclosing their visions and, as a result, failed to fulfill the spirits' commands,
even though they earned beatings from them for their disobedience. More
often, however, the spirits granted the visionaries signs verifying their apparition in order to ensure the accomplishment of the tasks they had assigned. When the Virgin told one woman to persuade her neighbors that
they must set their souls in order before an imminent epidemic, she pressed
the woman's fingers together in the shape of a cross and instructed her,
" 'Now, go with this sign so that they will believe you.' "[2] When the Virgin
told another woman to inform her neighbors that they must avert an on-
coming plague by building a new church, she marked the woman's shoul-
der with the impression of her fingers. After Saint Michael ordered a man
to inspire his community to construct a new chapel and form a religious
brotherhood, he crippled the man's legs, curing him only when he was
carried to the site where the chapel was to be built. Only after these seers
displayed the signs bestowed upon them by these saints did they expect
and receive the credence they sought.

For these late medieval visionaries, signs often if not always took the
form of material and indeed, corporeal transformations, such as twisted
fingers, imprinted skin, and enfeebled limbs, that could be examined and
recognized by all as objective evidence of superior interventions. According to Christian, "Signs . . . are phenomena that can be independently ver-
ified by the senses. They can be seen by anyone who looks, felt by anyone
who touches. Most late medieval apparitions are 'confirmed' by signs."[3]
Comparing the signs that these Iberian visionaries produced when obliged

to defend their assertions of visions to the responses that Joan made when similarly challenged, Christian concludes, "Jeanne had no sign."[4] Because she was unable to point to any bodily deformation or indeed to any empirical evidence at all of her allegations, Joan seemed to differ from these southern visionaries in her failure to provide external proof of her claims. Yet if Joan was unable to supply a sign, it is not clear whether it was because, as Christian puts it, she "had no sign" or because those who examined her could not see the sign she did have.

In the transcripts of Joan's trial, both the clerics who examined Joan at Rouen and Joan herself acknowledged that a visionary must be able to provide a sign of her contact with spirits before her claims to visions could be believed, yet they differed in their application of that requirement to Joan's case. The clerics denied that Joan had furnished any such sign, yet they did so assuming that the sign would exist objectively, separate from the thing it signified and separate from the person who perceived it. Joan, in contrast, insisted that she had furnished a sign, yet she did so assuming that the sign would exist subjectively, inseparable from the thing it signified and from the person who beheld it. Whereas the clerics protested that the sign was currently absent from the world and that it was Joan's responsibility to come forth with it, Joan maintained that the sign was already present in the world and that it was the clerics' responsibility to open their eyes to it. The clerics, convinced of the objective status of a sign, resembled other members of their ecclesiastical caste and, in particular, their fellow inquisitors, who stressed the necessity of collecting and evaluating evidence in the resolution of judicial cases, but Joan, persuaded of the subjective mediation of the sign, shared neither their judicial background nor the attitude toward evidence that it inculcated. If the clerics maintained that Joan failed to provide a sign while Joan affirmed that she did so, it was because the two parties held such radically different notions of what such a sign should be.

The clerics and Joan clashed on doctrinal as well as probatory matters, yet, here, Joan was the one who maintained control over the dialogue. As we saw earlier, when she spoke about theological and canonical matters, her words suggested that she often did not grasp the essential problems that the clerics saw in her replies. She did not understand, for example, that allusions to "fairy ladies" as such could not be reconciled with a belief in Christian monotheism, nor did she realize that the appearance of an angel of light could often disguise a demon. Though she perceived that dress and behavior at odds with one's natural social condition were to be reproached if undertaken out of personal desire, she did not grasp that the pleasure she seemed to take in her masculine persona might suggest that she had assumed it out of just such an inclination. Failing to apprehend the problems that so clearly disturbed her interrogators, Joan often repeated herself in her responses, insisting, for example, that she knew her voices were from God or that she was prevented from discarding men's clothes. When she spoke about these more judicial matters, however, her words suggested that though she did not share the clerics' unhappiness with her replies, she was readily able to understand and respond to their dissatisfaction with them. She spoke on one level when she acknowledged the objectivity of the sign and attempted to establish that objectivity and on another level when she continued to assert the necessarily subjective nature of any appreciation of the sign and thus remained true to her own convictions. Though the clerics and Joan may have disagreed in their conceptions of how one could go about proving an affiliation with God, it was Joan who, until the last day of the trial, made these conceptions seem not to conflict.

The King's Prayer

During the interrogations at Rouen, the clerics demanded that Joan show them a sign to persuade them of the divine nature of her mission. In his appeal to Joan on May 23, Pierre Maurice demonstrated most eloquently why they needed such a sign. Maurice asked Joan to imagine that her king had entrusted her with the protection of a fortress and had forbidden her from receiving just anyone who might arrive at its gates. If someone did arrive, claiming to come on the king's authority, he proposed that Joan would neither trust this stranger nor allow him into the fortress "unless he brings letters or another certain sign [*signum certum*]" (381). In refusing entry to any stranger without a "certain sign" of his legitimacy, he suggested, she would resemble Saint Peter and his ecclesiastical successors who, when Jesus Christ ascended into heaven, were entrusted with the government of the church and forbidden from receiving those who came in God's name "unless this is demonstrated sufficiently otherwise than by their own words." He concluded, "You should certainly not have faith in those who say themselves to have come in this manner, nor should we give faith in you, as God commands the opposite" (382). In demanding a sign of Joan's divine affiliation, Maurice, a Burgundian at Rouen, echoed the Armagnacs at Poitiers who had examined Joan two years earlier and who also demanded a sign from her.[5] Seguin de Seguin, the Dominican dean of the Faculty of Theology at the University of Poitiers, recalled having told Joan that "God did not want her to be believed unless something *how were they following Gods orders?*

appeared on account of which it seemed to them that she was lieved, and they would not advise the king, on the basis of her simpl. sertion, that soldiers be given to her and placed in danger unless she had something else to say."[6] Both Maurice and Seguin asserted that Joan's words, in and of themselves, were insufficient to convince them that she had been sent on the part of God, and both expressed concern for the dangers to which a reckless credence in these words would expose them. Both depicted themselves as following God's orders in demanding a sign of her.

In their appeals Maurice and Seguin both assumed the objectivity of the sign and of the process through which it would be recognized. To begin with, by their very act of demanding a sign, they assumed that a sign was a discrete entity, separate from the thing it signified, which Joan could provide for them if she were truly sent by God. The Faculty of Canon Law at the university shed light upon this assumption when, in their opinion on Joan's case, they too chastised Joan for not having provided a sign of her divine provenance and contrasted her to other visionaries who did furnish such signs. Moses, these canonists recall, could turn a staff into a snake and a snake into a staff, and John the Baptist could point to a passage in Isaiah, "I am the voice of he who cries in the desert, 'Prepare the way of the Lord'" (363), as a prediction of his advent.[7] Zanon, the bishop of Lisieux, who contributed an opinion to Joan's trial, similarly warned that a visionary should not be believed unless she could point to "the appearance of some signs and miracles or the special testimony of some passage in Scripture" (320) that would justify her claims. These clerics suggested that a sign of a divine mission would consist of a miracle, like that which Moses enacted, or a passage from Scripture prophesying one's arrival, like that which John the Baptist quoted. In addition, because for Maurice and Seguin a sign was something that existed as a sign and was recognized as such, it was supposed to contain within it an intrinsic ability to persuade the beholder of that which it signified. When Maurice referred to that which he demanded from Joan as a "certain sign," he indicated that certainty was an attribute of the sign, adhering to it as the king's seal might adhere to an envoy's letter, authorizing it and rendering its claims credible to all who read it. If one was persuaded by a sign, Maurice's phraseology implied, it was because the sign possessed a certainty that brought about this persuasion, and if one was not convinced, it was because the sign lacked the sufficient certainty to bring about that conviction. In either case, the responsibility for bringing about certainty lay with the sign or with its bearer and not with its interpreter. Finally, because the sign existed objectively and brought about certainty objectively, the thing signified by the sign, such as the truth or falsity of an individual's claims to be sent by God, was unaffected by the reading of the evidence. Just as the authorities who examined the alleged envoy's papers were presumed not to interfere with his status as envoy, the ecclesiastics who evaluated the miracles of an alleged visionary were presumed not to alter her status as visionary. Both sets of officials were thought to perform entirely supplementary tasks in interpreting the signs of these claimed affiliations. Though the clerics' assumptions about the sign may appear to be neutral and even academic nuances, they were not unrelated to their failure, as Burgundians, to see Joan as bearing a sign when the Armagnacs had succeeded in doing so.

As they investigated the sign through which Joan might prove her claims to have heard the voices from God, the clerics at Rouen could not but direct their attention to the seemingly miraculous act of recognition through which she proved these claims to those of her party. In response to their questions, Joan acknowledged that as she traveled from Vaucouleurs to Chinon, she had been concerned with how she would manage to persuade Charles, her king, of the legitimacy of her mission. En route, she stated, she sent her sovereign a letter announcing that she had journeyed more than 150 leagues to see him and that she knew "many good things for him." She added, "And it seemed to her that, in the same letter, it was indicated that she would recognize well the said king among all the others" (76). Continuing her account of her arrival at Chinon, Joan stated that she went first to an inn, where she ate a meal, and then ascended to the castle, which presided, and indeed which continues to preside, over the city. When she entered the castle, she went on, she was led into a large hall filled with more than three hundred knights and fifty torches, "without counting the spiritual light" (76). Despite the presence of so many sumptuously dressed noblemen in the hall, her report continued, "When she entered into the chamber of the said king, she recognized him among the others by the counsel of her voice, who revealed him to her" (51–52). The Armagnacs who testified to Joan's recognition of Charles upon her arrival often embellished her account with additional dramatic details. Simon Charles, the president of the *Chambre des Comptes*, maintained at the rehabilitation that the king receded from the crowd in order to prevent Joan from recognizing him as she had prophesied that she would do. He related that "when the king knew that she was coming, he withdrew to the side, separating himself from others. Nevertheless, Joan knew him well and made reverence to him."[8] Other sources affirmed that the king or his courtiers went so far as to attempt to persuade Joan that another lord was her sovereign. The chronicler Jean Chartier wrote that though various courtiers were far more richly clothed than the king, Joan approached the monarch and knelt before him in an act of homage. The king protested, " 'It is not I who am king, Joan,' " and, gesturing to another man, he added, " 'Here is the king.' "[9] Despite this effort at dissimulation, Chartier related, Joan replied, " 'In the name of God, gentle prince, it is you and no other.' "[10] Jean Moreau, a merchant from Lorraine who was not present in the hall and who thus spoke from hearsay at the rehabilitation, alleged similarly that "when she arrived, it was said to her that another was the king, seeing that she had never before recognized the king, but she said that this was not the case."[11] The *Journal du siège d'Orléans*, the *Chronique de la Pucelle*, and the *Miroir des femmes vertueuses*, in addition to Chartier's *Histoire de Charles VII*, all depicted various courtiers as pretending that they, and not Charles, were the king and Joan as seeing through these attempts to dupe her. Joan claimed in the minutes of the interrogations simply to have recognized the king, yet these other Armagnacs stressed the extraordinariness of her recognition by representing her as overcoming obstacles in doing so.

Though virtually all historians agree that Joan seems to have recognized Charles the first time she saw him, it is not clear how to read the additional allegations that she succeeded in this endeavor despite efforts to trick her. Henri Wallon and Claude Desama have pointed out that neither Joan nor the witnesses at the rehabilitation who were present at Chinon, such as Raoul de Gaucourt and Regnault Thierry, alluded to these attempted deceptions.[12] Given this evidence, these historians argue that the accounts of the courtiers' attempt to impede Joan from recognizing Charles constitute, as Desama puts it, "royal propaganda" aimed at making the feat even more remarkable than it actually was.[13] If Wallon and Desama are right and if Joan did recognize the king without having to overcome these various attempts at deception, however, the Armagnacs' embellishments, far from meaningless in themselves, can still be read as an indication of what exactly the adherents of this party found impressive in this act of recognition. In 1429, when Joan entered the great hall, Charles's identity as the rightful king of France had been in question for nine years, since his father, the mad King Charles VI, had signed the Treaty of Troyes naming Henry V of England as his successor and since his mother, Isabeau of Bavaria, had repudiated his legitimacy, perhaps as a result of English coercion, perhaps not. For all these years, the duke of Burgundy and his followers, who now numbered over half of his potential subjects, had withheld their fealty from him, citing his alleged bastardy. In the scene that these sources portray, Charles's identity as rightful king of France was denied by his courtiers, whose superiority of dress overshadowed his own poor attire and whose amusements involved not only disputing that Charles was king but usurping his role as sovereign. Even Charles himself denied he was the king, telling Joan, according to Chartier, " 'It is not I who am king.' " In this context, where the rightfulness of Charles's claim to the throne was contested both in actuality and in jest, Joan's gesture of kneeling before him and affirming, " 'In the name of God, gentle prince, it is you and no other' " took on a new meaning. At the same moment that Joan literally recognized Charles as the king, God, who was said to have sent her to him, could also be seen, more figuratively, to recognize him as the authentic ruler of France. Whether or not Joan's own sober account of her first meeting with Charles represented what "actually happened" in the castle, the witnesses' and the chroniclers' more elaborate accounts, with their playfully treasonous courtiers, their self-effacing monarch, and their insightful maid, may indicate faithfully the meaning of the events for the Armagnacs.

When one turns from Joan's recognition of Charles in the great hall of the castle of Chinon to the conversation between the maid and the monarch that ensued, one can observe a similar contrast between Joan's relatively simple narration of what happened and the Armagnacs' more extravagant version. On the first day of her public trial, when the clerics requested that she swear to speak the truth about all that she would be asked, Joan replied enigmatically that she would not tell them all that she knew because "as for the revelations which had been made to her on the part of God, she had never spoken of them or revealed them to anyone, except to Charles alone whom she says to be her king" (38). Later, after she recounted how she had recognized her sovereign in the hall, she described perhaps the same conversation with her king, perhaps another one, by stating plainly, "She told her king that she wanted to go wage war against the English" (52). The witnesses at the rehabilitation and the chroniclers of Joan's feats focused more on the mysterious "revelations" that Joan first said she discussed with the king than on the mundane plans to wage war that she later spoke of having mentioned. They indicated, in particular, that Joan spoke with the king in private and disclosed to him a certain "secret" that constituted a "sign" that she was sent to him on the part of God. Simon Charles testified at the rehabilitation that Joan "spoke with the king for a long space of time. And, having heard her, the king appeared joyful."[14] The *Miroir des femmes vertueuses* similarly depicted the king withdrawing to the end of a hall and ordering Joan to follow him. It continued, "She spoke to him for about an hour, without another person but those two knowing what she said to him, And the king wept most tenderly, which made the chamberlains who saw his face want to approach him to interrupt the conversation, but the king made a sign for them to draw back and let her speak."[15] Jean d'Aulon, Joan's squire, confirmed this testimony at the rehabilitation by affirming that "the said Maid spoke to the king our lord secretly and told him some secret things, which he does not know."[16] Other informants related a similar encounter between Joan and the king, though in semi- rather than absolute privacy. Jean, the duke of Alençon, who was present at Chinon at this time, asserted that during her second day in the city, "Joan came to the king's mass and, when she perceived the king, she bowed. And the king led her into a chamber, and with him were he who is speaking and the lord [Georges] de La Trémouille, whom the king retained, ordering that the others retire."[17] The *Chronique de la Pucelle* likewise showed the king sending away his courtiers, with the exception of Alençon, Robert Le Maçon, Christophe d'Harcourt, and Gérard Machet, and making those present swear, on Joan's request, that they would say nothing about that which would now happen. Whether Joan met with the king alone or in the presence of a small number of courtiers, these sources agree that she conferred with the king in an interview from which others were excluded and that she communicated to him at this time a certain "secret" that earned her his support. Jean Pasquerel, Joan's confessor, maintained that after Joan's interview with the king, "the king said to his assistants that Joan had told him certain secrets which no one knew or could know, except for God. For this reason, he had great confidence in her."[18] Though Jean Dunois, the Bastard of Orléans, kept silent about this exchange in his testimony at the rehabilitation, he is cited by Thomas Basin, in his *Histoire de Charles VII*, as having claimed to have heard the king say that Joan "had revealed to him, as proof of her words, things so secret and hidden that no mortal but himself could have had knowledge of them but by divine revelation."[19] All these sources speak of Joan's disclosure of a secret to the king, but only the chronicler Pierre Sala identifies the content of this matter.[20] According to Sala, Guillaume Gouffier, the lord of Boissy and an intimate of the king's, claimed to have heard Charles confide that in the days preceding Joan's arrival, he had been plagued with anxieties about the legitimacy of his birth and the consequent legitimacy of his claim to the French throne. Charles told his friend that on the eve of her appearance at Chinon, he had prayed to God to inform him if he were, in fact, the true king of France, to help him if he were, and to allow him to retreat to Spain or Scotland if he were not. When Joan spoke to Charles during their first meeting, she reminded him of this dream and presented herself as the messenger sent to convey this divine reassurance. Though Joan spoke simply of having transmitted to the king certain "revelations" that had been made to her, these other Armagnacs asserted that she had revealed God's own affirmation of the legitimacy of Charles's birth and rule.

Almost all historians concur that Joan succeeded in persuading Charles of the authenticity of her mission, at least for a time, but it is not clear how to reconcile the various accounts of how she accomplished this task. Numerous scholars, including Jules Quicherat, Régine Pernoud, Marie-Véronique Clin, and Pierre Duparc, have accepted Sala's report that Joan recalled to Charles a prayer he had recently made. Desama, once again, however, has pointed out that several important witnesses at the rehabilitation made no reference in their testimony to a secret encounter between Joan and the king and has deduced that whether these two parties spoke privately or not, whatever they said must not have been of a secret nature.[21] Far from recalling any revelation of the hidden matters to which he also alluded, Pasquerel, for example, quoted Joan as informing Charles at this time, " 'I tell you, on the part of *messire*, that you are the true heir of France and the son of the king, and he sends me to you to lead you to Reims,' " that is, as saying nothing that she had not said already and would not say again many times in public.[22] Other witnesses recalled Joan announcing to the king that she would lift the siege of Orléans and lead him to his coronation, demanding from him an army, horses, and arms with which to accomplish these deeds, and, thus, again saying nothing new, nothing occult, and nothing seemingly confidential. Yet even if Desama is again right and Joan revealed no genuine secret to the king, these embellishments of the Armagnacs remain telling. Joan might have reassured the king that he was "the true heir of France and the son of the king" without alluding to any prayer the king had made for such reassurance. But when she uttered these words, she nevertheless knew of his desire for reaffirmation and responded to that desire with an insight and a confidence that seemed beyond human scope. As her simple recognition of Charles in a crowded room was seen to reflect a divine recognition of him among various contenders for the throne, her simple declaration of Charles' legitimacy and her desire to support him was seen to reflect a divine declaration of that legitimacy and a divine desire to champion his cause. The acts of bowing to an uncertain king and of assuaging his unspoken anxieties, though they were not acknowledged as signs of godly affiliation by the clerics of Rouen, were acknowledged as such signs by persons open to their symbolic potential.

The Angel's Crown

As the clerics at Rouen continued their investigation, they demanded more details about the nature of the sign with which Joan persuaded those of her party that she heard voices from God. In her full account of the sign, Joan stated that one day she was in the house of the goodwoman of Chinon with whom she was then residing, praying, as she was almost always praying at that time, when an angel appeared before her. Beholding this spiritual being, Joan knelt, removed her cap, and thanked God for having sent her the sign that he had promised. Together Joan and the angel strolled to the castle of Chinon, accompanied by other angels, some winged, some not winged, some crowned, some not crowned, whom not everyone they passed was able to see. Joan and the angel ascended the steps to the king's chamber, which the angel entered first, followed by Joan. " 'Lord,' " said Joan to the king, " 'Here is your sign. Take it' " (136). The angel bowed before the king, reminded him of the fair patience that he, Charles, had shown during his great tribulations, and certified that he would possess the entire kingdom of France by means of God's help and Joan's labor. The king should put Joan to work and give her soldiers to assist her, the angel warned, or else he would not be so quickly crowned and anointed. As confirmation of these words, the angel also brought a sign that Joan described as something "in the manner of a crown" (140), and he gave it to Regnault de Chartres, the archbishop of Reims, who in turn gave it to the king. When Charles and those who were with him saw this sign and the angel who brought it, Joan added, she asked her lord if he were content and he responded that he was. Afterward, Joan reported, she heard that more than three hundred people saw the sign, including many notable knights, such as Charles de Bourbon, Georges de La Trémouille, and Jean d'Alençon. She stated that there were "several other knights who saw and heard [the sign] as well as Joan sees the men speaking to her and standing before her" (116). After these events took place, Joan went to a small chapel nearby, and it was in this chapel that the angel quitted her, leaving her "very upset at his departure." She explained, "she also wept and would willingly have gone with him, that is, have her soul go with him" (138). The sign, as Joan put it elsewhere, was the crown that this angel bore to her king and that persons both numerous and eminent beheld.

It may seem, at first glance, that Joan's depiction of the sign the angel brought to her king resembled the clerics' depictions of the sign that they required from her. To begin with, Joan represented the bearer of the sign and the sign itself as separate from herself and from her claims to be sent by God. The angel whom she portrayed escorting her to the castle and speaking with the king appeared to be entirely distinct from Joan, who was there by his side and hearing his words. The crown this angel carried appeared to be entirely distinct from the mission it was said to signify. In addition, Joan represented the sign as possessing within it an inherent certainty. The appearance of an angel bearing a crown could be agreed to be sufficiently remarkable to qualify as a miracle and, thus, to possess the intrinsic capacity to persuade its beholder characteristic of a "certain sign." Finally, Joan showed her contact with God as existing before it was acknowledged as existing by the king and his courtiers, so that the signification of the sign seems unaffected by those spectators' interpretation of it. The recognition that the king, his companions, and the clerics bestowed upon Joan when they witnessed the sign seemed merely to add external confirmation to a reality that had already achieved its definitive form. Though the clerics refused to be persuaded of the legitimacy of Joan's mission by her account of the sign, the fact that they ceased to question her about it after her narration of this episode and that they later summarized this narrative in the *libelle d'Estivet* suggests that the sign she depicted here corresponded to their conception of a sign and thus satisfied their demand.

Other indications in this text, however, prevent us from accepting Joan's account of the sign at face value. As we have seen, on the first day of the public trial, Joan refused to speak of "the revelations which had been made to her on the part of God" and that had been shared with her king, even, she added, "if they had to cut off her head" (38). Though the clerics asked Joan on February 27, March 3, and March 10 to tell them of what the sign consisted, she refused to grant their request because she had sworn to her voices that she would not do so. Even on March 13, immediately before she seemed to identify the sign, she made certain statements that put into question the value of this identification. When the clerics once again asked what sign she gave to her king, for example, Joan asked them in return, " 'Are you content that I commit perjury?' " and then reminded them, " 'I swore and promised not to speak of this sign, and on my own, because men would pressure me excessively to speak of it.' " The minutes of interrogation relate that at that moment, "she promised that she would speak no more about this to any man" (133). How is it possible that Joan would recall her oath never to name this sign, that she would recoil from the perjury that an infringement upon this oath would entail, that she would promise once again never to speak of the sign, and then, in her very next words, that she would speak of it? How is it possible that it is written, "She swore to say nothing about the sign given to her king" (133) in the margin of the very page of the minutes where she appears to begin the whole account of this evidence? These refusals to identify the sign cannot help but destabilize the meaning of the statement that follows, suggesting that this apparent identification of the sign ought not to be accepted simply and superficially and that these cryptic words may have constituted yet another, more secure means of preserving silence on this topic.

The mysterious quality of Joan's naming of the sign was effected not only by the accompanying promise never to name the sign but also by the ambiguous language with which she did seem to reveal it. For Joan described the sign, we recall, not as a crown but as something "in the manner of a crown" and thus distinguished the sign from a material crown in the very act of comparing it to one. She described the crown, or the sign "in the manner of a crown," as "so rich and opulent that she could not enumerate or estimate the richness which she found in it" (135), as so rich that "a man could not describe a thing as rich as is the sign" (117), and as so "fair and rich" that "there is not a goldsmith in the world who could make it" (139). By characterizing the crown as exceeding the capacity of a human being to grasp, to depict, or to fashion, Joan can be seen as portraying either a material object that transcended human understanding of the material or alternatively, an entity that is not a material object. She described the crown, or the sign that was "in the manner of a crown," as something that "will last for a thousand years or more" (116). By characterizing the crown as eternal or virtually eternal, she can be seen, again, as depicting either a crown whose divine origin renders it longer lasting than other crowns or, alternatively, one whose very immateriality renders it invulnerable to the passage of time. In brief, Joan's seemingly paradoxical refusal to disclose the true nature of the sign at the very moment when she appeared to disclose it, her observations that the sign was not a crown, but like a crown, and her mystical language when describing the crown all indicate that there may be more to this story than appears at first glance.

On the morning of May 30, a week after Maurice's appeal to her and the day of her execution, the two judges and seven assistants met with Joan in her cell for a final interview, and Joan took this time to inform at least four of the clerics, Martin Lavenu, Pierre Maurice, Jean Toutmouillé, and Nicolas Loiselleur, of that which these nuances in her account of the sign seemed to imply: the angel who appeared before the king was Joan herself, and the crown the angel presented to the king was Joan's promise of his eventual coronation.[23] Lavenu attested that

> spontaneously, without being constrained to do it, she said and confessed that, whatever she had said and boasted about this angel, there had been no angel who brought the crown, but, rather, Joan herself had been the angel who had said and had promised to him whom she calls her king that, if he put her to work, she would have him crowned at Reims. (417–18)

In a similar vein, Maurice, Toutmouillé, and Loiselleur remembered Joan saying that "she herself was the angel" (418, 419) or "she herself was the angel and that there was no other angel" (421). Toutmouillé testified that Joan confessed, "as for the crown, it was nothing but a fiction" (419), and Loiselleur testified that she said of the crown, "it was nothing other than a promise of the coronation of him whom she calls her king, which she made to him" (421).[24] If Joan was speaking metaphorically, if the angel was she and the crown was her promise of the king's coronation, then she was operating in a semiotic universe far different from the one to which the clerics at Poitiers and Rouen belonged. The clerics, as we recall, assumed that a sign was an objective entity independent from that which it signified. When, however, Joan confessed that the angel who proved she was sent by God was herself and the crown that proved she would bring about the coronation was her promise to achieve this feat, the line between sign and thing was blurred. For Joan depicted herself, on the one hand, as a human being who spent her time praying at the house of a goodwoman of Chinon, asking God for a sign that would deliver her from the clerics then arguing against her. She depicted herself as someone confronted with the daunting task of gaining the court's confidence, troubled by the persecutions of ecclesiastics, and in need of an assistance seemingly beyond her mortal powers. She depicted herself as someone who, after receiving this angelic assistance, pleaded with her comforter to take her with him and wept when he did not. Joan also represented herself, on the other hand, as an angel who arrived at the house of the goodwoman of Chinon where she was praying, who went with her to the king to announce that she would restore to him the kingdom of France and would lead him to his coronation, and who insisted that the king give her soldiers with whom she might accomplish these tasks. She represented herself as someone who handed over a crown so outstanding that it guaranteed the authority of her words. In brief, Joan portrayed herself both as a human being, unrecognized by the clerics who insisted upon signs of her divine affiliation and in need of heavenly assistance, and as an angel, commanding recognition and providing that heavenly assistance. She portrayed herself both as the thing signified by the sign and as the sign that signified that thing.

It is not surprising that Joan should depict herself both as a human being and as an angel. The author of "De quadam puella," for one, testified to Joan's very human aspects. In the first proposition of this treatise, the author wrote, "It must be asserted simply that she is a true maid and a true person of human nature.... This girl is found always to conform to other people in human acts, by speaking, by becoming hungry, by eating, by drinking, by staying awake, by sleeping, and by other acts of this sort."[25] In the years that followed the writing of this tract, Joan's humanity would continue to be perceived not only in her eating, drinking, and sleeping but in her military failures. Her battles after the king's coronation were not, in general, victorious. When she attacked Paris in September 1429, two months after the coronation, her army was beaten and she herself was wounded. When she was defending Compiègne in May of the following year, she was captured, incarcerated for months by the Burgundians, and then sold to the English. Like a human being, Joan endured defeats, frustrations, and suffering. Regnault de Chartres stressed that human fallibility, writing, shortly after Joan's capture, that God had allowed Joan to be captured because of her preference for wearing luxurious clothing and following her own will.[26] Yet, even if Joan was perceived to resemble a human being in her bodily habits and her moral weakness, she was also perceived to resemble an angel. Joan depicted herself as a messenger, or *angelos,* between God and the human race, the means through which God's identification of Charles as the true heir to the French throne was made known and through which his desire to return the kingdom to this heir was effected. The clerics who submitted briefs at the rehabilitation observed this resemblance between Joan's role and that of an angel when they justified her use of the term "angel" to describe herself. They wrote, "as the word 'angel' is the term for the office and has the sense of 'messenger of God' following the words of John the Baptist, 'See that I send my angel,' etc., Joan could say this of herself because the 'angel,' that is, herself as a messenger of God, bóre the 'crown' to the king, that is, the palm of victory of which the crown is the fruit."[27] If Joan resembled an angel in her mission to convey news from God to men, she also resembled an angel in her success at performing feats that no mortal was held capable of performing at that time. Jean Luillier, a burgher of Orléans, recounted at the rehabilitation how, when Joan entered his city, she "was received with as much joy and applause by all, of both sexes, great and small, as if she had been an angel of God, for they hoped, through means of her, to be rescued from their enemies, just as later happened."[28] After five months of siege at Orléans, when the highest military commanders despaired of holding the city, Joan relieved it in ten days. In the seemingly divine origin of her mission and the remarkableness of her achievements Joan was, for her Armagnac contemporaries, easily assimilable to an angelic typology.

The relationship between the human Joan and the angelic Joan bears little resemblance to the simple opposition of entities that one finds in the clerics' contrast of sign and thing. The human Joan is constant, praying at the goodwoman's house in Chinon as the account begins and weeping in a chapel of the castle as it ends, whereas the angelic Joan arrives and departs. The human Joan appears to all, but the angelic Joan appears to a select few, as Joan made clear by stating that the angels accompanying her from her lodgings in Chinon to the king's castle were unseen by those en route but were seen by the king. The human Joan is an earthly creature who cannot convey her divine affiliations to the clerics arguing against her; the angelic Joan is a spiritual being who shows the human Joan to be infused with a meaning and a significance not immediately perceptible to those around her. In brief, the human Joan is to the angelic Joan as the literal level of a text is to an allegory. Whereas the letter of the text remains perpetually exposed even to the most obtuse of readers, allegory, like the angel, is not always present and not always visible to all spectators even when it is present. Allegory infuses the literal level of the text with meaning but remains apart from it, like the angelic Joan who validates her human counterpart and then retires. For a medieval audience, to grasp the literal level of a text without grasping its allegorical content was to restrict oneself to a poorer, less powerful, less meaningful version of the text's true possibilities. From the time of Saint Paul, the letter constituted that which kills, the spirit that which gives life. The letter represented the Old Testament, and, by extension, Judaism, which acknowledged only the Old Testament, while the spirit represented the New Testament and Christianity, which recognized the New Testament as well. According to this tradition, as John Freccero summarizes, he who perceives only the letter falls prey to "blindness, hardness of heart, darkening of the mind, senselessness," whereas he who perceives the spirit beyond the letter achieves a "vision" that corresponds to "the eternity of things that are not seen."[29] To apprehend the human Joan without recognizing her angelic level is to see a peasant girl without perceiving the divine agent that operated through her. Through the use of an allegory that preserves the manifest content of her responses, Joan was able to evoke a self divided between a mundane, constant, human presence, vulnerable to the vicissitudes of fortune, and an impermanent spiritual force that bestowed upon this human form a potency far beyond its own expected limitations. By shifting the opposition between the sign and the thing to an opposition between the allegorical and the literal level of her speech, Joan suggested that the sign was not an entity separate from the thing but, rather, another level of the same thing. While the clerics demanded something new and external to Joan's responses before they would be persuaded of them, Joan implied that this newness and externality would be found not by looking outside her speech but by opening oneself up to further aspects of her speech, as the king and his courtiers were able to do.

Joan's account of the angel and the crown undermined not only the clerics' assumption of the objectivity of the sign and the processes through which it was recognized but also their assumption of the priority of the thing's being to the recognition of its being through the sign. In her responses to the clerics about the sign, Joan emphasized the presence of the king and dignitaries of high rank at the encounter with the angel in the castle chamber and the recognition they accorded her as a result of that encounter. When Joan arrived before the king with the angel, she said to him, " 'Here is your sign,' " and then she asked if he were content with it, to which the king replied that he was. Joan affirmed that Alençon, Trémouille, Bourbon, and the archbishop were present at this encounter and that they all saw the angel, adding that others who did not see the angel nevertheless saw the crown he bore. She explained that "for the love of her and so that men cease to interrogate her, God wanted to permit that those of her party who saw the sign saw it" (118). If one takes Joan's statements literally, then Charles and his courtiers saw an angel enter his chamber to present a crown and heard the angel prophesy the imminent restoration of the kingdom to the king. They recognized Joan as an emissary of God through her connection with the angel and the crown. If one takes these statements figuratively and accepts that the angel was Joan and the crown her promise of the king's coronation, then the king and his courtiers perceived in Joan at once a human being and an angel. They apprehended not just the surface, human form of the young woman before them, with her men's clothes and her peasant origins, but her latent, angelic capacity to accomplish deeds beyond human scope and to reverse the losses their party had for so long suffered. Whereas the human Joan who accompanied the angel to the king's chamber represented the actuality of what the men saw, the angel and the crown symbolized the potentiality that they also perceived. It was because of this recognition that the Armagnac clerics finally ceased to dispute her claim to have been sent by God and allowed her to proceed to Orléans.

Once Joan was recognized by the king and his courtiers, she became capable of performing what was perhaps her most direct accomplishment, the revival of the morale of the Armagnac party. Though Joan was respected as a military strategist, it is often thought that her greatest power as a leader lay neither in her strength at arms nor in her strategies but in her ability to revive the confidence and the idealism of her armies.[30] From the opening years of the Hundred Years' War, the French and then the Armagnacs had regularly succumbed to the English forces, often despite considerable numerical advantages on the field at battle. At Crécy in 1346, at Poitiers in 1356, at Agincourt in 1415, and at Verneuil in 1424, well-disciplined English yeomen, barricaded behind stakes and armed with longbows, pierced not only French armor but French conviction in the invincibility of Gallic knights. Even on February 12, 1429, a few days before Joan's departure for France, when a convoy of Lenten foods was making its way from Paris to the English armies outside Orléans, the Armagnac troops sent to disrupt it once again failed miserably in the inglorious "Battle of Herrings." Examinations of the number of English soldiers actually posted in France and of the funds actually dispensed to support them indicate that the English were able to persist in their occupation not because of their strength but because of the Armagnacs' weakness. Even at Orléans, the number of English soldiers maintaining the siege has suggested to some historians that it was more nominal than real. In a context in which self-doubt and discouragement played a stronger role than any material disadvantage, it is not surprising that the arrival of a maid who proclaimed the righteousness of Charles's claim to the throne and the inevitability of an Armagnac victory should prove to be so instrumental. By counterbalancing the negative judgment of God, seemingly symbolized by the history of defeats, with her own divine inspiration, Joan persuaded her people of the justice of their cause, gave them hope that with her arrival losses would be transformed into victories, and recharged and mobilized their flagging energies. In his chronicle, Perceval de Cagny connected Joan's success at restoring to Armagnac hands seven fortified cities and numerous towns and castles and at leading the king to his coronation within the space of four months to the shift she brought about in the soldiers' willingness to fight. Under Joan's leadership, he wrote, "all knights and squires and other men of war were content to serve the king in his army even though they were poorly paid."[31] Unlike the ability to swing a sword or plan an attack, however, the ability to restore morale that Joan exemplified exists only at the moment that its possessor is recognized as legitimate. Joan's conviction that God was on the Armagnac side became militarily significant only at the moment that others began to look upon her as sent by God and, as a result, began to believe her message. In being recognized by the king and his companions, Joan's angelic potentiality ceased to function merely as a private fantasy and entered into the world where it could play an active role, whether or not it had possessed any reality prior to that recognition. The recognition of Joan's ability to rout the English can be said to have preceded the existence of this ability to rout the English, and, hence, the recognition of the thing to have preceded the existence of the thing.

Joan's understanding of the sign undermined Maurice and Seguin's understanding of the sign as distinct from the thing it signifies, yet it no less undermined their understanding of certainty as a quality inherent within the sign. If the truth about Joan was to be found not by seeking something else but by seeking a deeper level in that which had already been seen, then it is clear that it was not just the sign itself but the willingness of the beholder to seek a deeper level that brought about certainty. Indeed, though the Burgundian clerics were still demanding a sign from Joan in the spring of 1431, the Armagnacs appear to have ceased demanding such signs after her relief of the siege of Orléans two years earlier. At Poitiers, Joan indicated that the sign that she was sent by God to relieve the siege of Orléans would be the relief of the siege of Orléans. Seguin recalled at the rehabilitation that when he had demanded a sign from Joan at Poitiers, she replied, " 'In the name of God, I did not come to Poitiers to make signs, but lead me to Orléans. I will show you the signs for which I am sent.' "[32] Raoul de Gaucourt likewise remembered Joan responding to the clerics that "the sign that she would show them would be the lifting of the siege and the succor of the city of Orléans," and François Garivel confirmed his testimony.[33] Joan promised that the relief of the siege of Orléans would furnish the sign that her clerical interrogators sought, and Armagnac sources do afterward refer to the relief of this siege as a sign. The treatise "De mirabili victoria," for example, is dated on the eve of Pentecost, "after the sign experienced at Orléans in the driving off of the English siege."[34] At the rehabilitation, Basin declared of Joan that "it can be said that she showed sufficiently fair signs of her mission in that, through her work and through that of her company, the fortresses of the English, so very mightily established around the city of Orléans, were destroyed and the English were in part fallen and in part set to flight, something that was almost despaired of before the arrival of this Maid."[35] Pierre Duparc summarizes, "The judicial memoirs of the rehabilitation trial insist on this point: the success before Orléans is a sign which allows one to place faith in the visions, revelations, and the entirety of the mission."[36] Armagnac authors who did not refer to the relief of the siege with the term *signum* referred to it with other terms that also indicate a divine intervention in human affairs, such as *monstrum, prodigium, portentum,* and, most interestingly, *miraculum.* Guillaume Girault, the notary at the Châtelet of Orléans, wrote in his *Histoire du siège,* for example, that "on Wednesday, the eve of the Ascension, the fourth day of May, ... as by miracle, the fortress of the English at Saint-Loup at Orléans was taken by force of arms" and that "the following Saturday, after the Ascension of our Lord, the seventh day of the said month of May, and also by the grace of our Lord, and also as by the most evident miracle which has appeared since the Passion ... the siege which the English had set at Les Tourelles at the end of the bridge of Orléans was lifted."[37] Mathieu Thomassin, a general procurer and *président des comptes* from the Dauphiné, writes similarly in his *Registre delphinal,* "by means of the grace of God, by evident miracle, the very strong and unconquerable fortresses that the English had made were assailed most valiantly and taken and all the siege was lifted."[38] Christine de Pizan penned, simply and strongly, in her *Ditié de Jehanne d'Arc,* "no miracle, as I hold, was clearer, for God helps his own."[39] The fact that all these Armagnac authors and witnesses agreed that the "sign" or "miracle" of Orléans proved the divine origin of Joan's mission and that the Burgundian clerics, in contrast, acted as if they were ignorant of the events that took place at that city, suggests that the recognition of a sign is determined not only by the objective certainty of the sign but by the subjective considerations of political allegiance. It is this necessity, not just that Joan produce a sign of her divine affiliation but that the potential beholders of this sign open themselves up to recognizing it as a sign, that Joan suggested through her use of a trope whose allegorical meaning the literal-minded clerics were unable to discern.

Through the discussion of the sign that proved the authenticity of Joan's mission to Charles, two conceptions of judicial proof emerged. According to one view, shared by most fifteenth-century sources, the sign exists objectively, possessing within itself its power to establish certainty. If Joan was, in fact, sent by God, this view maintained, she would have a sign from God of this divine mission, such as a passage from Scripture that predicted her advent or a miracle that she had performed, and this passage or miracle, possessing in and of itself the power to persuade, would convince others that Joan was sent by God. According to the other view, however, the sign does not exist objectively as a sign and does not possess within it a power to establish certainty. Even if Joan was, in fact, sent by God, this view held, a passage from Scripture need not be read as predicting her particular advent, nor need any event in which she was involved be read as a miracle. For those who adhere to the first opinion, one's identity, whether as an emissary of God or as a king, is established exclusively by oneself. For those who adhere to the second opinion, one's identity is determined by an interaction between oneself and one's beholder. If the clerics believed Joan failed to produce a sign of the authenticity of her mission, and Joan believed herself to have succeeded in doing so, it was because the two parties conceived of such a sign in such different ways.

5 | The Inquiry at Rouen

When one considers the clerics participating in Joan's trial not as scholastics, interested in the speculative truths of theology, but as inquisitors interested in the practical truths of legal matters, one discovers a paradox in their treatment of Joan's speech during these proceedings. On the one hand, as we have seen, Pierre Maurice compared himself and his fellow clerics to captains-at-arms because he viewed it as their duty to protect the church by refusing to believe people who claimed to have come in God's name "unless this is established sufficiently otherwise than by their own words" (382).[1] Maurice and his colleagues expressed skepticism toward Joan's allegations that she had heard voices from God because they saw her as providing no "certain sign" (381) to support her assertions. Words, the clerics suggested, are easily spoken, easily misleading, and, for that reason, unreliable as proof in a judicial trial. On the other hand, as we have also seen, Maurice and the other clerics spent twelve days interrogating Joan, and they depended upon her responses during these sessions in formulating their charges against her and their eventual condemnation of her. They do seem to have sought testimony about her aside from her own statements and to have used it in developing their interrogatories, but they did not incorporate this evidence into the trial documents or rely upon it as direct proof about Joan, as they might have done and as officials in other trials of the day regularly did. Though the clerics regarded Joan's words as of dubious veracity and value, they also treated them as the sole grounds upon which their judgment was to be based.

For an illumination of the contradictory status of Joan's speech in the transcripts of her trial for heretical depravity, it is helpful to turn, temporarily, to the transcripts of her rehabilitation. The transcripts of this later trial, like the transcripts of the trial for condemnation, are a text composed at a specific historical moment in response to specific historical pressures and therefore represent the truth of what happened in the castle of Rouen in the first five months of 1431 no more than the earlier record represented the truth of that event. At the same time, the transcripts of the rehabilitation and, in particular, the depositions of the clerics who participated in the earlier proceedings that are included in these transcripts inform our understanding of the judicial status of Joan's speech during her interrogations in three contradictory ways. First, the witnesses portrayed the interrogators at Rouen as violent, not because they submitted Joan to torture, because they did not, but because they questioned her in a hostile manner. By highlighting and decrying this violence, they implied that such hostility was aberrant to the norms of interrogation then, as we assume it to be aberrant to such norms today. Second, even as the witnesses expressed outrage about the manner in which Joan was questioned, they provided details that demonstrate, to the reader familiar with medieval and modern manuals of interrogation, that her interrogation was, in fact, far from irregular. They showed that the interrogators, through the very aggressiveness of their questions, sought to transform Joan's speech from one whose meaning she consciously controlled and could thus use to deceive, though it would be valueless in a judicial trial, into another sort of speech, one whose significance she no longer mastered and could no longer employ to mislead yet which would be probatory in a court of law. Finally, the witnesses depicted the interrogators as extraordinarily abusive in pursuing an ordinary interrogation, yet they also depicted Joan as deflecting their abuse. They showed that although the interrogators sought to transform Joan's speech to serve their purposes, they failed in doing so and Joan continued to preside over what she said. If in chapter 4 we saw how the clerics, as inquisitors, sought to circumvent Joan's conscious intention by securing evidence against her outside her speech, in this chapter we see how the clerics, again as inquisitors, seek to circumvent her conscious intention by turning her speech into evidence against her. If, in the last chapter it became evident that Joan thwarted the clerics' aims, here, the same outcome manifests itself.

Captious Questions

Two decades after Joan's death, when the Armagnacs had reconciled the Burgundians to their party and were completing the expulsion of the English from French territories, they turned to the rehabilitation of the maid who had played such an important role in altering their fortunes. In February 1450, three months after his seizure of Rouen, Charles requested that his counselor Guillaume Bouillé open an inquiry into Joan's trial and submit its results to the royal counsel. Bouillé's investigation was never completed, but because it was royal rather than canonical, it could not have overturned the sentence that had condemned Joan, whatever its finding had been. In May 1452, two years after Bouillé's aborted investigation, Jean Bréhal, the inquisitor of France, and Guillaume d'Estouteville, a papal legate and close relative of the king, initiated a second inquiry, canonical this time but still destined not to come to any definitive end. Finally, in June 1455, three years after the start of Bréhal's investigation, Pope Calixtus III ordered a third, final inquiry into Joan's condemnation. As part of these investigations, the judges and their assistants heard the testimony of 116 persons in Domrémy, Orléans, Paris, and Rouen who had known Joan at various stages of her brief life. When these witnesses appeared before the officials of the rehabilitation, the latter read to them a series of articles proposing, among other matters, that the principal Burgundians at Joan's trial had borne mortal hatred against her for having turned the tide of the Hundred Years' War against their interests, that they had conspired with the English from the very beginning of the trial to condemn her, and that they had crafted interrogatories designed to elicit avowals that would justify a conviction. After the witnesses provided testimony substantiating these suspicions, on July 7, 1456, in the great hall of the archbishop's palace in Rouen, the reviewers announced the annulment of the earlier sentence condemning Joan for heresy and destroyed one copy of the transcripts of the earlier trial to symbolize this act.

Among the witnesses who testified at the rehabilitation were many clerics who had participated in Joan's earlier trial and had contributed to her condemnation, as well as various additional observers of the proceedings. It is true that several of the most important personages in the trial were no longer available for examination by the time of the inquest. Of the two judges, Pierre Cauchon had died in 1442 and Jean Le Maître, always a mysterious figure, failed to appear at the first two inquiries, disappearing from all official records after 1452. Of the most important assistants, Pierre Maurice, the theologian who had made the last appeal to Joan prior to her condemnation, had passed away in 1436; Jean d'Estivet, the prosecutor who had prepared the *libelle d'Estivet*, had been found dead in a ditch outside Rouen in 1438; Nicolas Midi, the cleric who had addressed the crowd before Joan's death at the Vieux Marché, had expired a leper in 1442; and Gilles de Durémort, the abbot of Fécamp, whose example in condemning Joan for heresy was followed by so many of the clerics, had died in 1444. Seventeen clerics from the trial at Rouen did, nevertheless, appear before rehabilitation officials, namely, the bishop Jean de Mailly; the archdeacon André Marguerie; the prior Pierre Miget; the canons Jean Beaupère, Nicolas Caval, Thomas de Courcelles, Guillaume Du Désert, and Richard de Grouchet; the friars Jean Le Fèvre, Isembard de La Pierre, and Martin Lavenu; the notaries Guillaume Manchon, Guillaume Boisguillaume, and Nicolas Taquel; the physicians Guillaume de La Chambre and Jean Tiphaine; and the usher Jean Massieu. Nicolas de Houppeville, a cleric who seems to have clashed with Pierre Cauchon over the legality of Joan's trial and to have withdrawn from the proceedings, also testified. In addition to the assistants, several persons who had had only brief contact with Joan during her stay in Rouen, including Pierre Cusquel and Pierre Daron, two citizens of the town who had spoken to Joan out of curiosity, and Jean Monnet, a future professor of theology at the university who had attended the trial as Beaupère's secretary, added their recollections to the rehabilitation's records. Several residents of Rouen, including the priest Pierre Bouchier, the burgher Jean Marcel, the prior Thomas Marie, and the merchant Jean Moreau, also testified, though they knew Joan only from what they heard of the events within the castle walls and from what they saw of the events at the cemetery of the abbey of Saint-Ouen, where Joan was threatened with the stake and persuaded to abjure, or at the Vieux Marché, where she was burned. All together, about 13 percent of the clerics from the earlier trial as well as other bystanders spoke of their recollection of the accused in a political and judicial context far different from that in which they had once known her.

Though all eleven of the assistants from the earlier trial who had taken part in the final vote, namely, Caval, de La Chambre, Courcelles, Du Désert, de Grouchet, Lavenu, Le Fèvre, Marguerie, Miget, de La Pierre, and Tiphaine, had a quarter-century earlier condemned Joan to the secular arm, virtually all now objected to the "difficulty" or the "subtlety" of the questions

ed. The documents of the rehabilitation charge that Joan's
pursued her with difficult and involuted interrogations and
nd, for the most part, ... interrogated her on points about
vas entirely ignorant of what they were" (193). Nearly all of
the clerics from the condemnation trial attested, with a syntax seemingly
suggested by their interviewers, that the questions Joan had been asked
were so subtle that even a learned man would have struggled to answer
them. Monnet stated, for example, that "they asked Joan very difficult questions to which a master in theology would have responded with difficulty"
(360). De Grouchet recalled the abbot of Fécamp stating that "a great
cleric would have failed to respond to the difficult questions asked of her"
(229), and Tiphaine declared that "there is no doctor so great and subtle
that, if he had been interrogated by so many lords and before such an assembly as was Joan, he would not have been well confused and exhausted"
(349). Lavenu twice claimed that "they asked Joan difficult questions which
were not appropriate for such a simple woman" (235). In these character-
izations of Joan's interrogations, the clerics presumably alluded to inquiries such as whether Joan apprehended her voices "corporally and really," whether she believed them to have been created "in the manner and
form" in which she perceived them, and whether she was in a state of
grace, questions that are grounded in theological understandings of the
bodies of separated spirits and the limits of human knowledge.[2] By identifying the questions Joan was asked with those a master of theology, a
cultivated man, or a great or subtle doctor might encounter, these deponents compared the *quaestiones* with which Joan was confronted to the
quaestiones disputatae and *quaestiones quodlibetales,* the public debates that
dominated the medieval university and that provided the formats for
scholastic writing. When Joan's interrogators asked her these questions,
these witnesses implied, they were well versed in both the public debates
from which the inquiries arose and the orthodox answers articulated in
the course of the debates. When Joan answered these questions, however,
she was ignorant both of the context from which these interrogations
sprang and of the Catholic responses developed by doctors to these inquiries. Though Joan's interrogators knew the full signification of the
questions they asked, a signification attained through academic disputations, Joan was unaware of this meaning, unable to respond to that meaning, and unable to control the meaning that her answer would assume to
university-trained ears. By asking Joan questions whose resonances she
only partially grasped, the clerics argued, her interrogators had encouraged her to respond with theologically or canonically incorrect answers.

Cusquel claimed that Joan's interrogators sought "to seize her [*ad capiendum eam*] in her speech" (220) or "to seize her [*ad capiendum eam*] in her words" (453), and de Grouchet depicted Joan as "interrogated with difficult, involuted, and captious [*captiosis*] questions, in the intention that she be seized in her speech and, it seemed to him, be distracted from her theme" (229). By insisting upon the verb *capere* and the adjective *captiosus*, the clerics portrayed the Burgundian interrogators as aiming to seize Joan, to trap her, to capture her, not in her body, as the Burgundian soldiers had seized her outside Compiègne several months before, but in her speech. Just as soldiers setting up a trap entice their enemies to enter into the snare through their own advance and thus bring about their own capture, so did these interrogators set up their captious questions so that Joan would provide evidence against herself and cause her own conviction. According to these witnesses, the interrogators aimed not simply to condemn Joan for heresy but to encourage her to condemn herself through heterodox responses.

It is not only the difficulty of Joan's interrogations that the witnesses at the rehabilitation censure but also the disruptive behavior of the interrogators. Numerous witnesses claimed that the interrogators often asked Joan several questions at once. According to Massieu, "when Joan was being interrogated, there would be six assistants with the judges who would be interrogating her, and, sometimes, when one was interrogating her and she responding to his question, another would interrupt her response" (432). De La Chambre similarly recalled that once, when the abbot of Fécamp was interrogating Joan, "Master Jean Beaupère intervened with many and diverse questions" (351). Like Massieu and de La Chambre, Moreau remembered that Joan "often entreated those interrogating her that she might respond to only one or two of them and that they greatly troubled her with so many interrogations made at the same time" (463). Even when Joan's examiners were not cutting in on each other's lines of inquiry, they still showed a predilection for interrupting her responses. Manchon attested that "the first day of her interrogations, in the chapel of the castle of Rouen, there was a great tumult, and almost every single word of Joan's was interrupted when she spoke of her apparitions" (416), and Le Fèvre stated that "sometimes those who were interrogating her cut in on her interrogations, to the point where she could hardly respond" (448–49). When Joan's interrogators questioned her all at once or interrupted her answers, it was not a desire to clarify her response to the matter under discussion that motivated them. Manchon stated that "many times there would be a shift from one interrogation to another, changing the theme" (421), and Le Fèvre claimed that "they sometimes interrupted the interrogations, passing from one to another" (237). Other clerics testified that the interrogators not only moved rapidly from one topic to another but introduced topics irrelevant to the trial. Boisguillaume related that "Joan very often complained that they asked her subtle and irrelevant questions" (438), while both Bouchier and de Houppeville recalled hearing Le Maître cite Joan's protests against questions that were "not at all relevant" (204) and "about matters not concerning the trial" (446). Joan's interrogators, the clerics agreed, confronted her with multiple questions at the same time, interrupted her when she attempted to respond, shifted rapidly from one subject to another, and badgered her with impertinent inquiries and, if they did so, it was, at least according to Le Fèvre, in order "to see if Joan would change her theme" (448). By preventing Joan either from grasping a coherent theme in their questions or from providing, in turn, a coherent theme in her responses, the clerics insisted that she address each matter under consideration in itself, without any surrounding context that might give it meaning. With their "fractured interrogations" (208), as Massieu described them, they strove to elicit fractured responses. Disconnecting Joan's individual responses from any overarching line of defense, the interrogators aimed to lead Joan to contradict this defense and, thus, to provide testimony against herself. The interrogators are seen, once again, as conspiring to turn Joan the speaker against Joan the defendant.

Captious in their content and chaotic in their form, Joan's interrogations were also, the clerics attested, exhausting in their length. Manchon related that Joan was questioned for three or four hours in the morning and often, after the clerics had reviewed her answers to come up with "some difficult and subtle interrogations" (421), for two or three hours in the afternoon. He concluded that "during the trial, she was fatigued by many and diverse interrogations" (421). Le Fèvre confirmed Manchon's testimony, reporting that the sessions were so long "that the doctors assisting were much fatigued by them" (237). Other clerics recalled the sufferings that Joan endured as a result of these lengthy sessions. De La Pierre claimed to have heard Joan complain often that "they asked her questions excessively" (223), and Taquel noted that "Joan, sometimes wearied by many interrogations, would ask for a delay until the next day" (198). If Joan's interrogators subjected her to lengthy interrogations, it was not because they had so many different questions to which they needed answers. According to de La Chambre, at one point in her interrogations Joan told those questioning her "that they did her a great wrong in troubling her thus, and that she had already responded to these interrogations" (351). The clerics directing the rehabilitation suggested a motive for these long sessions in their allegation that Joan's interrogators "fatigued her for a long time with interrogations and examinations so that she became afflicted with weariness and so that they might take some unfavorable words from this prolixity" (94). The interrogators insisted upon prolonged sessions, the clerics suggested, because they sought to tire Joan and perhaps to lower her vigilance in regard to that which she said. They insisted upon "prolixity" because they expected that out of this abundance of words some of them would be unfavorable to Joan's case. Just as they did in their choice of subtle questions and their disordered manner of questioning, the interrogators aimed to turn Joan against herself.

Since the rediscovery of the transcripts of Joan's trials, commentators have echoed the words of the witnesses at the rehabilitation in condemning the nature of the interrogations. In 1841, Jules Michelet glosses the minutes of these sessions by characterizing one query as "an insidious and perfidious question, such a question that it is sinful to ask of any living human creature," others as "hostile and unseemly," and still others as "bizarre questions, intended to make her confess to some devil's work."[3] He reports that at one moment, the interrogators "attacked on a delicate, perilous point" and that at another, "they attacked her anew, with fiercer hatred, and they asked her in quick succession questions which might have led to her undoing."[4] He concludes of these recorded dialogues, "Terrible indeed was that Church in the persons of logicians, schoolmen, enemies of personal inspiration."[5] Six years later, in 1847, Thomas De Quincey concurs with Michelet's condemnation of the interrogations as malicious in their attempt to trap Joan in her own words. He states, "General questions were proposed to her on points of casuistical divinity; two-edged questions, which not one of [the interrogators] could have answered without (on the one side), landing himself in heresy (as then interpreted), or, on the other, in some presumptuous expression of self-esteem."[6] Whereas Michelet and De Quincey take exception to the scholastic difficulty of the questions with which Joan was confronted, Vita Sackville-West, writing in 1936, and Marina Warner, writing in 1981, take exception to the disorder with which these questions were presented. Sackville-West protests that "her judges did their utmost to confuse her by a bombardment of inconsecutive and apparently irrelevant questions, whose drift must have been exceedingly difficult for her to perceive."[7] Warner compares "the nightmarish ambiguity, formlessness, confusing menace" of Joan's interrogations to that of Kafka's novels and complains that Joan "has no means of knowing where the interrogation is driving, what the concealed charge is. She has to defend herself for her life, but was never told where lay her wrong."[8] Michelet and De Quincey see the interrogators' tendency to ask questions whose theological subtleties Joan could not detect as evidence of their intent to lead Joan into responses whose full consequences she also could not detect and whose repercussions could well be unfavorable to her. These later biographers see the examiners' tendency to ask questions whose connection to each other Joan likewise could not grasp as even stronger evidence of their nefarious intentions. All of these commentators, though aware that the witnesses at the rehabilitation spoke within a judicial context already oriented toward censuring Joan's interrogations as irregular, follow their lead in censuring the interrogations themselves.

By criticizing the subtlety, disorder, and lengthiness of Joan's interrogations at Rouen, the medieval witnesses and the modern commentators reveal a presupposition that these qualities do not characterize a normal interrogation but, rather, mark, as officials of the rehabilitation put it, an "unusual and extraordinary manner of interrogating" (11). These various parties assumed, first, that in a more conventional interrogation the suspect would not be confronted with subtle questions, unclear questions, questions designed to seize her, to trap her, or to capture her. If the questions Joan was asked possessed two meanings, one apparent in the inquiries made to her during the trial and the other latent in their scholastic ramifications, in a proper interrogation, these various parties intimate, questions would possess only one meaning evident to the individual being interrogated. The interrogator would ask questions whose implications were transparent, and the suspect would then appraise those implications and respond with them in mind. Addressing the questions in their full meaning, she would be able to control the meaning that the answers would assume for the interrogators. These parties took for granted, second, that in a more customary interrogation the suspect would be able to follow the order of the questions and to respond to them in that fashion. Instead of several interrogators asking questions at the same time, one interrogator would ask one question. Instead of interrupting the respondent, they would listen to her full answer. Instead of leaping from one topic to another in their interrogations or reaching into topics irrelevant to the trial, they would pursue one subject for a reasonable length of time and would restrict their questions to those pertinent to the trial. Whereas Joan was unable to apprehend where the interrogators were going with their questions and, hence, was unable to defend herself against what they were indirectly attempting to prove, in a more normative trial, the witnesses indicated, the suspect would know where the interrogators were headed and would be able to protect herself against their implied accusations. These parties imagined, finally, that in a more conventional interrogation the interrogators would question the suspect for a limited period of time. While Joan's interrogators questioned her for several hours, sometimes both in the morning and in the afternoon, and presumably dulled her concentration through the lengthiness of these sessions, more traditional interrogators would allow the suspect to remain well rested, alert, and in control of her faculties throughout the interrogations. Instead of asking the same questions numerous times, these interrogators would ask one question once and, having received an answer, would be satisfied. Eschewing all attempts to dupe, confuse, or dull the suspect, these ideal interrogators would spurn the verbal violence said to characterize Joan's trial.

The ideal interrogation, as the witnesses at the rehabilitation depicted it, would entail a transmission of knowledge. The interrogator, presumed to be seeking certain information from the suspect, would use his questions to request a transferal of the information. The respondent, presumed to possess the information, would transfer it to the interrogator in the answer. The interrogation of a suspect, as the witnesses envisioned it, would be identical to the examination of a witness. When an investigator interviews a witness, he seeks certain information about a crime; he asks questions that make clear to the witness what information he seeks, and the witness gives the desired information to the investigator. There is no conflict between the two parties, no struggle, and hence no recourse to ambiguous, chaotic, or repetitive questioning. The interlocution occurs on a single level and hence does not involve attempts to turn the suspect against herself by providing disadvantageous answers or otherwise contributing to her condemnation. The interlocution consists in the representation, not in the production, of knowledge and thus takes place on the surface of the suspect's psyche in her conscious intention. The dialogue is pure, sunny, Apollonian, devoid of the verbal violence so often perceived in Joan's interrogations. The only question is whether such a dialogue could possibly fulfill the judicial role of an interrogation.

Ruses of Inquisitors

Though the minutes of Joan's interrogations at Rouen give little explanation for the subtlety, disorder, and lengthiness attributed to their sessions by the witnesses at the rehabilitation, treatises on interrogation, both medieval and modern, do provide an explanation for these apparently unmotivated characteristics. In the thirteenth and fourteenth centuries, as the Inquisition surfaced and spread in western Europe, several inquisitors composed works that provided not only information about the various heretical sects, as the earlier summas *summae hereticorum* did, but advice about how to interrogate the members of these different groups. Such manuals for inquisitors, analyzed by Antoine Dondoine, include Pseudo-David of Augsburg's *De inquisitione haereticorum* of 1150–1200, the treatise of the Passau Anonymous of the 1260s, and the two best-known manuals, Bernard Gui's *Practica inquisitoris haeretice pravitatis* of 1323–1324 and Nicolau Eymerich's *Directorium inquisitorum* of 1376.[9] Between the midnineteenth and midtwentieth centuries, legislators both in Europe and in North America, wary of interrogation's ability to coerce confessions from reluctant and occasionally innocent suspects, passed laws regulating this procedure, and numerous police officers and intelligence specialists drafted works advising their peers on how to obtain confessions they needed within these ever tighter restrictions. In France, the law of December 8, 1897 (now incorporated into Article 114 of the *Code de procédure pénale*), obliged the *juge d'instruction* to refrain from interrogating the suspect during their first encounter and instructed him, rather, merely to inform the suspect of the crime of which he stood accused and of his right to have an attorney present at all future interrogations. The treatises of Louis Lambert, a professor at the Ecole Normale Supérieure de Police, and Robert Borel, a police commissioner, reflect what is generally felt to be the effect of this law in shifting the task of interrogation from the *juge d'instruction* to the police officer, and strive to prepare the officer for his new duties by instructing him in techniques of questioning.[10] In the United States, the Supreme Court spent thirty years refining the "voluntariness" test used to evaluate a confession before ruling in the 1966 *Miranda* brief that all suspects must be read their rights to remain silent; to secure legal counsel, even if they do not have the resources to pay for it; and to know that anything they say may be held against them. The interrogation manuals deemed most influential in police academies since then, namely, those of Arthur S. Aubry Jr. and Rudolph R. Caputo, Fred E. Inbau and John E. Reid, Charles E. O'Hara and Gregory L. O'Hara, and Robert F. Royal and Steven R. Schutt, all former police officers, testify to the judiciary's confidence that with the help of appropriate stratagems investigators can elicit the confessions necessary to secure convictions for crimes despite the inhibiting influence of the *Miranda* ruling.[11] In international law, the Geneva Convention of 1864 banned the use of torture to facilitate interrogations, even of prisoners of war, yet manuals from the U.S. Army Intelligence Center and School at Fort Huachuca, Arizona, propose techniques of questioning that will ensure that this prohibition does not prevent officers from obtaining information from captured enemy soldiers.[12] Though thirteenth- and fourteenth-century manuals for inquisitors are obviously based in historical circumstances far different from those of their modern counterparts, the techniques recommended to interrogators in a text such as Eymerich's *Directorium inquisitorum* resemble the techniques recommended to interrogators in these recent writings. This resemblance suggests that these medieval and modern texts share a similar understanding of the logic of interrogation and that the texts of one era may thus shed light upon those of the other. In both the medieval and the modern manuals, the authors demonstrate how the processes of interrogation can transform the respondent's speech into evidence, and in doing so they demonstrate that the processes of Joan's interrogations may have been less arbitrary and less aberrant in their violence than they otherwise appear.

As we have seen, the witnesses at the rehabilitation reproached Joan's interrogators for asking her questions so "subtle" and "difficult" that even a great cleric would have found it hard to answer them. Though interrogators, whether medieval or modern, do not regularly ask questions with scholastic resonances, the witnesses' underlying implication that Joan's interrogators were more familiar with the subject of the interrogations than she was and that they used this discrepancy to their advantage is far from irrelevant to general interrogative practice. In his manual, Eymerich recalled that by the time the inquisitor interrogated a heretic, the investigator had already collected considerable information about him, information to which the accused, in accordance with the customs of the Inquisition, was allowed only the most limited access. He advised the inquisitor to exploit this superior knowledge by reading aloud from the depositions against the heretic and by urging him, " 'Tell me the truth because you will see that I know all about your case. Tell me so that people will know that I have excused you and you will not lose your good reputation.' "[13] He advised the inquisitor to exploit his exclusive familiarity with the evidence by suggesting that it was far more extensive and more damning than it actually was, so that the heretic would believe he had nothing to lose by confessing to heresy. The inquisitor should leaf through the heretic's file, Eymerich suggested, declaring as he did so, " 'It is clear that you are not speaking the truth and that it is as I say it is. Tell clearly, therefore, the truth about your case.' "[14] When the heretic denied a particular matter, the inquisitor should pull a paper out of the file and ask with surprise, " 'How can you deny it? Is it not clear enough to me?' "[15] Eymerich continued, "And let him read from this statement and pervert it and read it aloud."[16] If the inquisitor should take advantage of his privileged knowledge of the contents of the heretic's case by giving the accused the impression that his file was already complete and sufficient for conviction, regardless of whatever the accused might now confess, he should also protect himself from the gaps and weakness in his knowledge by hiding his uncertainties from the heretic. As Eymerich put it, he should resemble the civil investigator who asks, not whether the accused has killed the murder victim, but what he has done and thus hides his own possible doubt in the suspect's guilt. Though Eymerich's inquisitor does not necessarily enjoy a knowledge of theology or canon law greater than that of the respondent, he does enjoy a knowledge of the evidence against the respondent greater than that which the heretic possesses and does profit from this advantage.

Modern interrogation manuals, no less than their medieval counterparts, stress the superiority of the interrogator's knowledge to that of the respondent and the importance of benefiting from this advantage. Like Eymerich, Inbau and Reid remind interrogators that they are familiar with the extent of the evidence against the suspect, whereas the suspect is not. They know, for example, what clues at the site of the crime point to this suspect, what witnesses have contributed information unfavorable to the accused, and what codefendents have implicated this individual in their own confessions, while the suspect remains ignorant of these matters. Like their medieval predecessor, these authors point out that interrogators can use their superior knowledge to give the suspect the impression that they possess far greater evidence against him than they actually do and can take advantage of this impression in order to elicit a confession. They recommend that when interrogators have only limited information against the suspect, they tell him of it in a manner that suggests that it is only part of the evidence against him. Like the inquisitor, Inbau and Reid propose that interrogators dramatize their greater knowledge about the case by consulting a file in the suspect's presence. They suggest that the interrogator keep a large folder on his table in the interrogation room, that he flip through this folder at the beginning of the interrogation and at other moments during the session, and that if he does possess evidence against the suspect, he mention it in the course of these references to the file. "All this is done in a manner which conveys the impression that the particular bit of information of material is only a small part of the incriminating data embodied in the complete file," they instruct.[17] Finally, they too advise interrogators who are reasonably certain that the suspect must have committed a certain act in relation to the crime to inquire not whether this act was performed but how or when it was perpetrated: "With the question phrased in such a way as to imply a certainty of [the act's] existence, . . . it [becomes] difficult for the subject to make a denial," they explain.[18] Just as Joan's interrogators used their far greater knowledge of theology and canon law against her, asking her questions derived from a scholastic learning she had never acquired, so do these modern interrogators use their greater knowledge of the evidence against the suspect, asking him questions and uttering interjections that give an incorrect impression of the likelihood of his conviction. In both cases, the interrogators' questions possess two levels, one apparent to the suspect and one hidden. In both cases, the interrogators use this duplicity to provoke the suspect into making incriminating statements.

Neither the medieval inquisitors nor the modern interrogators are ashamed to advocate recourse to deception in order to elicit a confession. Repeating stereotypes of heretics that go back to Pseudo-David of Augsburg and Bernard Gui, Eymerich reminded his reader that heretics, especially Waldensians and beghards, were renowned for the ruses with which they deflected the interrogations of inquisitors without resorting to outright lies. He recalled that they responded to particular questions by feigning surprise that they should be asked about such a matter, by asking the inquisitor how he would respond to such a question, by answering the question with an equivocal expression or a condition that imperceptibly altered the meaning of what they were saying, or by feigning illness, stupidity, madness, or extreme sanctity. He told of a prostitute who, by using such tricks, was once able to evade the interrogations of several illustrious doctors and to escape conviction for her heresy until she was found later collecting the bones of a burned heretic to venerate as relics. Repeating recommendations to inquisitors that, again, go back to earlier centuries, Eymerich advised that, in order to avoid such humiliations in the future, "when the inquisitor sees a tricky and dexterous heretic who does not want to uncover his error but to lead the inquisitor around in tergiversations, he must pay him back in kind. He must use precautions, so that he may lay hold of him in the error of the heretics."[19] When the inquisitor has dealt with a heretic in such a manner, Eymerich proclaimed, he can say with Saint Paul, "Wily, I have taken you by wiles."[20] Modern interrogators show themselves no less inclined to trickery. The U.S. Army advises that "direct interrogation," which is distinguished by forthright questioning, be restricted to low-level prisoners deemed to possess little valuable information and that "indirect interrogation," which is "characterized by obtaining information through deception," be used with all higher-echelon sources.[21] Lambert encourages the use of "wiles," "ruses," "perfidious questions," and "traps" in order to "ensnare the suspect."[22] These modern authors, like Eymerich, defend the use of deception by contrasting the extraordinary conditions within which they are employing this technique with ordinary conditions. Discussing one case in which the interrogator employed trickery to obtain a confession, Inbau and Reid remark, "the interrogation was 'unethical' according to the standards usually set for professional, business, and social conduct, but the pertinent issue in this case was no ordinary, lawful, professional, business, or social matter."[23] They explain, "criminal interrogators must deal with criminal offenders on a somewhat lower moral plane than that upon which ethical, law-abiding citizens are expected to conduct their everyday affairs."[24] While a sincere moral lecture or an appeal to the suspect to confess will almost always fail with such populations, they report, deceptive approaches, like those they recommend, will lead to a confession and conviction. Lambert inquires in a similar vein, "To interrogate skillfully, that is, in a manner to obtain the truth, is it not necessary, by virtue even of the laws of the intellect, to use artifices toward him who seeks to trick you? Intellectual disloyalty is indispensable against such a person."[25] That very perfidy that the witnesses at the rehabilitation protested in Joan's trial is here presented as a legitimate, indeed, essential characteristic of interrogation.

As we have seen, the witnesses at the rehabilitation reproached Joan's interrogators for the chaotic form of the interrogations. Though these witnesses chastised the interrogators for repeating questions and for asking multiple questions simultaneously, Eymerich recommended that the inquisitor "multiply the interrogations."[26] By thus confusing the heretic, the inquisitor would disarm him, leading him to make either confessions that he did not mean to make or contradictory remarks with whose illogicalities he could then be confronted. Eymerich urged, "when he is found having made different statements, let it be exposed to him how he said one thing in one manner while he said another in another manner... and let him be urged to speak the truth entirely."[27] The U.S. Army similarly recommends a "rapid fire" technique wherein one or more interrogators ask "a series of questions in such a manner that the source does not have time to answer a question completely before the next question is asked."[28] A source faced with simultaneous questions, the army hypothesizes, will become confused, contradict himself, and when confronted with these contradictions, fall back upon forbidden information in order to justify them. It maintains, "in attempting to explain his answers, the source is likely to reveal more than he intends."[29] While the witnesses at the rehabilitation reproached Joan's interrogators for having interrupted her with different questions, the army again suggests that such a technique is basic to interrogatory procedures. The recourse to interruption, it states, "involves a psychological ploy based upon the principle that everyone likes to be heard when he speaks and it is confusing to be interrupted in mid-sentence with an unrelated question."[30] When military interrogators interrupt their source, as when they ask him numerous questions at once, they seek to confuse the respondent in the hope that such confusion will lead to an avowal. Finally, the witnesses reproved Joan's interrogators for having asked her questions irrelevant to her trial, yet the army once more indicates that it is standard practice to ask questions unconnected to what one seeks to learn, again in order to confuse the source and to catch him in his lies. "Since a person must concentrate to lie effectively, the interrogator can break this concentration by suddenly interjecting a completely unrelated question, then switching back to the pertinent topic," it avers.[31] It is useful to break the respondent's chain of thought by asking unrelated questions, the army teaches, not only in order to confuse the respondent and thus lead him to contradict himself, so that he is unable to sustain an invented story, but also in order to distract the respondent from the true object of the interrogator's interest and thus lead him to speak of the object unawares. Virtually all the police manuals affirm, with Aubry and Caputo, that "confusing the subject can be a very effective technique" because such confusion leads the suspect to contradict himself and, when exposed to these contradictions, to relinquish his claims to innocence.[32] These modern interrogation manuals reveal that the seemingly chaotic format of Joan's interrogations, traditionally attributed to her judges' unrestrained animosity toward their prisoner, was and is the standard format of interrogation.

As we have seen, finally, the witnesses at the rehabilitation criticized Joan's interrogators for conducting lengthy and repetitive sessions in which Joan was asked the same questions for several hours. Eymerich, however, stated that "the interrogations will be as frequent as the inquisitor wants them to be," and Lambert insists upon the necessity of prolonged interrogations, like those Joan underwent, in eliciting a confession. "It is known how effective the prolonged interrogation is," he asserts, "when, for an entire day followed sometimes by an entire night, the guilty person hears himself repeat the same answers, sees himself opposed by the police officers' same unshakable conviction in his guilt, to the point that, in a sudden release of tension, in a true 'mental vertigo,' he lets slip the liberating confession."[33] Lambert writes elsewhere, "Let us always presuppose in the individual whom we are interrogating a state of tension, of fatigue and of fear, and let us systematically exploit these dispositions by opposing him with our conviction and by imposing upon him, if necessary, a prolonged interrogation."[34] As Lambert defends the lengthy interrogations as instrumental in extorting a confession, other authors defend repetitive interrogations for the same reason. Robert Borel advises "a constant repetition of varied questions under different forms, by different officials familiar with the file of the case."[35] The army likewise recommends a "repetition" technique in which the interrogator, after hearing the source's answer to a question, repeats the question and receives the same response several times. After several such exchanges, the army projects, the source "becomes so thoroughly bored with the procedure that he answers questions fully and candidly to satisfy the interrogator and to gain relief from the monotony of this method of questioning."[36] In addition to providing a mental pressure conducive to confession, the repetition of questions is also believed to help in identifying the source's deceptions. The army counsels, "Since a lie is more difficult to remember than the truth, especially when the lie has been composed on the spur of the moment, the interrogator can establish errors by rephrasing and disguising the same questions which the source has already answered."[37] That is, not only does the length of the interrogation wear down the suspect's resistance to confession, dull his mental acuity, and make him long for relief from this session, but the repetition of questions takes advantage of that exhaustion, insensibility, and craving for rest by encouraging him to contradict himself and thus take the first step toward acknowledging the falsity of his claims to innocence and the truth of his guilt. Just as Joan's interrogators subjected her to lengthy and repetitive sessions, hoping to fatigue her, to diminish her vigilance over what she said, and to take unfavorable words from the prolixity of her speech, so do these modern interrogators subject suspects to long and repetitive sessions, and for the same reasons.

Both medieval inquisitors, like Eymerich, and modern interrogators, like Inbau, Reid, Lambert, Borel, and the anonymous authors from the U.S. Army, assume that the accused does not wish to confess at the onset of the interrogation. They assume that he is consciously aware that confession will bring about or at least facilitate conviction and that he seeks to avoid this conviction and the punishment that would ensue from it. In order to bring the suspect to confess, despite his resistance to doing so, they reason that they must overcome him, through the use of various interrogatory techniques, so that he no longer controls his own speech.

They reason that they must compel truth, located within him but in opposition to him, to speak out in his stead. If Joan's interrogators were violent, as the witnesses at the rehabilitation and as later commentators on the trial claim that they were, it was in their rejection of Joan as subject, master of her speech, in favor of the truth that resides within her.

Sancta Simplicitas

At first glance, the witnesses at the rehabilitation appear to have depicted Joan as overcome by the interrogations. The officials of the rehabilitation affirmed to the deponents at Rouen that "the said Joan was a girl of nineteen years of age or thereabouts, simple, ignorant of the law and of judicial procedure, nor was she, of herself, without a director or instructor, competent or skillful enough to defend herself in such a grave and difficult case" (193), and the deponents, to a large extent, confirmed the officials' portrayal of Joan's simplicity and ignorance. De Houppeville and Cusquel both maintained that Joan was so simple and ignorant that she was not able to handle herself well during the trial. Lavenu affirmed, "as for her simplicity, he says truly that she was very ignorant and hardly knew the Our Father" (234). Manchon reported that "Joan . . . occasionally responded simply enough" (216) and that "as it seemed to him, she was very simple" (416). The witnesses agreed that Joan was simple specifically in the medieval sense of this term: she was not familiar with the law and judicial procedures, and her education was limited, at most, to some prayers. By protesting that this simplicity prevented Joan from defending herself in such a difficult case and, in particular, from answering her interrogators' difficult questions appropriately, the witnesses recalled the traditional division between the learned and the people in medieval culture. Whereas the clerics spoke Latin, the people spoke the vulgar tongue. Whereas the clerics were *litterati*, at once literate and learned in a distinctive scholastic culture, the people were deemed ignorant of both the written word and that culture. By calling Joan "simple," by identifying this simplicity with her ignorance of theology and canon law, and by imagining that this simplicity would prevent her from defending herself against learned interrogators, these witnesses adhered to this conventional division of medieval society.

A closer glance at the witnesses' responses reveals, however, a more complex view of Joan's rapport with her interrogators. Though the witnesses did affirm the rehabilitation officials' declaration of Joan's simplicity, virtually all qualified that declaration. De Houppeville and Cusquel protested that Joan was simple and incapable of defending herself in the trial, but they both went on to speak highly of her responses. Cusquel stated that Joan was ignorant of the law, but he also maintained that "she spoke very prudently" (220). Lavenu stated that Joan was simple and ignorant, yet he added, "although he heard her at one time or another responding faithfully and prudently" (234) and, elsewhere, "granted that sometimes, when she was interrogated, she responded prudently" (440). Though Manchon affirmed that Joan seemed to him very simple, he said this, "granted that she sometimes responded with great prudence...as can be seen in the trial" (416). Most of these clerics contrasted Joan's simplicity to her wisdom, stating, as Lavenu did, that she was ignorant "although [*quamvis*]" she responded faithfully and prudently, or as Lavenu and Manchon did, that she was simple, "granted [*licet*]" that she answered prudently. Yet Le Fèvre does not contrast these seemingly opposite qualities. When this cleric claimed that "Joan was...very simple and [*et*] responded prudently" (447), his use of the conjunction *et* suggests that Joan's simplicity was not opposed to her prudence but, rather, was connected to it. With this conjunction, he evokes an alternate medieval semantics of simplicity that opposes simplicity not to a desirable learnedness but to a false erudition. In the New Testament and the writings of the church fathers, the "simplicity" of Christianity is set against the sophistries of the pagan philosophers, so that it becomes identified with the presence of Christian truth rather than the absence of a desirable teaching. Saint Paul, for example, wrote that "Greeks desire wisdom, but we proclaim Christ crucified,...a foolishness to the Gentiles" and counseled, "you should become fools so that you may become wise. For the wisdom of this world is foolishness with God."[38] The officials at the rehabilitation depicted Joan's simplicity as hindering her, insofar as it prevented her from responding with sufficient sophistication to the difficult questions she was asked, but numerous witnesses from her earlier trial depicted this simplicity as aiding her in giving her greater access to God. According to Manchon, the wisdom of Joan's simple answers convinced him that she received divine assistance. In two depositions, he asserted, "he believes that in such a difficult case she would not of herself have been adequate to defend herself against so many doctors unless she had been inspired" (216, 416). According to the friars de La Pierre and Le Fèvre, this unexpected sagacity led them to similar conclusions, in part or for a time. The one brother commented, "when she spoke of the kingdom and the war, she appeared moved by the Holy Spirit, but, when she spoke of her person, she imagined sometimes" (186), and the other remarked, "she responded prudently to such a point that for three weeks he believed her inspired" (447). If simplicity means the absence of those qualities that make one powerful in the world, then when this quality is routed through the Gospel's transvaluation of values, its absence becomes a presence, its negative lack a positive plenitude, its ignorance wisdom. If the interrogators succeeded in compelling an other to speak through Joan, then this other who spoke was not a part of Joan turned against herself but God speaking through her voice.

Indeed, even if one presumes that interrogators undermine a suspect's image of his ego in order to elicit the truth that they seek, it cannot be said that it was Joan's ego that was destabilized during her trial. The witnesses at the rehabilitation recalled that though Joan was presented with questions that would have taxed a learned cleric, she was not befuddled by them. As we have seen, Monnet claimed that Joan was asked questions so hard that a "master of theology" would have answered them with difficulty, and de Grouchet claimed that according to the abbot of Fécamp, she was asked questions so hard "a great cleric" would have failed to answer them. Tiphaine asserted that she was asked questions so hard that a "great" and "subtle" doctor would have been confused and exhausted by them. Boisguillaume recalled that Joan replied to the question as to whether she was in a state of grace by asserting, " 'If I am, may God keep me there, and if I am not, may God put me there. For I would like better to die than not to be in God's love' " (438) and that "those who were interrogating her were very stupefied by this response and they left her then, without interrogating her any more at that time" (438). Throughout this testimony, the witnesses compared the questions Joan answered to those that "a master of theology," "a great cleric," and a "great" and "subtle doctor" might be expected to answer. They compared Joan's performance during her interrogations to the hypothetical performance of an ideal cleric, who is, it seems, an idealized version of themselves, yet in doing so, they grew uncertain. Though Joan answered these subtle questions prudently and wisely, they feared that their idealized counterpart would hardly be able to respond to such questions, would become confused and exhausted, or would even fail to answer them. These clerics were appointed to assist at Joan's trial on account of their clerkly training in theology and canon law, but Joan, through her wise responses to theological and canonical questions, proved that wisdom did not rely upon such training, that a simplicity illuminated by divine grace could be wiser than any *clergie*, and that a self-perception grounded in the identity of clerkliness and wisdom was deluded. The clerics were "stupefied," rendered silent, by this performance.

Joan's prudence in answering difficult questions was not the only quality the witnesses admired in her responses. In depicting the chaotic format of Joan's interrogations, the simultaneous questions, the interruptions, and the shifts from one topic to another, the witnesses portrayed Joan as undaunted by the interrogators' attempts to confuse her. Massieu twice testified that when numerous interrogators questioned her at once or when an interrogator interrupted her, "she spoke several times to those interrogating her with these words: 'Fair sirs, go one after the other'" (432). Moreau similarly recalled, "she often beseeched those interrogating her that she might respond to only one or two of them and [she said] that they troubled her greatly with so many interrogations made at the same time" (463), while de La Chambre remembered that when one interrogator interrupted another in order to ask other questions, Joan "told them that they did a great wrong to her in troubling her thus" (351). In a context in which Joan was expected to answer the questions that she was asked, she refused to accept the simultaneous questions thrown at her, refused to succumb to the confusion her interrogators were attempting to instill, and demanded that they ask one question at a time. Instead of accepting the format of the interrogations, she demanded that the interrogation be conducted on her own terms. Instead of addressing these learned men, these ecclesiastics, these judges with deference and obedience, she called them "'fair sirs [beaux seigneurs]'" and bade them to follow each other, thus displaying the same combination of gentility and authority that the chronicles portrayed her as having displayed earlier at the court of France. When one considers that the interrogators appear to have followed Joan's orders, to have gone one after the other when she insisted, to have checked their records when she demanded, and to have ended the session when she requested, it appears that Joan was able, in this instance, to disrupt the customary hierarchy between judges and an accused, clerics and a layperson, men and a woman.

Just as the witnesses at the rehabilitation depicted Joan as unvanquished by her interrogators' subtle and disordered questions, so too did they depict her as resolute under long and repetitive interrogation. Nearly all of the witnesses declared that when the interrogators asked her questions they had asked before, Joan remembered the date when she had previously responded to the query and the content of her response. Manchon reported, for example, that "she very often said, 'I responded to you at another time about that,' saying, 'I refer to the cleric,' meaning he who is speaking" (421), and Boisguillaume added that she would have her answers read aloud to refresh their memory. So great was Joan's memory, the clerics claim, that in cases where Joan disagreed with a cleric about her responses, it was often determined that she was in the right. Marcel recalled, "when the notary had written something and repeated what he had written, Joan told the notary that she had not responded thus and referred to the assistants, who all said that Joan had spoken well, and a correction was made of her response" (379–80). He added that another master told him "that he had never seen a woman of this age give so much trouble to those who were examining her, and he admired greatly the responses of this Joan and her memory, because she remembered what she had said" (379). Daron remembered an incident in which Boisguillaume said that Joan had not replied to a particular question and she said that she had; the clerics read aloud from the minutes and found that Joan was correct. He attested that "Joan was joyful, telling Boisguillaume that, if he failed another time, she would pull his ear" (469). Though the clerics were able to transcribe the interrogations, whereas Joan was not, though they were able to consult this record, whereas she was not, and though they possessed the authority of those who know how to read and write, the illiterate Joan, by virtue of her prodigious memory, recalled more accurately than they what was said in earlier sessions, corrected their accounts, and thus outdid the mnemonic devices of the learned clerics. When she exulted at being proven right, she made clear that these disputes with the clerics over what she had said constituted a battle between their clerkly egos and her own and that she had won this round. When she threatened to pull Boisguillaume's ear should he err again, she declared that though it was they who were deciding whether to condemn her for heresy and to abandon her to the secular arm, it was she who would punish them and who would cause them physical pain. In brief, just as Joan responded to her subtle interrogators with a subtlety greater than theirs, just as she interrupted their interruptions with demands that they proceed in order, so did she call attention to the lapses in their memories and reproach them for this weakness. Far from losing her mastery over her responses, Joan caused the interrogators to lose mastery over their interrogations.

Although the witnesses at the rehabilitation attributed the violence of Joan's interrogations to the political prejudice of her judges, the details they provided about the interrogations showed that this violence was ultimately due to the belief implicit to interrogation that truth is revealed only when an other within the self speaks. By locating this violence not in the political circumstances within which the interrogations took place but in the very structure of interrogation itself (in what they showed, if not always in what they said), the witnesses reinforced Joan's own depictions of her experience of being interrogated. Joan recalled in the minutes of the interrogations that clerics at Poitiers had questioned her before permitting her king to place his faith in her, yet she did not contrast that Armagnac interrogation to the Burgundian one in which she was now immersed, even though her earlier interrogators had been members of her party, not opponents of it, and even though they had concluded their interrogations by announcing they had found nothing of evil in her, not by condemning her for heresy. She related at various places in the minutes that when she was among the Armagnacs, God sent a sign establishing the legitimacy of her mission "in order to remove her from the pain caused by the men who were finding fault with her," "so that men put off finding fault with this Joan," or "so that men cease to interrogate her."[39] After this sign appeared, she added, she thanked God because "he freed her from the pain caused her by the clerics of her party who were finding fault with her."[40] If Joan spoke unfavorably of her past interrogations at Poitiers, she spoke no less unfavorably of her current interrogations at Rouen. She recalled that the Armagnac clerics ceased to interrogate her once they had received a sign of her authenticity in the context of the Burgundian clerics' own interrogations and their own demand for a sign. She stated repeatedly, in response to particular inquiries, that she had already answered these questions at Poitiers and that her answers were recorded in "the register of Poitiers," thus stressing the resemblance between the one interrogation and the other.[41] She asked that if she were to be brought to Paris for further interrogation, she be given a copy of the minutes of interrogation with which she could show her future examiners how she had been questioned and how she had replied "so that she would no longer be troubled with so many demands." She thus connected the past interrogation at Poitiers, where she had been asked certain questions, with the present interrogation at Rouen, where she was asked the same questions, and a possible future interrogation at Paris, where she might be asked the same questions a third time.[42] Throughout these passages, Joan compared her experience of interrogation in Poitiers with her experience of interrogation in Rouen and thus connected the pain she felt during these sessions not with the political biases of those questioning her but with the process of questioning itself. She spoke of the "pain [pena or paine]" of the interrogations by clerics who "find fault [arguent or arguent]" with her and of being "troubled [vexetur or travaillee]" by so many questions. Though Joan was never subjected to the rack, the strappado, or other medieval tortures during her interrogations at Poitiers or

Rouen, she nonetheless connected the experience of interrogation with the experience of pain, the experience of *quaestio,* or "the question," with the experience of what is still today known in French as *la question,* "torture." By protesting the "pain" she endured on account of those who "find fault" with her, Joan revealed herself to associate interrogation, whether by political friends or by political enemies, with a suffering analogous to physical anguish.

Though the witnesses showed Joan to suffer under the symbolic violence of *la question,* they also showed her to surmount this violence. They demonstrated through their testimony that despite the agreement between medieval inquisitors and modern interrogators as to the techniques that will bring about a decentering of the subject, these techniques can backfire and disconcert the questioners rather than the respondent. Indeed, it is the triumph of Joan, not the triumph of the interrogators, that modern readers of the trial transcripts have consistently observed. Jules Michelet writes, for example, "Tested by Pharisees who sought in vain to catch her in her words, she resisted wholly in this last combat; she rose above herself and burst into sublime words, which will eternally make people weep."[43] Pierre Champion notes similarly, "In wishing to destroy Jeanne, to publish to all the world the errors of her doctrine, and her 'lies,' the judges at Rouen worked greatly to preserve her memory.... It is thanks to them that we are become judges in our turn, witnesses at the marvelous drama wherein strategy and ruse played with virtue and simplicity."[44] Warner likewise comments on the irony of the fact that though "the trial sought to prove her falsehood and, indeed, succeeded in doing so to the satisfaction of some of the most learned men of the time, ... the quite extraordinary quality of directness in the trial document ... has, since the 1840's and its first publication, made Joan of Arc an unforgettable source of inspiration."[45] If the clerics attempted to transform Joan's controlled, legally worthless self-defense into an uncontrolled, legally valuable admission of guilt, through their interrogations, their success in this endeavor was short-lived.

6 | The Confession of Conscience

The clerics who tried Joan for heresy approached her not just as scholastics, trained at the university in theology or canon law, and as inquisitors, experienced in the evaluation of evidence, but also as pastors devoted to the *cura animarum,* or the care of souls, and it is from this angle that Joan might seem to have been most likely to satisfy them.[1] In the course of their interrogations, the clerics asked Joan about her sacramental practices and received altogether orthodox answers to their questions. When they inquired whether Joan had been in the habit of confessing her sins every year, as the Fourth Lateran Council required all Christians to do, she replied that as a child, she confessed "to her own curate and when the curate was hindered, she confessed to another priest" (46), thus echoing the stipulations of the bull *Omnis utriusque sexus.* She stated that, in addition to her annual Easter duties, when she was living in Domrémy, she confessed two or three times to mendicants in nearby Neufchâteau and that later, when she was traveling through France, she received the sacraments of penance and communion "from time to time" (102) in large towns. At the rehabilitation, Joan's childhood friends and companions at arms recalled that she confessed frequently throughout the year, while her personal confessor, Friar Jean Pasquerel, in fact maintained that she confessed almost every day. Correct in the regularity of her confession, Joan might also appear to have been correct in her recognition of the need for this sacrament. Joan's voices had promised her that she would go to heaven, yet when the clerics asked if she believed it necessary for her to confess, given her assurance of ultimate salvation, she answered that "she believes that one cannot cleanse one's conscience too much" (150). When the clerics inquired whether she was in a state of grace, she replied, as we have seen, "if I am not, may God put me there, and, if I am, may he keep me there" (62). At the times when she saw Saint Michael, she conveyed, "it seems to her that ... she is not in a state of mortal sin" (87), and "if she were in a state of sin, she believes that the voice would not come to her" (62). She denied knowing whether she had ever been in a state of mortal sin and wished, " 'would that it be pleasing to God that I have never been in it and that it be pleasing to him that I have never done nor will do acts through which my soul would be burdened' " (87). With these hypothetical and subjunctive clauses, she acknowledged, in accordance with Catholic doctrine, that, whatever celestial voices might speak to her and whatever assurance they might give her of her salvation, she remained ultimately ignorant of the present or future status of her soul, so that she could always be aided by confessing her sins. In contrast to the heretics of the Free Spirit, who were thought to believe themselves capable of ascending to spiritual heights that freed them from vulnerability to sin and from dependence upon the church's sacrament of reconciliation, Joan avoided both an admission of a blameworthy sinfulness and an assertion of sanctity for which she could also be reproached. Uncertain as to whether she was in a state of grace and eager to confess because of that uncertainty, Joan appears to have been not only orthodox but unusually pious in her penitential practices.

As much as the confessional literature of the Middle Ages stressed the importance of the regularity and the voluntariness of confession, it also stressed the importance of the quality of the relationship between priest and penitent. The church sought for confession to be understood not merely as an annual obligation necessary for the parishioner's salvation but as the primary locus of the parishioner's spiritual direction. If pastors questioned parishioners, it was because they wanted them to open up their hearts to ecclesiastical scrutiny, and if they instructed and counseled them when they had uncovered their sins, it was because they sought to lead them back to the true path of sanctity. It is only when one considers the confessor not merely as an administrator of the keys but as a spiritual director of this kind that Joan's conduct becomes suspect. When she recounted a spiritual crisis that she underwent while imprisoned in a Burgundian tower, she made clear that, as avid a penitent as she might have been, it was not to a confessor that she had turned for guidance at this time. Similarly, when she responded to the judges' and assistants' efforts to contribute to her salvation during the trial, she showed that, as eager a supporter of the church as she might be, it was not to clerics that she would entrust the care of her soul. Though Joan might have appeared most Christian in the regularity and the fervor of her confession, she clashed with the clerics who tried her in her refusal to rely upon mortal men, in general, and upon these mortal men, in particular, as the regulators of her inner life.

Charitable Admonitions

In their first words of the first day of interrogation, the clerics at Joan's trial set what would become the confessional tone of their interactions. On February 21, 1431, in the royal chapel of the castle of Rouen, Cauchon had the citation for Joan to appear and to respond to interrogations on this day read aloud to the assistants and then ordered Joan to be brought into the chapel. The minutes then relate, in Cauchon's voice,

> we first of all charitably admonished and requested the said Joan, then seated before us, that, for the acceleration of the present affair and the unburdening of her own conscience, she speak the entire truth as to that about which she would be interrogated in matters of faith, seeking neither subterfuges nor ruses that would separate her from the confession of truth. (37)

After this exhortation that Joan speak the truth about that which she would be asked, the minutes continue, again in the bishop's voice, "we judicially requested Joan to take an oath in the due form, touching the Holy Gospels, to speak the truth, as it had just been indicated, about the points about which she would be interrogated" (37–38). Having registered the appeal that she swear to speak the truth, the minutes add, "we, the said bishop, forbade this same Joan from leaving the prisons assigned to her in the castle of Rouen without our permission, under penalty of being convicted of the crime of heresy" (42). With these demands that Joan answer the clerics' questions faithfully, that she commit herself to answering them faithfully, and that she resign herself to remaining within her castle prison for the duration of her trial, Cauchon set the framework within which the interrogations were to take place.

When Cauchon urged Joan that, "for . . . the unburdening of her own conscience, she speak the entire truth as to that about which she would be interrogated," he made a number of assumptions about the interaction that would take place between himself and his prisoner. First, when he referred to "the unburdening of her own conscience," he assumed that Joan's conscience was already encumbered, that is, that she had already committed sins sufficient to weigh it down. This presupposition of Joan's guilt was not new to the trial. In an earlier letter sent to both Philip the Good and Jean de Luxembourg, the bishop had described Joan as "suspected and defamed of having committed several crimes, such as spells, idolatries, invocations of demons, and several other acts concerning our faith and opposed to it" (9), and he had alleged that through these crimes, Joan had scandalized Christian communities in his diocese and in other areas. In this current appeal to Joan herself, however, Cauchon spoke not of any such crimes but of a weight that he imagined to afflict her. He referred not to a Christian community endangered by her errors but to a conscience endangered by her sins. As his frame of reference shifted from external imperiled communities to an internal imperiled "conscience," he moved from an exclusively judicial to a pastoral register. This shift from outer danger to inner crisis and hence from judicial to confessional rhetoric holds important consequences for the trial. Though a particular individual may or may not be guilty of having committed crimes, all Christians are considered guilty of having committed sins, as the clerics themselves recalled when they cited the scriptural warning "The just succumb seventy times a day" (239). In presupposing the heaviness of Joan's conscience, Cauchon resembled a Paschal confessor who presupposed the heaviness of his parishioner's conscience and who dismissed any claim to innocence as a theological impossibility. In addition, when Cauchon advised Joan to speak the truth "for... the unburdening of her own conscience," he assumed not only that she had committed sins sufficient to encumber this conscience, but that she experienced these sins as a burden. In his choice of the term "unburdening" (*exoneracione* in Latin, *descharge* in French) the bishop compares Joan's presumed recollection of her sins to an onus, a charge, pressing upon her. Through this choice of metaphor, he recalled a pastoral tradition that considered sin, however freely chosen, to be a weight and considered the sinner, however adamantly erring, to be suffering under the burden of her wrongful actions. According to other metaphors from the confessors' manuals, sin constituted an illness from which the sinner ailed, infected matter to be ejected from the body by vomiting or bloodletting, or pus to be drained from a ruptured blister.[2] Whether regarded as a weight or a disease, sin was understood to be intrinsically vile and oppressive, so that the sinner, prior to the intervention of the confessor, was believed to lie in a state of torment from which she sought to be rescued. Finally, when Cauchon urged her to unburden her conscience by "speak[ing] the entire truth," he connected her potential relief from the weight of her heavy conscience with her own speech. According to medieval theology, *oris confessio* constituted one of the three components of the sacrament of penance, alongside *cordis contritio* and *operis satisfactio,* not only because the penitent's verbal representation of sins enabled the confessor to gauge the state of the soul and hence to absolve and assign penance appropriately, but also because the verbal representation of sins caused the sinner to feel shame, because this shame led to humility, and because these twin emotions of shame and humility helped transform sinners into true penitents, worthy of God's forgiveness. "Confession of the mouth" was thought to inspire tears of remorse, which helped to cleanse the sinner of the sin, and it is this very type of confession that Cauchon appealed to Joan to make. By representing Joan as suffering from a heavy conscience and by suggesting that Joan might relieve herself of its weight through answering truthfully what the clerics ask her, Cauchon depicted Joan as a penitent, the clerics as her confessors, and the interrogations as the verbal arena of her confession.

When Cauchon urged Joan to swear to speak the truth and abandon hope of leaving her prison, he reinforced the confessional character of the clerics' interaction with the suspect. In requesting that Joan swear to speak the truth, Cauchon requested that she function not as a passive and unwilling object of the clerics' interrogations but as an active and engaged participant in the imminent dialogue. He requested, in other words, that she establish an internal monitor to regulate the veracity of her responses, to eliminate possible "subterfuges" or "ruses" in her speech, and to compel her to reply fully and accurately to the clerics' questions. He recommended that by taking this oath, Joan ally herself with the clerics in a united search for truth. As Michel Foucault discusses in his volume on confession, the confessor operates best when he appoints in the conscience of the parishioner a deputy who will apply the same force internally that he applies externally.[3] It was such a deputy that Cauchon was advising Joan to nominate by swearing to speak the truth. In recommending that Joan refrain from leaving her prison, he was demanding that she commit herself to the trial not only by swearing to tell the truth during her interrogations but also by agreeing to remain in her prison, even if the opportunity to escape should arise. Warning Joan that she would be judged guilty of heresy should she escape, he warned her that heretics were not just those who held heterodox views and who persisted in holding them even when corrected, but also those who refused to look upon their judges as charitable priests, eager to help save them from their sins, and their trials as the frameworks within which they could be reconciled with the church. To look upon one's judges as one's adversaries and one's trial as an adversity was to reveal oneself to be not only guilty but unwilling to confess and atone for one's guilt. In the *libelle d'Estivet,* the clerics confirmed the implications of the bishop's requests when they reproached her for "supporting impatiently and hating to have to be placed in judgment of ecclesiastics and to be brought before them" (246). In the same way that penitents were expected to engage themselves in the three steps through which they would be cleansed of sin, Joan was expected to engage herself with good faith in the process through which she would be confessed, absolved, and assigned penance for her sins.

Despite the spiritual benefits Cauchon suggested Joan would reap by engaging herself in her trial, Joan refused to swear to speak the truth about all that she would be asked. Joan distinguished between her father, her mother, and her activities since her departure for France, all of which she was willing to discuss, and "the revelations which had been made to her on the part of God" (38), which she was not willing to discuss even if they threatened to cut off her head. Throughout the trial, Joan appears to have spoken readily about factual, external occurrences, such as the festivities of her childhood, the details of her voyage to the king, and her conduct as a military captain, yet, as we have seen, when the clerics turned the discussion to the voices and, in particular, to the revelations made to her king, Joan resisted replying. Both on the first public day of her trial and on the days that followed, Joan retained this distinction between issues she would and would not discuss with the clerics. In accounting for her refusal to speak of the revelations to the clerics, Joan explained on the first day of the interrogations that "she held from her visions or her secret counsel that she should not reveal them to anyone" (38). Later she demanded, "If the voice prohibited me from it, what do you want me to tell you about it?" (60) and stated, "she does not want to reveal that which has been revealed to her without the permission of God" (238). While the clerics pressured Joan to respond to their questions and to commit herself, through an oath, to their interrogations, Joan testified that her voices applied a contrary pressure for her not to speak of certain matters, whether by prohibiting her from disclosing them or, as she later clarified, by withholding their permission for Joan to speak. By contrasting the clerics' demand that she speak with the voices' possible preference that she remain silent and by acquiescing to this inner counsel, Joan showed that she respected the authority of her voices more than she respected that of the clerics. While the bishop promised that, should Joan respond truthfully to all of the clerics' questions, she would unburden her heavy conscience, Joan maintained that, should she do so, she would stand to offend these alternate spiritual directors and thus, perhaps, add weight to her conscience.

As Joan refused to swear to speak the truth, she also refused to abandon all hopes or plans of escape. When Cauchon forbade her to leave the castle, the minutes recount "she would not accept this prohibition, saying that, if she escaped, no one could reproach her for having broken or violated her faith, because she had never given her faith to anyone" (42). Faced with the bishop's accusation that she had attempted to flee from previous prisons, she affirmed that " 'It is true that elsewhere I wanted and that I would like to escape, as it is allowed to whomever is incarcerated or imprisoned' " (42). By appealing to the rights of prisoners of war, Joan appealed implicitly not to a pastoral code, which assumed that penitents welcomed their penances and those who administered them, but to a chivalric code, which assumed that prisoners desired to flee their prisons and those who ensured their captivity. She cited a discourse in which she, as an Armagnac prisoner, would be acknowledged to have interests contrary to those of her English and Burgundian captors and in which this conflict of interest would be not only recognized but respected. According to Honoré Bonet, whose work on warfare and chivalry was popular at the time, if a prisoner had not given his faith to his captor, as Joan insisted she had not, he was not obligated to remain in prison. Bonet wrote, "It is beyond argument that every man desires to have his liberty and freedom, for liberty comes of the law of nature, and we assert that natural law is at all times good and just. So, if he goes, he acts according to the law of nature and offends in no point."[4] In reminding the bishop of the chivalric code, Joan asked him not to attempt to co-opt her desire into his own by forbidding her from escaping her prison but to recognize her desire as at once opposed to his and legitimate in that opposition. Whereas the bishop asked Joan to recognize her own interest in attempting to restore her spiritual health as identical to the interest of the clerics, Joan asked the bishop to recognize her interest in attempting to regain her freedom as different from that of her jailors.

In both of these conflicts, whether over Joan's proposed oath or over her intention to escape from her prison, Cauchon attempted to construct a relationship with his prisoner that Joan resisted. When he requested that Joan swear to answer truthfully any question they might pose to her, he asked that she prepare herself to share with them all of her secrets, all of her private experiences, all aspects of her personality, so that she might be exposed before them in all her nakedness. When he demanded that she forsake any plans to flee her captivity, he demanded that she forsake her own intuition of how she might best secure her life and happiness and, instead, trust his judgment in determining her future. In both of these requests, Cauchon asked that Joan accept the clerics as her spiritual directors, that she place her faith in them, and that she willingly abandon her will to them. Despite the forcefulness of Cauchon's demands, Joan refused to enter into the relationship with the clerics that he sought. When the clerics inquired, on March 14, if she had ever committed a mortal sin, Joan replied, "It pertained to God and to the priest in confession to review this" (152). With this remark, Joan distinguished between the information appropriate to share with a confessor and that appropriate to share with judicial authorities, and she reproached the interrogator for overstepping the boundaries between these two roles.

The Leap from the Tower

After Joan fell from her horse into captivity during a skirmish outside Compiègne in May 1430, she was kept in a series of Burgundian fortresses, including that of Beaurevoir, thirty miles southeast of Arras. At first, Joan's stay in the tower of this castle does not appear to have been entirely unpleasant. Though the household was dominated by the Burgundian knight Jean de Luxembourg, it was softened by the presence of the "three Jeannes": Jean's aunt Jeanne de Luxembourg, onetime lady-in-waiting to Isabeau of Bavaria and godmother to Charles VII; his wife Jeanne de Béthune, widow of Robert de Bar, a nobleman slain at the battle of Agincourt; and her daughter Jeanne de Bar. All of these ladies, though linked through present familial and marital ties to followers of the Burgundian party, were attached through previous alliances to members of the French royal family or defenders of this house and were thought, as a result, to be Armagnac in their sympathies. At Rouen, Joan told the clerics that Jeanne de Luxembourg and Jeanne de Béthune had offered her women's clothes while she was staying in the tower and that though she had refused to accept this attire, "she would have done it more quickly at the request of these two ladies than of any other woman living in France, except her queen" (95). After Joan had been a month in this large and pleasant castle, in the company of ladies for whom she expressed such evident affection, however, her fortunes took a turn for the worse. For some time, the citizens of Compiègne had displayed remarkable loyalty to the Armagnac party, willingly accepting Charles's rule after his coronation, refusing to forsake this allegiance even when Charles conceded the city to the Burgundians, and holding off the Burgundians who were attempting to impose their rule upon them by force. It was on account of this loyalty that Joan had come to their aid with her men and had fought to repel the troops outside their walls, though finding herself only taken prisoner for her efforts. Now, in mid-August, Philip the Good, duke of Burgundy, decided to intensify his efforts to conquer Compiègne and assigned Jean the task of putting this plan into action. Now, rumors began to circulate that the Burgundians would not only succeed in taking Compiègne but would massacre all of its inhabitants when they had done so. Around the same time as the renewal of the attack upon Compiègne, the negotiations over Joan's sale to the English, which had been stalled since not long after her capture, began to make progress. Jeanne de Luxembourg, who was known to have resisted this transferal, left Beaurevoir in order to visit the tomb of her sainted brother Pierre in Avignon, as she did every year, and died there in mid-September, so that whatever protection she had once extended to Joan came to an end. If, for some time, Joan had known Compiègne to be suffering under Burgundian assault and herself to be suffering under Burgundian imprisonment, now she understood the city to be in even worse straits than it had been in before and herself to be falling into the far more menacing hands of a foreign enemy. It was in response to this situation that Joan performed the sole action mentioned in the transcripts that she acknowledged to have been a sin and that she believed herself to have been obliged to confess.

Joan leaped from the tower of Beaurevoir because of her fears for the people of Compiègne and for herself, she claimed, yet her explanation for this leap during the interrogations suggested another reason for this action as well. When the clerics at Rouen inquired as to why she leaped, Joan stated, first, "that she had heard said that all those of Compiègne who had attained seven years of age were supposed to be put to death by fire and by sword and that she preferred to die than to live after such a destruction of good people" (144). She recalled having asked her voices, " 'How will God leave to die these good people of Compiègne who have been and are so faithful to their lord?' " (145) and thus revealed her assumption that if these people were to die, it would be because God had allowed them to perish. Historical events occurred, her words suggested, not only because empirical contingencies brought them about but because a central, divine consciousness allowed them to happen. Contrasting the goodness and loyalty of the people of Compiègne with the prospect of their extermination, Joan revealed her belief that God, who is all-just as well as all-powerful and all-knowing, normally rewarded the virtuous and did not allow them to undergo such grief. Joan's question to Saint Catherine showed that she was distressed not only because she expected the people of Compiègne to be slaughtered but because this anticipated massacre upset her belief in God's presence in historical events and in the consequent justice of those events. It showed that she was troubled not just because she feared that the inhabitants of Compiègne would suffer but because their suffering struck her as undeserved. Joan explained that she had leaped from the tower, in addition, because "she knew herself to have been sold to the English, and she would have preferred to die than to be in the hands of the English, her adversaries" (144). Speaking of herself, Joan did not contrast the unfortunate fate to which she appeared to be destined with her loyalty to her lord, as she did when speaking of the people of Compiègne. She mentioned neither her devotion to her king in leading him to his coronation nor her obedience to God in quitting her village, assuming arms, and waging war on his behalf. Despite this silence, just as Joan had affirmed her preference for death over life after the destruction of Compiègne, she affirmed her preference for death over life in English captivity and thus suggested, through the parallel structure of these utterances, a parallel perception of these events. Joan leaped from the tower not only because she and the people of Compiègne were about to suffer but because it was unjust that they should suffer and because her faith in a God who does not allow such injustices to take place had been undermined by this apparent future.

At this time of spiritual crisis and confusion, it was not a priest but Saint Catherine who instructed and counseled Joan, though Joan was not always receptive to her words. When Joan expressed anxiety about the people of Compiègne and about herself, Saint Catherine attempted to reassure her by informing her of the plans God had made for them. During her interrogations, Joan related that "Saint Catherine told her almost every day... that God would help her and also those of Compiègne" (144). She related that the voice told her that she would not be delivered from her imprisonment until she had seen the king of the English and thus, implicitly, that she would be delivered after this encounter with the enemy monarch. While Joan had perceived Jean de Luxembourg's decisions to massacre the people of Compiègne and to sell Joan to the English as endpoints in the histories of this people and of herself, Saint Catherine taught her that these were not endpoints but mere temporary tribulations on the way to happier outcomes. She intimated that meaning revealed itself only with the conclusion of a narrative and that if history appeared to be unjust and hence not divinely ordained, it was only because one's reading of this narrative had not yet reached its end. Refocusing Joan's attention on a point beyond the current danger, she taught that God would not allow good and loyal people to die but, instead, would always ultimately come to their aid. As Saint Catherine instructed Joan about God's intentions, she also counseled her as to the wisest plan of action, given these intentions. Joan reported, "the voices . . . prohibited her from leaping from this tower" (107) and "Saint Catherine told her almost every day not to leap" (144). Because God would eventually come to the aid of the people of Compiègne and Joan, Saint Catherine bade Joan not to try to save them or herself by leaping from the tower but, rather, to be patient, to have faith in God, and to await his divine assistance. Yet when Saint Catherine informed Joan that God would help the people of Compiègne, Joan protested, "as God would help those of Compiègne, she wanted to be there" (144). When Saint Catherine informed Joan that she would not be delivered until she had seen Henry VI, Joan objected, " 'Truly, I would not like to see him, and I would prefer to die than to be put into the hands of the English' " (144). With these retorts and with her leap from the tower, Joan rejected Saint Catherine's lessons that God would eventually aid the people of Compiègne and herself, and she rejected her counsel, based upon these lessons, that she not leap but wait for God's help. Though Saint Catherine functioned like a priest, teaching and advising Joan, her lessons were not always heeded and her recommendations not always followed.

Saint Catherine functioned as an intermediary between God and Joan, yet Joan's actions showed she doubted Saint Catherine's capacity to act as such an intermediary at this time and turned to God instead as she leaped from the tower. Readers of Joan's responses about the leap from the tower at Beaurevoir, from the clerics to modern historians, have expressed uncertainty as to whether Joan meant to save herself and the people of Compiègne or to commit suicide. On the one hand, when the clerics inquired if she had intended to kill herself by throwing herself from her window to the ground sixty feet below, Joan denied having had such an intention. She asserted that she meant, "by means of this leap, to escape being delivered over to the English" (145) and that " 'I did that, not out of despair, but in the hope of saving my body and going to help many good people who were in need' " (153). She leaped, she affirmed, not in order to destroy her body but in order to save it from destruction at the hands of the English. She leaped, she claimed, not out of despair at the future she foresaw for the people of Compiègne but out of hope that she might help them. On the other hand, Joan gave indications that it was not just a desire to protect herself and the people of Compiègne that motivated this deed. She leaped, she stated, because "she would prefer to die" rather than to live after the destruction of the good people of Compiègne or than to be delivered over to the English. In these explanations, Joan stressed not her desire to save herself or others but her desire to die, and she connected this desire to her leap from the tower. Joan also conceded that "she believes that it was not well done to have made this leap, but it was badly done" (153) and that, aware of the wrongfulness of her action, she confessed to a priest. If she were leaping in order to escape her prison, her action would have been morally justifiable according to the chivalric code that she cited when defending the right of prisoners of war to attempt to escape. It was only if she were leaping not in order to escape but in order to kill herself that her action would have been sinful and that she would have thus felt beholden to confess. When the clerics asked again whether Joan had meant to kill herself by leaping from the tower, she replied, "no, but in leaping she recommended herself to God" (145). Maintaining at once that she leaped out of a desire to save her body from destruction and that she exposed her body to precisely that destruction through this leap, Joan showed herself to have asked God to determine which fate would be hers. By "recommend[ing] herself to God" as she leaps from the tower, she acknowledged that as she floated through the air, it would be not herself but a force outside herself who would determine how she fell. To leap is to abandon one's control over one's body and to allow an external power to exercise that control. To leap is to abandon, willingly, one's will. Fearful of the dangers under which she and the people of Compiègne lay, skeptical of the instruction and the counsel she had received, uncertain of God's true volition, Joan provided the deity with a clean slate, her body hurtling through space, on which to reveal his inclination. She provided God with the opportunity to disclose his desire by determining whether, upon landing, she would be able to jump to her feet and return to Compiègne to help in the city's defense or whether she would shatter her body and expire. Though she temporarily rejected Saint Catherine, who claimed to communicate God's will to her, she appealed to God to communicate his will directly by fixing the outcome of her fall.

Joan's disregard of Saint Catherine's promises suggested a skepticism toward this being who claimed to mediate her rapport with God, but the outcome of this leap reaffirmed her faith in Saint Catherine's instruction and counsel. After having leaped from her window, Joan did not land safely and flee to friendly territory, yet neither did she die. Instead, according to Pierre Rocolle's reconstruction of these events, she was knocked unconscious when she struck the earth.[5] Awakened a few moments later by the dawn, she dragged herself to the foot of another tower where she remained, stretched out on the ground and semiconscious, until her guards found her later that morning. If divine will was reflected in the outcome of Joan's leap, God desired at that point neither for Joan to escape her imprisonment nor for her to perish from her fall but, rather, for her to remain imprisoned a while longer, as Saint Catherine had told her. Through the result of her leap, God showed that when Saint Catherine bade her to remain in the tower, she bade her to accept a continued captivity and a sale to a foreign crown, neither of which could be avoided. If Joan's failure to escape her captivity confirmed the fate that Saint Catherine predicted for her, the events of October 1430 likewise confirmed the saint's predictions. During that month, Jean de La Brosse, lord of Boussac and of Sainte-Sévère and marshal of France, came to the aid of Compiègne, routing the forces of Jean de Luxembourg and obliging the Burgundians to abandon the city. Both in the prevention of Joan's escape and in the relief of the siege of Compiègne, God could be seen as confirming the truth of Saint Catherine's teachings and the wisdom of her counsel.

If it was Saint Catherine who taught and advised Joan when she was in spiritual crisis, it was also Saint Catherine who saved and rehabilitated her when she sinned. Though it was to God, and not to the voices, that Joan recommended herself as she leaped, she attributed the preservation of her life to the voices, who, she stated, "preserved her so that she did not kill herself" (161). She added, by way of commentary, that "in whatever she did, in her great undertakings, the voices always succored her, and this is a sign that they are good spirits" (161). It was the voices who softened her fall so that she did not break her bones, just as it was they who had always helped her. After she leaped from the tower, Joan related, "she was in such a state that, for two or three days, she did not want to eat, and she was oppressed by this leap to such a point that she could not eat nor drink" (145). Joan depicted herself as suffering when she lay ill after this attempted escape, as she depicted herself as suffering when she feared being transferred to the English, but now her suffering consisted of the shock she experienced as a result of her fall and of the inability to eat or drink she experienced afterward. No longer portraying herself as an innocent unfairly made to suffer, she portrayed herself as one who had acted "badly" and who performed a "penance" for her unworthy action. Her suffering was no longer meaningless, the proof of the absence of divine will and justice in human events, but was now meaningful, a deserved punishment of someone who had doubted Saint Catherine's teachings and had disobeyed her counsel. Joan benefited not only from Saint Catherine's preservation of her life but also from her consolation as she recuperated from the fall. Even though she could neither eat nor drink, Joan continued, "she was comforted by Saint Catherine, who told her to confess and to seek pardon from God for having leaped, and without fail those of Compiègne would have succor before the feast of the blessed Martin in the winter. Thus she started to enter into convalescence and began to eat, and was shortly thereafter cured" (145). Once again, Saint Catherine instructed Joan, telling her once more that the people of Compiègne would be saved, as she had told her, before her leap, that they would be saved. Yet though Saint Catherine taught Joan almost exactly the same lesson about the future of the people of Compiègne as she had taught her earlier and though the previous lesson seemed to have made little impression upon its auditor, Joan indicated that she now learned from it. Joan's paratactic speech, which connected Saint Catherine's promise of the rescue of the people of Compiègne with the "comfort" that she received from Saint Catherine, suggests that she now felt consoled by this promise. Once again, Saint Catherine advised Joan, urging her to confess and to ask pardon of God, and this time she obeyed. "It was on the counsel of Saint Catherine that she confessed" (153), Joan announced during the interrogations. Joan stated that " 'after the leap I confessed and requested pardon from the Lord,' " that "she had pardon from the Lord," and that "she knows herself to have had pardon by the revelation of Saint Catherine after she confessed" (153). If Joan connected the teachings and the counsel that Saint Catherine offered her with the "comfort" she now experienced, she also connected her renewed trust in Saint Catherine's teachings and her renewed obedience to Saint Catherine's counsel to her convalescence and her cure. Suffering from her fall as a form of "penance" for her sin of leaping, Joan recuperated because, through her restored acceptance of Saint Catherine as her spiritual advisor, she rid herself of her sin. The very being whose teaching Joan had doubted and whose counsel she had rejected came to her aid, saving her from the death of the soul just as she had saved her from the death of the body.

As the episode at Beaurevoir ended, Joan acted as all repentant sinners are bidden to act by Christian theology. She sought out a priest, confessed her sin, and asked forgiveness of God. On the surface, Joan appears to have conformed to church precepts by recognizing the necessity of confessing her sins before a priest. On another level, however, Joan undermined the intention behind the church's reform of confession when she refrained from adopting her confessor as her spiritual director. When she was in spiritual turmoil, confounded by God's apparent acceptance of the destruction of good and loyal people, it was not a priest but Saint Catherine who attempted to instruct her in God's ways. When she was tempted to sin by leaping from the tower, it was not a priest but Saint Catherine who counseled her to resist her impulse, who later urged her to confess, and who still later informed her of God's pardon. The priest who heard Joan's confession appears to have had no influence upon her inner life but, rather, merely to have provided the formal means, in his administering of the sacrament of penance, through which Joan could ask the forgiveness of God. In her account of the episode at Beaurevoir, Joan made clear that her true spiritual teaching, counsel, and salvation took place without the participation of church personnel.

Penitential Appeals

According to the Gospel of Matthew 18:15–17, a Christian should reproach an erring brother, first, in solitude, then, if he continues to sin, in the presence of one or two other persons, and, finally, if he persists in his wrongdoing, in the presence of the church itself. After the interrogations had been completed and the flaws in Joan's responses had been discovered by the various consultants to the trial, Cauchon and the clerics spoke to Joan on three occasions. First, on Wednesday, April 18, the bishop and a half-dozen or so assistants entered Joan's tower cell, where she lay ill, and presented themselves as "visiting her for her consolation and comfort" (152) during her malady. Cauchon informed Joan of the defects that learned clerics had found in her responses and urged her to accept the assistants who accompanied him as men willing to assist her in correcting these defects; he offered to designate other men — even, in the Latin version of the minutes, those of Joan's choosing — to provide her with such instruction and counsel. On Wednesday, May 2, two weeks after this first, private appeal, Cauchon and sixty-three assistants addressed Joan again in the chamber near the great hall of the castle. In front of this large audience, the bishop reiterated much of what he had said during the previous admonition, yet he used a more elaborate rhetoric. He recalled to those in attendance that learned clerics had found problems in Joan's responses and that though he and the assistants had spoken to Joan in private, so that she could amend these problems, they had had no success in persuading her to do so. Now, he stated, they had decided to face her again, in public, in the hope that this large crowd might bend her to submission. Jean de Châtillon, the archdeacon of Evreux, took upon himself the tasks of explaining to Joan six principal areas of her error and urging her to abandon these various positions. Finally, on May 23, three weeks after the second, public admonition, Cauchon and nine other clerics confronted Joan once more in a chamber near her cell. In this session, Pierre Maurice, the Parisian theologian, assumed the duty of delivering the principal address to Joan, explaining to her twelve principal areas of her error and beseeching her to distance herself from them. It was only the day after this final, third admonition that the clerics proceeded to condemn Joan for heresy at the cemetery of the abbey of Saint-Ouen.

In the course of these three appeals to Joan, the clerics stressed, first, their role as her instructors. They frequently reminded Joan of their degrees in theology and canon law and of their access to the truths to be found in these fields. Cauchon described the assistants and consultants to the trial as "learned and knowledgable men" (328), "wise people who know divine and human law" (335), and "doctors in holy theology and canon law and also licensed scholars in the same law and others graduated from the said faculties" (327). As experts in theology, the clerics explained to Joan that when Jesus Christ had left this world, he had entrusted the church to Saint Peter and his successors; that even after this transferal from divine to human hands, the church had continued to be guided by the Holy Spirit; and that this Holy Spirit prevents the church from ever erring in its judgments. As experts in canon law, the clerics taught Joan that the Church Triumphant, with God, the Virgin Mary, the saints, and the saved souls, was indivisible from the Church Militant, with its popes, prelates, and clerics, and that as a result all Christians must submit their words and deeds to the Church Militant just as they would to the Church Triumphant. As theologians and canonists, the clerics perceived the truth of what they taught as existing in its own right, independent of their articulation of it. The clerics instructed Joan not only in the indivisibility of the holy Roman and apostolic church and the duty of Christians to submit to this church but also in the ways in which she had strayed from these church teachings. On April 18, Cauchon informed Joan that the ecclesiastics who had considered her responses had "noted many things said and confessed by her to be dangerous for the faith" (328). On May 2, de Châtillon related that Joan's "words and deeds were for many days diligently examined by doctors and clerics who found in them many and grave defects" (337). According to the clerics, the assistants to the trial "noted" or "found" these deviations when examining Joan's responses. That is, the deviations already existed, as deviations, and were simply apprehended by the assistants. Having discovered differences between church dogma and the content of Joan's responses, the clerics disclosed these differences to Joan. Cauchon represented the clerics' ministry when he stated, "we show her charitably that which in her words and deeds differs from faith, truth, and religion" (335). He averred, "it seemed ... expedient that we labor in all manners to instruct this woman in those things in which she seemed deficient and to lead her back to the path and perception of truth" (334–35). As teachers communicating their theological and canonical learning to Joan, the clerics perceived themselves as merely showing and instructing something that existed apart from their teaching. As the clerics turned from exposition of pure dogma to analysis of Joan's responses, they retained the pedagogical detachment that had characterized their earlier teachings. Not only did the clerics perceive the infallibility of the church and the indivisibility of the Church Triumphant and the Church Militant to be truths that existed independent of their representation, but they also saw Joan's deviation from these truths to be objectively ascertainable. The clerics understood their role, whether in expounding dogma to Joan, in detecting her divergence from this dogma, or in exposing this divergence to her, to be an external and nonintrusive depiction of something already there.

The clerics' instruction of Joan did not end with communicating her errors. Having informed Joan of church teachings and of her deviations from them, the clerics went on to inform her of what would befall her should she continue in these errors. Cauchon told Joan that her "great and grave defects ... exposed her to great perils" (327) and that if she did not correct these defects, "it would be necessary for us to abandon her" (329). De Châtillon told her of "the grave penalties that canonical laws inflicted on those deviants who separated themselves in this way" (338). Maurice reminded Joan that "the damages of soul and body, which you risk if you do not correct and amend yourself in submitting yourself and your deeds to the church and in accepting its judgment, have been declared to you" (380) and added, "Know then, if ... you persevere in this error, your soul will be damned to eternal torture, perpetually tormented, and, as for your body, I fear greatly that it will come to perdition" (382). When Cauchon, de Châtillon, and Maurice recalled to Joan the "great perils," "the damages of soul and body," and the "perdition" that she faced, none of them acknowledged any responsibility, on their part or on the part of the other clerics, for these threats. On the contrary, they saw themselves not as causing Joan to be endangered but merely as "exposing" or "declaring" those predetermined dangers to her. They depicted the hazards she confronted as existing before and apart from their intervention in her case. When Cauchon warned Joan of the punishment that would follow if she did not correct herself, he used the words "it would be necessary for us to abandon her," emphasizing that an impersonal force would compel them to this action. Similarly, when Maurice reminded Joan of this threat, he did not recognize that he, as a cleric participating in the trial, belonged to the forces creating that threat, but, rather, he pointed to this bodily perdition as something that he "fears" for Joan. Because the clerics understood themselves as in no way causing Joan's anticipated sufferings, they depicted them as they depicted church dogma and Joan's deviation from it: all constituted objective truths whose reality the clerics did not cause but merely perceived and communicated to Joan.

The clerics accepted no responsibility for the sufferings Joan endured and appeared about to endure, yet they clearly identified the party responsible for these sufferings. On May 2, Cauchon informed Joan that she "exposes herself to grave perils which could put her soul and body in danger" (335), and a week later, he referred to "the salvation of her soul and her body... which, by her lying inventions, she exposed to grave perils" (349). Two weeks later, on May 23, Maurice reminded Joan of "the damages of soul and body which you risk if you do not correct and amend yourself in submitting, yourself and your deeds, to the church and in accepting its judgment." Repeatedly they stated that it was Joan who had exposed herself to grave perils, grave dangers, and damages, both of soul and body, and it was Joan who would bear responsibility for her fate. Maurice informed her, "when you do not want to submit yourself to the church, in fact, you withdraw yourself from it" (382) and "you separate yourself from the church and the faith which you promised in holy baptism and you thus strip the authority of God from the church" (382), stressing, in this succession of second-person pronouns and second-person verbs, Joan's activity in the current situation. Maurice provided what is perhaps the strongest depiction of Joan's agency when he portrayed her at a crossroads, choosing between two contrary paths. As he saw it, Joan could, on the one hand, opt to amend her allegedly defective positions, submit to the church, and thus save her soul and her body. He advanced that "in acting thus, you will save your soul, you will buy back, as I think, your body from death" (383). On the other hand, Joan could choose to remain obdurate to the clerics' appeals, not amend her positions, and not submit to the church. If she followed this route, Maurice warned Joan, "your soul will be damned to eternal torture, perpetually tormented, and, as for your body, I fear greatly that it will come to perdition" (383). It was Joan, the clerics maintained, who had already actively endangered her soul and body, who was actively persisting in keeping herself in this peril, and who would ultimately decide whether to save or condemn her soul and body. Just as God, having granted human beings free will, merely knows the difference between sinfulness and virtue, detects the relative sinfulness of each soul, and consigns these souls to heaven, hell, or purgatory based upon what he perceives, so did the clerics deem themselves merely to know the difference between heresy and orthodoxy, to detect the heretical leanings of those accused, and to assign penance or abandon the accused based upon what they detected. In both cases, the sinner determines whether he or she shall fall prey to infernal or inquisitorial flames, while the judges merely furnish the means through which this fate is achieved.

If the clerics portrayed themselves, first, as instructors who taught Joan Christian dogma, the ways in which she had erred from it, and the sufferings that she would undergo if she continued in her present path, they portrayed themselves, second, as advisers who counseled her to recant her error and thus to save her body and soul from the flames of earthly and spiritual punishment. Recognizing that it was Joan's will that would determine her fate, the clerics applied themselves to attempting to influence that will. On April 18, Cauchon decided "to exhort [*exhortari*] her charitably and to admonish [*admonere*] her sweetly and to have her admonished [*admonere facere*]" (327). He urged that his companions "give Joan a profitable counsel" (328), and he had Joan "summoned, exhorted, and requested [*sommata, exhortata, et requista*] to take the good counsel of the clerics and notable doctors" (331). On May 2, he appointed de Châtillon "to induce her to want to recede from these defects and crimes and to perceive the path of truth" (335). Even as de Châtillon was given the primary role in this appeal, the minutes noted that "the said Joan was cautioned [*monita*] abundantly and anew by all" (346) and that "several doctors and experienced men . . . cautioned [*monuerunt*] her and induced her charitably and exhorted [*exhortati*] her" (347). Finally, on May 23, Maurice reminded Joan that his fellow clerics had devoted themselves to "beseeching, exhorting, and cautioning [*rogantes, hortantes et monentes*] you, by the entrails of our Lord Jesus Christ who wanted to suffer such a cruel death for the redemption of the human race, that you correct your words and submit them to the judgment of the church" (381). He stated, "I caution, beseech, and exhort [*moneo, rogo et hortor*] you, that, by the piety which you bear for the passion of your Creator and by the love which you have for the salvation of your soul and your body, you correct and amend all that has been said and you return to the way of truth, in obeying the church, and in submitting yourself to its judgment and determination" (383). The clerics' repeated choice of the perlocutionary verbs *monere, admonere, hortari, exhortari,* and *rogare* to represent their speech acts toward Joan shows that they perceived themselves as no more capable of directly rescuing Joan from the hazards she faced than a confessor would be capable of directly rescuing a sinner from perdition. All they could do, as all any confessor can do, was to attempt to bend the will of the sinner through these speech acts, to persuade the sinner to repent of her sins, and, as Cauchon put it, "to induce her to want" to distance herself from her deeds. With Joan retaining sole power over her will and hence over her fate, all that the clerics saw themselves capable of doing to affect that fate was to put pressure upon her will.

Because the clerics saw themselves as instructing Joan in the dangers she faced and as pleading with her to distance herself from these dangers, it is not surprising that they should have viewed themselves not only as her teachers and advisers but as her potential saviors as well. Cauchon informed Joan that "we were . . . ready . . . to apply ourselves to procure the salvation of her soul and body by all means possible" (328–29), while Maurice depicted Joan's judges on two occasions as "seeking [her] salvation as much in soul as in body" (381). The clerics grounded this duty and desire to bring about Joan's salvation in their status as clerics. Cauchon reminded Joan that "we were ecclesiastics whose vocation, will, and inclination was to do this" (328–29) and that for such men, "to accomplish this especially we have wished and wish with all our desires" (335). Though historians have traditionally ascribed the most malicious of intentions to the participants in Joan's trial, these clerics never ceased to address Joan as their "most dear friend" (380), to characterize their words to her as "sweetly and charitably" (335) spoken, and in other ways to express the most beneficent of emotions toward their prisoner. Indeed, when Cauchon told Joan that if she refused to correct herself "it would be necessary for us to abandon her, from which she could consider what peril would arrive to her" (329), he was reminding her that the Inquisition merely "abandoned" impenitent heretics to the secular arm, with conventional appeals to the civic magistrates' mercy, and that it was the secular arm that condemned them to the stake. In accordance with the rhetoric of salvation that filled inquisitorial trials, it was not the acts of these clerics but, rather, the cessation of these acts that Joan had most to fear.

As the clerics asked Joan to accept them as her teachers, counselors, and potential saviors in the course of their appeals, they did not merely demand that she accept their instruction and advice as a route to salvation. If Joan was to acknowledge the clerics as her teachers, she had to also acknowledge herself as someone in need of their teaching. She had to recognize that she was, as the clerics put it, "a woman unlearned and ignorant of Scripture" (329) who should not rely upon "her own sense and her unskilled head" (329). She had to recognize that the stances she had so far maintained were in disagreement with "faith, truth, and religion" and were characterized only, as the clerics insisted time and again, by "defects" and "errors." If Joan was to accept the clerics as her rightful counselors, she had to agree that what she had done up to that point had constituted merely a deviation from a unique and well-defined path of truth and that they alone were capable of returning her to that path. She had to look upon the beliefs she had held, upon the actions she had committed, and, indeed, upon the person she had been prior to this reconversion in the purely negative terms that the clerics used when referring to them. The clerics' demand that Joan renounce her earlier inner life became particularly concrete when Maurice informed her that the "enemies of God" were capable of "transforming themselves sometimes into the appearance of Christ, angels, and saints, saying and affirming themselves to be thus, as is amply contained in the lives of the Fathers and in Scripture" (381). The angels and saints Joan claimed to have seen were not necessarily angels and saints, Maurice warned. Appearance is not necessarily reality; sensory experiences do not necessarily lead to the apprehension of truth. Because of this, Maurice advised Joan to disregard her own experience and to rely instead upon the texts of theology and canon law, which alone give sure access to truth, or, in the absence of training in these texts, upon the judgments of clerics acquainted with such works. Recalling Joan's voices, Maurice recommended, "whatever may have thus appeared to you, do not believe it. Rather, wholly repel the belief or imagination which you have had about these things, acquiescing to the words and the opinions of the University of Paris and of other doctors who know the law of God and Holy Scripture" (381). Cauchon likewise advised that Joan "not hold excessively to her own judgment, but believe in the counsel of worthy and wise men who know divine and human law" (335). The clerics agreed that because scholastic study provided the only solid basis of knowledge, an unlearned woman like Joan could only gain access to truth by dissociating herself from her lived experience and, in particular, from her lived experience of her voices, and by filtering her experience through the instruction and counsel of learned men like themselves. In order to welcome that which these clerics offered in their instruction and counsel, Joan had to clear a space for these gifts by rejecting that which she has previously thought and done.

But just as Joan refused to confess to the clerics who interrogated her during her trial in the same manner she might confess to her pastor, she also refused to accept either the instruction and counsel these clerics offered or the salutary intentions they attributed to these appeals. Though the clerics repeatedly taught Joan about the defects their learned colleagues had found in her statements, she stood by her original utterances. On May 23, for example, she affirmed, " 'As for the words and the deeds that I spoke of during the trial, I refer to them and want to support them' " (383). Though the clerics repeatedly advised her to amend these defects and to submit to the church in order to preserve her life and her soul, Joan retained her original defiance. Even if she saw the wood piled up and the executioner ready to light the fire, even if she saw herself in the midst of the flames, she announced, she would neither say nor do anything different from what she had already said and done. Though the clerics repeatedly portrayed themselves as seeking to save her, Joan identified her true salvation as coming not from them but from God himself. On May 2, she stated, " 'I await God, my Creator, for everything. I love him with all my heart' " (337). She added, " 'I have a good master, that is, God, from whom I await all, and not from another' " (343). Far from absorbing the teachings Cauchon offered her about the sins supposedly burdening her conscience, she instructed him about the weight he placed upon his own soul. On February 24, she informed him, " 'I tell you this: take good care in calling yourself my judge, because you assume a great burden and you burden me excessively' " (55). Far from accepting the counsel Cauchon offered her about the perils she risked by ignoring their teachings, she warned him of the dangers he hazarded by encumbering her with such an onus. She cautioned, " 'You say that you are my judge. Take care with what you do, because, in truth, I am sent on the part of God and you place yourself in great danger' " (59). Later, when asked about this threat, she repeated and clarified her statement: " 'You say that you are my judge. I do not know if you are, but be careful that you not judge me badly, because you would put yourself in great danger' " (147–48). Just as, in Joan's view, it was not herself but the bishop who remained unaware of the potential sinfulness of his action, it was not herself but he who remained vulnerable to divine punishment. Finally, far from accepting the clerics as her potential saviors, Joan depicted herself as aspiring to save Cauchon. On March 14, after informing him of his danger, she stated, " 'And I warn you so that, if God punishes you for this, I do my duty in telling you' " (148). Though she made no pretense that she looked upon the bishop as her "most dear friend" or that she spoke to him "sweetly and charitably," she did nonetheless acknowledge "a duty" toward him, which made her warn him to act so as to avoid the rightful vengeance of God. Refusing to respect the authority of the clerics as ecclesiastically appointed pastors or to accept their instruction and counsel, Joan asserted, in contrast, the legitimacy of her authority as a divinely appointed emissary and her power to teach and advise them instead. Even though Joan confessed frequently and ardently, according to her own responses and the testimony of her contemporaries, she did not depict these Burgundian clerics as intermediaries between God and herself but, on the contrary, presented herself as intermediary between God and them.

7 | The Prison Cell

According to the transcripts of Joan's trial, the judges and their assistants clashed with the accused until the very last week of the proceedings. As scholastics, the clerics expected Joan to think logically, analytically, and objectively, while Joan insisted upon thinking intuitively, synthetically, and subjectively. As inquisitors, they required her to provide them with a sign whose inherent certainty would establish the authenticity of her mission, while Joan indicated that it was not simply the sign she provided but the clerics' capacity to recognize the sign as such that would determine whether or not they were persuaded of her calling. As confessors, they encouraged her to confess her sins to them as she would confess them to her parish priest and to accept their guidance in undergoing penance as she would accept that of her pastor in such matters. Yet Joan made clear that she looked upon her voices from God, and not upon the Burgundian clerics trying her for heresy, or indeed any clerics, as her true spiritual directors. Throughout these exchanges, the clerics expected Joan not only to conceptualize truth as they conceptualized it, from their scholastic, inquisitorial, or pastoral points of view, but to recognize that as an illiterate laywoman, her comprehension of the truth was necessarily inadequate. They urged her to cease to rely upon "her own sense and unskilled head" (329) and to begin to rely, instead, upon their authority, as her intellectual superiors, her judicial arbiters, and her spiritual counselors, in apprehending the truth. Throughout these exchanges, Joan refused either to envision truth as the clerics envisioned it or to treat the clerics as the mediators through whose assistance she might gain access to it. It was only in the last week of the trial, as it is depicted in the transcripts, that Joan underwent a transformation of the kind the clerics had long recommended. First, she began to blame herself as the clerics blamed her. She renounced her mission and the voices who had inspired it, and even when she rescinded that abjuration a few days later, she still renounced herself for having briefly made that renunciation. Second, she began to adopt the critical perspective upon her voices that the clerics had long encouraged her to assume. Regarding them with this new eye, she came to judge them as she had never judged them before, to detach herself from them as a result of that judgment, and to attach herself, instead, to the clerics. The Joan portrayed in the minutes of the trial's last week stopped resisting the clerics, as she had resisted them all along, and started accepting truth as they had always wanted her to accept it.

The Abjuration at Saint-Ouen

According to the minutes of the trial, on the morning of Thursday, May 24, 1431, Joan was led up onto a platform in the cemetery of the abbey of Saint-Ouen. From this vantage point she could see the large crowd gathered in the graveyard, the forty or so clerics assembled on the platform opposite her, and the third platform, built only for one person, with firewood beneath it and a stake above. Guillaume Erard, master of theology at the University of Paris, opened the proceedings by delivering a sermon based on John 15:4, "The grain cannot bear fruit by itself if it does not remain attached to the vine" (386), in which he demonstrated the need for every Catholic to remain attached to the mother church. After his sermon, Erard informed Joan that the judges had found numerous errors in things she had done and said. At first, Joan responded boldly in this dialogue with Erard. She declared, as she had declared throughout the trial, that she had spoken and acted "on the part of God" (386) and demanded that an account of her be sent to the pope.[1] At this point, however, she said that, "as for her deeds and words, she does not burden any person with them, neither her king nor anyone else, and if there is any defect, it is in her and not in any other" (387). Here, for the first time, Joan spoke of her deeds and words as capable of "burdening" someone in general and as capable of "burdening" her king in particular. Here, for the first time, she spoke of what she had said and done as capable of possessing some "defect." The minutes do not record any words from Erard that provoked this response, though several witnesses at the rehabilitation recalled the preacher lamenting that despite the traditional orthodoxy of the French royal house, the king had attempted to regain his kingdom through "a schismatic, heretical, and sorcerous woman" and Joan crying out, in defense of her sovereign, " 'Oh, preacher! You speak badly! Do not speak of the person of the lord King Charles because he is a good Catholic and he did not believe in me.' "[2] The minutes of the original trial do, however, record that Joan accused herself in an effort to protect her king from such accusations. It was after this initial recognition of the possibility that she had committed crimes, as Cauchon began to read the sentence in which he condemned Joan as an unrepentant heretic and abandoned her to the secular arm, that Joan interrupted him and announced that she would observe what the church had ordered:[3] The minutes convey, "She said several times that, as the ecclesiastics said that the apparitions and revelations which she said herself to have had were not to be supported nor believed, she did not want to support them, but in all things she referred to our holy mother the church and to us, the judges" (388–89). Saved from the stake by this submission to the church and by the statement of abjuration that attested to it, Joan was consigned, as a penance, to drink the water of sorrow and to eat the bread of distress in prison for the rest of her days and was then led down from the platform and back to her prison cell. During the afternoon following this ceremony at the cemetery, a few clerics, including Jean Le Maître, Thomas de Courcelles, Nicolas Loiselleur, Nicolas Midi, and Isembard de La Pierre, visited Joan in the tower and informed her of the great grace that God had shown her in inspiring her to abjure and the great mercy that the church had shown her in readmitting her into her bosom. When these clerics then told Joan that she must exchange her men's clothes for women's dress, she replied, "that willingly she would accept this women's dress and that in everything she would yield and obey the ecclesiastics" (394). After changing her clothes, Joan is said to have "wanted and permitted that her hair, which she earlier wore cut bowl-fashion, be shaven and removed" (394). Joan's abjuration was preceded by her acknowledgment of a possible "defect" in that which she had said and done and by her attempt to protect her king from association with that "defect" and was followed by her "willing" assumption of the women's clothes she had for so long rejected.

If Joan was disturbed enough in the course of the abjuration to cease reproaching the clerics and begin reproaching herself, her disturbance was all the more evident on Monday, May 28, four days after the ceremony at Saint-Ouen, when the two judges, Pierre Cauchon and Jean Le Maître, and seven assistants, including Courcelles, de La Pierre, and Nicolas de Venderès, appeared in Joan's cell in order to verify rumors that she had relapsed into the heresy she had so recently abjured. The clerics found Joan wearing a tunic, a hood, and a doublet, even though, as the minutes state, "she had earlier, on our order, put off these clothes and taken up again women's clothes" (395). Asked about her return to masculine attire, Joan responded in a series of different ways. At first, she only partially answered the clerics' question. The minutes record, "we interrogated her 'when and for what reason had she taken anew these men's clothes?' And Joan responded that she had taken these clothes not long ago and had put off the women's clothes" (395). Though she responded to the first part of the clerics' inquiry, offering that she had taken men's clothes "not long ago," she refrained from responding to the second part. She stated not why she had abandoned feminine garments, but only that she had done so. When the clerics asked her a second time why she had returned to masculine attire, Joan alleged a personal preference for men's clothes. "Interrogated why she had taken the men's clothes . . . , she responded . . . that she likes these clothes better than women's clothes" (396). Finally, when the clerics asked a third time, Joan maintained that it was appropriate for her to wear men's clothes when living in a secular prison among male guards. "She responded that she did this because it was more permitted or suitable to have men's clothes when she was among men than to have women's clothes" (396). Reluctant at first to answer the clerics' questions about the reason for her return to men's dress, Joan ultimately provided explanations that are discontinuous at best, citing, first, a personal desire to wear men's clothes and, second, an impersonal need to conform to social circumstances. When in the course of this dialogue the clerics reminded her of her oath or promise never to return to men's clothes, her responses were no less puzzling. She stated, on the one hand, that "she never understood that she had made an oath not to take back these men's clothes" (396), and then, on the other hand, that "she had taken them back because what she had been promised had not been observed, namely, that she could go to mass, receive the body of Christ, and be put out of the iron shackles" (396). She claimed that she had not understood herself to have sworn never to return to men's clothes, yet she also claimed that she was justified in breaking that oath, though this would seem to imply that she knew herself to have made it. As she had done at the abjuration, Joan continued to shift her position from one remark to the next throughout this exchange, as if she were no longer sure what position she wanted to assume.

In speaking of her return to men's clothes or of her alleged infringement of her oath not to return to these clothes, Joan defended her actions, however contradictorily, yet in other remarks during the conversation, she undermined these self-defenses. Joan asserted, for example, that "she likes better to die than to be in iron shackles, but if it were permitted that she go to mass and be put out of the iron shackles and be given a gracious prison [and if she have a woman], she will be good and will do what the Church wants" (396–97).[4] She asserted that "she likes better to do her penance at once, that is in dying, than to support her suffering in prison any longer" (399). In offering "to do what the Church wants," Joan acknowledged that the clerics before her were to be identified with the church, which she had resisted acknowledging all along, and she agreed that she had not done what these clerics and therefore the church wanted. When she promised "to do her penance" and to "be good," she acknowledged her sinfulness all the more clearly. Accusatory toward the clerics for keeping her in iron shackles and in a prison whose male guards necessitated her choice of masculine attire, she was also accusatory toward herself. Suffering from the presence of the male guards, the weight of the iron shackles, and the other distressing aspects of her imprisonment, she also sought to escape this suffering through her death. Joan's recriminations against herself and her desire for death, in addition to her self-contradictions, all evoke, in the text, a Joan considerably less confident than that depicted before.

Joan's disturbance is highlighted by the interlocutory context within which she spoke. Though two months had gone by since the end of the interrogations and though there was no formal need to interrogate her again, the dialogue between Joan and the clerics took the form of another interrogation. Once again, the clerics dominated the conversation. They initiated the encounter, coming to Joan's cell and speaking first. They selected the issue to be addressed, namely, Joan's change of clothes. They determined the angles from which the issue was to be approached, that is, the time she undertook this action, the possible instigator who tempted her to do it, and most of all, the reasons for which it was done. Once again, Joan spoke only in response to the clerics' questions and within the parameters the questions set up. The minutes relate that the clerics "interrogated her" once as to when and three times as to why she had resumed wearing men's clothes, and that Joan was "interrogated" as to whether she had not sworn to cease wearing such clothes. Even when the clerics made a rare declarative statement, "telling" Joan that she had sworn not to take back men's clothes, the utterance functions as a question: the transcripts, interpreting Joan's statement after this remark, note that she "responded" to it. Yet though the form of this interrogation echoed those of February and March, its function differed from that of its predecessors. In general, an interrogation, as part of an investigation into the state of the accused party, is designed to enable the judges to obtain information on the basis of which they may later deliberate. In accordance with this purpose, the clerics not only examined Joan during the earlier interrogations, but they cross-examined her, returning to the same points time and again in an apparent pursuit of the truth. Her responses to these questions provided the source of the charges against her, each of which was bolstered by lengthy quotations from the minutes of interrogation. Now, however, though the clerics interrogated and Joan responded, the clerics did not treat her answers as they had treated her earlier ones. There were no subsequent sessions in which they cross-examined her about her change of clothes. When they judged her the next day, in the archbishop's manor, they made no reference to the information uncovered during this interview. Joan's allusions to the suitability of wearing men's clothes when living among male guards and to the sufferings that she endured in prison, sufferings so great that they made her long for death, may seem to suggest that she had been subjected to a sexual assault, and the clerics' recollections at the rehabilitation of other, more explicit remarks she made that went unrecorded might seem to confirm this point, yet there was no investigation of any such possibility noted in these transcripts.[5] Instead of discussing Joan's reasons for returning to men's attire and the validity or invalidity of these reasons, the clerics referred to her simply as "seemingly not content with women's clothes" (402). Joan and the clerics both participated in a genre of dialogue designed to provide the foundation for a judgment, but the clerics never used this final interrogation for its conventional purpose. They opened up, brought to the surface, but then did nothing with what they uncovered.

If the clerics made clear that Joan had to respond to their questions but they were not obligated to respond to her responses, either literally or figuratively, they also made clear that though she was responsible for adhering to promises she made to them, they were not responsible for keeping promises they made to her. When Joan answered the clerics' allegation that she had broken her oath to cease wearing men's clothes by pointing out that "what she had been promised had not been observed" or when she offered, at the end of the passage, to be "good" and to do that which the church wanted if they would relieve her of her shackles, move her to a "gracious" prison, and give her a woman guard, she implied that if the clerics did not fulfill their promises, she was not obliged to fulfill hers. If she had gone back on her word, it was only because they had gone back on theirs; if they kept their word, she would keep hers. In making these connections between the clerics' actions and her own, Joan assumed that her relationship with the clerics was contractual, that one party had to do X only if the other party did Y. She assumed that both parties would make concessions to the other, whether they be a change of clothes or a change of prison, and that both would reap benefits from the other, whether they be the preservation of one's own life or the submission of another's will to oneself. When the clerics declined to respond to Joan's accusation or offer, they implied that, as they were not obliged to respond to Joan's utterances during the interrogation, neither were they obliged to bear responsibility toward her. They refused to acknowledge that their relationship with Joan was anything but a one-way, interrogator-respondent relationship. Joan spoke as if the conditions of her penance were negotiable, yet the clerics' reference to Joan having broken "our order" in returning to men's clothes indicated that they did not see these conditions as subject to negotiation. Throughout the dialogue, the clerics refused to respond to what Joan said, both in the superficial sense of being positioned to ask, not to answer, questions and in the deeper sense of refusing to react to Joan's answers.

Confused and distressed in speaking of her return to men's clothes, Joan displayed confusion and distress also in speaking of Saint Catherine and Saint Margaret, who, she acknowledged in response to the clerics' questions, had spoken to her again since her abjuration. When the clerics asked what Saint Catherine and Saint Margaret had told her, she replied that "her voices told her, when she was on the platform or scaffold, before the people, to respond boldly to this preacher who was preaching then. And Joan said that he was a false preacher and that he had said that she did several things that she had not done" (397). In depicting her voices as instructing her to respond to Erard "boldly" (*audacter* in Latin or *hardiement* in French), Joan echoed other times, recalled in the minutes, when they gave her the same advice or when she gave this advice to others. As she first headed off to her king, for example, the voices bade her, " 'Go boldly! When you are before the king, he will have a good sign to receive you and believe you' " (117). As she fought outside Orléans, she urged her soldiers, " 'Enter boldly among the English!' " and, we are told, "she herself entered"

(97). One morning earlier in the trial, as she had awakened from sleep in her prison cell, the voices had encouraged her to respond "boldly" (58) during that day's interrogation. In each case, Joan evoked aspects of the situation that might have alarmed her or her companions, such as the fear that the king would not believe she was sent by God, the fear that the English soldiers would destroy their forces, or the fear that the clerics would condemn her, and in each case, the adverb "boldly" indicated the manner in which she or her men surmounted their trepidation and pursued their desire. Yet, despite the voices' instructions, Joan made clear she had not responded boldly to this preacher. Instead, she admitted the "enormous treason to which she, Joan, had consented in making the abjuration and retraction in order to save her life" (397) and the "great wrong [she had done] in confessing that she had not acted well in doing what she had done" (398). Instead of telling Erard, as she told the clerics now, that he was a false preacher and that he spoke wrongly, she "consented" to making the abjuration and retraction and she "[did] a great wrong" through that act. The crime Joan committed at Saint-Ouen lay in her not acting boldly and instead succumbing to her fear. "Whatever she said or revoked on that Thursday, she only did and said it out of fear of the fire" (398), and she explained "all that she did, she did out of fear of the fire" (399). If boldness is that which would have enabled her to inform Erard that he was a false and lying preacher, fear was that which held her back and made her tolerate and even consent to his falsehoods. If boldness was that which would have enabled her to affirm that God had sent her and that she had acted well in doing what she did, fear was that which made her deny the divine origin and rectitude of her mission. For Joan, boldness was that which propelled the self forward, while fear was that which held the self back. Had she acted boldly, as the voices told her to do, she would have lost her life but saved her self; by acting out of fear of the fire, as she put it, "she damned herself to save her life" (397). On the one hand, with these remarks Joan distinguished the Joan who now saw the virtue of boldness from the Joan who had succumbed to fear at Saint-Ouen and thus demonstrated that she was returning to the boldness she had abandoned at the cemetery. On the other hand, even as she insisted upon the necessity of affirming her self, she reproached the Joan of four days earlier, with whom she continued to identify her self, and thus counterbalanced the affirmation of self that she extolled with the denigration of herself that she performed. She had committed a great wrong, she repented of that wrong, yet she still held herself to be blameworthy for that wrong.

In the very dialogue in which Joan chastised herself for having temporarily valued her life over her self, she also claimed she had not been aware of what she was doing during her abjuration at Saint-Ouen. Even though she had just stated that she "had consented [*consenterat*]" to a notorious treason in making the abjuration and retraction, that she "had damned herself [*dampnaverat*]" in order to save her life, and that she "had done a great wrong [*fecerat magnum iniuriam*]," employing past tenses that affirm her actual completed performance of these actions, she went on to maintain that she never understood herself or intended to perform such actions. At first, she turned to the conditional. "If she said that God had not sent her," she said, "she would damn herself and . . . , in truth, God did send her" (397–98). With this hypothetical clause, Joan referred to her denial that God had sent her not as something actually performed but as something she might have done, and she referred to her damnation of herself not as something that she had accomplished but as something that she would have accomplished if she had made this statement. The abjuration, so recently affirmed as having happened, was now placed in doubt. Shortly thereafter, when she stated that "whatever she said or revoked on Thursday, she only did and said it out of fear of the fire," she referred to her declarations at the cemetery vaguely, as if she was not entirely sure of what she had said. Finally, and most importantly, when the clerics asserted that she had confessed on the scaffold before her judges and the people to having "mendaciously . . . boasted" (398) in identifying her voices as Saint Catherine and Saint Margaret, she replied that "she did not understand herself [*intelligebat* or *entendoit*] to do or say this. . . . she said that she did not say or understand [*intellexit* or *a . . . entendu*] that she was revoking her apparitions, that is, that they were Saint Catherine and Saint Margaret" (398). She added, "she never did anything against God or the faith, whatever she had been bidden to revoke, and that which the statement of abjuration contained, she did not understand it [*intelligibat* or *entendoit*]. . . . [S]he did not have the intention [*intendebat* or *entendoit*] to revoke anything, except providing that it was pleasing to God" (399). In these responses, Joan did not deny that she had revoked her apparitions, as many interpreters of this passage have claimed she did.[6] As she shifted from claiming she had not said this to claiming she had not understood herself to say this, Joan put into question not so much the objective content of her utterances as her subjective consciousness when making them. She may have revoked her apparitions, she acknowledged, but she had not understood herself or intended to do this. She suggested a split between her action and her consciousness, intimating that whatever she might have done, she was not entirely there when doing it.

At first glance, Joan may appear to have been contradicting herself in insisting that she was not aware of having acted badly and reproaching herself for having done so. As was mentioned earlier, since the reform of ethics in the twelfth century and of confession in the thirteenth, an action's sinfulness was determined not objectively, by what was done, but subjectively, by what the subject meant to do. An individual who killed without meaning to do so, it was maintained, was less to be blamed than one who killed intentionally. An individual who renounced her voices without understanding or meaning to renounce them, it appears, would be less to be blamed than one who did so with understanding and intention. On another level, however, to sin at this time meant not to act without full consciousness or understanding of one's actions, for if one were fully aware of what one was doing, one would not sin. Thomas Aquinas wrote, for example, that "ignorance can be the cause of a sinful act, for it is the privation of knowledge which enables reason to prohibit sin inasmuch as it directs human acts."[7] For Joan to assert at once that she committed a great crime and that she did not understand herself to have committed this crime thus makes sense. Her crime, as she depicted it, lay not only in having acted fearfully rather than boldly, in having effaced rather than affirmed herself, but also in having absented herself from herself so that she said things she did not understand or mean herself to say.

The minutes of Monday, May 28, reveal a Joan far different from the Joan of the minutes of the previous four months. This Joan failed to respond directly to the clerics' questions and, instead, offered a series of contradictory assertions. She stated that she never took an oath not to resume wearing men's clothes; that she did take the oath and that she broke the oath but was justified in breaking it; and that she took the oath, broke the oath, and failed to be "good" through failing to keep her word. She stated that she did not remember renouncing her voices at Saint-Ouen and that she did renounce the voices, committing a great wrong and damning herself through doing so. This Joan accepted her sinfulness, blaming herself at once for her past actions in the cemetery of the abbey of Saint-Ouen and for her present actions in her tower cell. Though half of Joan still struggled against the clerics, defending her choice of men's clothes and affirming the holiness of her voices, half of her blamed herself for not always having struggled against them. Her reproaches merge with the clerics' reproaches, so that when she speaks of "being good," of "doing what the church wants," and of "fulfilling her penance," there is little distinction made between the grounds of her own self-excoriation and the grounds of the clerics' excoriation of her.

The Final Interview

On Tuesday, May 29, the day after this interview in Joan's cell, the clerics met in the chapel of the archbishop's manor to decide how they would react to what they had heard. Cauchon summarized how the clerics had admonished Joan numerous times to submit to the church, how she had at first refused but then had later seemed to consent to these appeals, and how she had now returned, like a dog to its vomit, to that heresy so recently forsaken. After this prologue, the bishop opened up the floor so that the assistants might offer their opinions as to what should happen next. Nicolas de Venderès spoke first, recommending that Joan be abandoned to the temporal powers with the plea, customary to the Inquisition, that these powers act gently with her. Gilles de Durémort spoke next, supporting Venderès's recommendation and suggesting that the statement of abjuration be read and explained to Joan anew. Of the forty other assistants who then offered their opinions, thirty-seven cited and seconded the views of this second speaker and all voted to abandon Joan to the secular arm. A few, such as Thomas de Courcelles and Isembard de La Pierre, urged that Joan "be charitably admonished about the salvation of her soul and that she be told that she has no more to hope for as regards her temporal life" (407), thus manifesting concern for her soul even as they ceased to manifest concern for her body. After the expression of these various sentiments, the judges then concluded the session by thanking these advisers for their help and by announcing that they would proceed against Joan as against a relapsed heretic.

According to the testimony of the posthumous documents of the trial, early on the morning of the following day, Wednesday, May 30, the two judges and the assistants Thomas de Courcelles, Jacques Le Camus, Nicolas Loiselleur, Jean Toutmouillé, Pierre Maurice, Martin Lavenu, and Nicolas de Venderès gathered in Joan's cell in the castle of Rouen with the intention of exhorting Joan to save her soul. Loiselleur, instructing Joan as to how she should speak during this final interview, stated that "she must no longer hide the truth, for nothing must be thought of any longer but the salvation of her soul" (421). With these words, Loiselleur suggested that now—as the platforms were being set up in the Vieux Marché, as the stake was being raised and the wood piled up around it, as the crowds were collecting to watch the spectacle—a change would have come over Joan that would affect how she spoke. If life was normally characterized by the possibility of change, by contingency, by futurity, now that the text of Joan's condemnation was already written and now that these possibilities were no longer there, Joan was no longer living. She was no longer on the edge of her life's narrative, no longer experiencing each episode ignorant of how it would end, no longer fighting and struggling to make it conclude as she wished. She knew how the narrative would terminate and as a result, she was already detached from it. Yet even though the tale of Joan's material existence had already been written, Loiselleur suggested, the same was not true of the tale of her spiritual existence. Now, though she could no longer save her body from the temporal flames of the Vieux Marché, she could still save her soul from the eternal flames of hell. Now, with her earthly life already lost, she had nothing to gain by continuing to tell the falsehoods that he suggested she had told up until this point. Now her speech should consist not of lies but of the truth because she should speak not to human beings, capable of being deceived by such lies, but to God himself, incapable of enduring such deception.

If Loiselleur recommended that Joan now conceive of her life as a narrative whose conclusion she apprehended, it would not be the first time in the trial that Joan imagined her life in such terms. She related during the earlier interrogations that from the time she was fighting in the trenches of Melun her voices had told her that she would be taken before Saint John's Day and "that it must be thus, and that she must not be struck with stupor from it, but must take it willingly and that God would help her" (112). Through this prediction, the voices had prepared Joan for her capture, so that she was able not only to delegate tasks to her captains, as she stated she had, but to withstand the shock her capture would otherwise have produced and to retain her wits during this event. However much the disaster taught her that she had no mastery over her circumstances, this anticipation gave her a sensation of mastery over them all the same. In bracing Joan for the shock of the capture, the voices helped her all the more in teaching her that "it must be thus." Because she knew that the capture would happen before it did, she knew that it was planned by a central consciousness, that it was intended, and that it was necessary. She knew, when she was overpowered by Burgundian forces outside Compiègne, that her defeat was not the result of a quirk of fortune or a reflex of an arbitrary universe but, rather, that it was a planned and necessary eventuality. When the clerics asked Joan if her angel had not failed her when she was taken, she replied, "she believes, as this is pleasing God, that it was for the best that she be taken" (122). Foreknowledge of disaster enabled Joan not only to steady herself against it but to accept it as one element in an ordered world.

If the voices aided Joan in teaching her of the eventuality and the necessity of her capture, they aided her also in teaching her that "God would help her." As Joan told the clerics, the voices " 'told me that I would be freed, but I do not know the day or the hour, and that I should boldly put on a good face about it' " (93). Saint Catherine told her, she clarified two weeks later, that she would have help, most likely either by a deliverance from her prison or by a disturbance during her execution that would enable her to be freed. "And most often," she stated, "the voices told her that she will be freed by a great victory, and then the voices tell her, 'Take everything willingly. Do not concern yourself with your martyrdom. You will come finally to the Kingdom of Paradise.'. . . And she calls this martyrdom because of the pain and adversity she suffers in prison" (148). In these messages to Joan, the voices suggested two narratives. In the first, they informed her that her suffering in prison would end in her physical liberation from captivity, either during her confinement itself or during her execution. In the second, they told her that her suffering or "martyrdom" would end in her arrival in the kingdom of paradise. The clerics, attentive to the ambiguity of the term *martyre*, which at this time signified both death for the sake of one's religious beliefs and any general distress, inquired as to which meaning she was employing. Though she claimed to evoke only the second, more general sense of the term, her depiction of this martyrdom being rewarded by an ascent to the Kingdom of Heaven cannot but recall legends like those of Saint Catherine and Saint Margaret as well. It was typical of Joan that though she seemed to suggest the possibility that she would undergo a martyrdom like those of the female saints who appeared to her, she did not expand upon this possibility and when questioned about it, denied that it had occurred to her. She never identified herself with the martyrs rendered blessed through their endurance of persecution and never came to interpret the "great victory" that would free her from prison as her death and reception of a martyr's crown, though others would later do so. For Joan, liberation was liberation from prison, not from life, and the victory through which this would come about was a military conquest. In both of these narratives, however, the voices depicted Joan's current travails in prison as a mere prelude to future glory. They reminded her that the narrative of her life was not yet complete and promised her that when it was over, she would perceive these current tribulations as mere temporary inconveniences prior to great delights. They reassured her that however much those who served God might be tested by misfortunes, when the narrative was complete these servants would be vindicated. Teaching her to experience her life not as a series of incidents, each in isolation, each poised on the abyss, but as a complete narrative in which each incident takes on its appropriate importance, the voices taught her that that which happened in the world would ultimately prove to be not only preordained and necessary but just, as well.

In their instructions to Joan about her capture outside Compiègne, the voices addressed Joan as they are depicted as having addressed her since the start of her career. When she was first heading to Robert de Baudricourt to ask him for men to lead her to the king, the voices told her that this captain would refuse her two times and on the third appeal would give her that which she wanted. When she was heading to the king to inform him that she had been sent by God to raise the siege of Orléans and to bring him to his coronation, the voices told her that the king would have a sign through which he would know the merit of her claims. Later, the voices had forewarned her that she would be wounded by an arrow in her neck in the course of relieving the siege of Orléans and had assured her that she would soon after be healed. In each of these cases, the voices prepared Joan for an event that stood to cause her anxiety and reassured her that it would end successfully. Joan asked one of the voices, we recall, "How could he fail me when he comforts me everyday?" (122), and she stated elsewhere that "she would be dead were it not for the revelation which comforts her everyday" (186). With these responses, Joan appeared to describe the voices' prophecies and reassurances as acts by which they "comforted" her or, in the etymological sense of this word then current, as acts by which they "made her stronger." It is with such acts, acts that comfort and strengthen her in reassuring her of the ultimate order, meaning, and justice in the world, that one can identify Joan's "spirituality" and that one can fathom the source of her resilience.

Now, however, on the morning of Joan's execution, the clerics reminded her of the voices' prophecy of her deliverance from prison, pointing out that it was clear that it would not come true and suggesting that she had been misled. Though the clerics differed in their later testimony as to which of them drew attention to the contradiction between what the voices had promised and what was about to happen, all agreed that she responded to this contradiction by acknowledging that she had been deceived. According to Loiselleur, "in these revelations she had been deceived, and she recognized and saw this well, because she had been promised by these revelations her liberation from prison, of which she perceived the contrary" (422). Venderès reported, "given that the voices coming to her promised that she would be liberated from prison and that she saw the contrary, she perceived and knew that she was and had been deceived by them" (416). Lavenu relates that Joan stated that "she knew and recognized that she had been deceived by the voices and apparitions coming to her...she had been deceived, because the said voices promised Joan that she would be liberated and extricated from prison, and she perceived well the contrary" (417). The clerics contrasted the narrative as the voices had promised Joan it would end and the narrative as it was about to end, and Joan conceded that these narratives did disagree. Joan admitted that she had been deceived by the voices, yet she responded to this deception, according to most of the clerics, neither by blaming the voices for their betrayal nor by defending them despite it but, rather, by submitting to the clerics' opinion of these apparitions. Loiselleur, for example, recalled Joan saying that "as for whether these spirits were good or bad, she referred to the clerics, but she did no longer and would no longer place faith in these spirits" (422). Lavenu remembered her announcing that "as the ecclesiastics held and believed, if there were spirits coming to her, they came and proceeded from evil spirits, she also held and believed what the said ecclesiastics held and believed about this, and she did not want to place faith in these spirits any longer" (417). Maurice testified to having heard her declare that "as for whether they were good or evil spirits, she referred to the ecclesiastics" (418). After so many months of insisting upon her ability to discern good from evil spirits, when she was confronted with the falsity of her voices' prophecy, she responded by abandoning her belief in her own ability to discern good from evil spirits and thus to see through her experience to the meaning of that experience. If in the past she had not been capable of telling false revelations from true ones, she reasoned, in the present she was still not capable of doing so and must defer to the men of the church who were capable of such discernment.

Having ceded to the clerics the ability to make sense of her experiences, Joan described her voices without attempting to make sense of that which she perceived and thus provided a testimony remarkably different from her previous depictions of these beings. Joan replied, first, to the clerics' inquiry as to whether it was true that she had voices and apparitions. According to all witnesses, Joan responded to this question in the affirmative. Lavenu stated that, in response to this question, she acknowledged that "it was [true] and in this belief she would persevere to the end" (417). Venderès affirmed that she claimed that "she had seen and heard, with her own eyes and ears, the voices and apparitions of which there was mention in the trial" (416). Toutmouillé alleged that she said that "she really heard the voices" (419), and Loiselleur likewise asserted that she said that "she really had revelations and apparitions of spirits" (422). With these responses, Joan echoed her earlier assertions about her voices in her emphasis upon the actuality of her perceptions. Even now, when she had lost faith in that which the voices told her, she insisted to Toutmouillé and to Loiselleur that she "really" experienced these voices and to Lavenu that she would persist in this stance until the end. In telling Venderès that she had perceived these voices "with her own eyes and ears" she echoed her statement earlier in the trial that she saw Saint Michael and Saint Gabriel "with [her] eyes" (92). Here, as before, she appealed to her organs of perception to strengthen her remark. With these responses, however, Joan also diverged from her previous answers. During the interrogations proper, she had customarily moved from insisting upon the actuality of her perceptions to insisting upon the identity of that which she perceived. Now, however, though she again stressed the reality of her perception of the voices, she did not go on to affirm their identity. Maurice testified to this shift when he recalled that when he asked her if her apparitions were real, "she responded that they were and that they really appeared to her, whether they were good spirits or evil ones, saying thus in French, 'Soient bons, soient mauvais esperils, ilz me sont apparus,'" (418). While she still expressed certainty in the actuality of her sensations, she expressed no certainty in her interpretation of these sensations, even contrasting the confidence with which she proclaimed the one with the doubt with which she spoke of the other.

After asking Joan about the reality of her voices, the clerics questioned her, once again, about their appearance. Maurice inquired about the angels who she had earlier alleged had accompanied her as she went from her lodgings in Chinon to the king to announce her mission. In the interrogation transcripts, Joan stated simply that, at that time, she was accompanied by an angel, who "was accompanied by other angels," yet in the libelle d'Estivet, the clerics accused her of having boasted that Saint Michael came to her "with a great multitude of angels" (254) and that Saint Michael and Saint Gabriel sometimes came to her with "a thousand thousand angels" (254). After hearing this charge, Joan claimed not to remember having spoken of so many beings. Now, however, when Maurice asked about the multitude of angels who had brought the crown to her king, Joan responded that "they appeared to her in the appearance of certain very small things" (418). Lavenu recalled, similarly, that when Joan was asked what her voices looked like, she stated that "they came in great multitude and in minimal size" (417). Toutmouillé likewise cited her having said to have had "apparitions that came to her at one time or another in great multitude and in minimal quantity or in minimal things" (419). In response to no particular question, Joan also asserted to have heard the voices especially at matins and at compline, when the bells were rung.[8] She expanded a detail of her earlier responses, her perception of the angels who accompanied the angel at Chinon, so that this plurality comes to characterize not just the angels at this one instance but her perception of her voices in general, and she added observations about the smallness of the voices and their association with bells.

In these responses, Joan showed a new willingness to discuss the physical appearance of the voices. Earlier she had refused to provide details about their hair, clothes, and rings and had responded to the clerics' questions about these details by insisting upon the identification of these voices as saints and angels. Asked about the parts, she had pointed to the whole. Now, however, in providing a physical description of the voices, she consented to the clerics' demand and portrayed the parts without the whole, the accident without the essence, the empirical perception without the emotion attached to the perception. By informing the clerics of the minuteness and the multiplicity of the voices without attempting to make sense of what she was describing, Joan spoke like the ideal patient describing her symptoms to the physician. She provided the details of her symptoms without hazarding a diagnosis of her illness and even without presenting them in a manner that would lead to a particular diagnosis. Because of the neutral, "scientific" mode in which she portrayed her voices, Maurice was able to respond like a physician responding to a patient, developing his own interpretation of her sensations and suggesting that she might have mistaken the bells for mystical voices. Because of this neutral, "scientific" mode, legions of physicians and psychologists, following Maurice's lead, have relied upon Joan's utterances here in forming their own diagnoses of her auditory and visual hallucinations as the result of vertigo, hysteria, epilepsy, or any of a host of other medical conditions. Joan differed from a modern patient in a doctor's office, however, in that her turn to this "scientific" discourse was the result not of cultural norms demanding the patient's submission to the doctor but of a loss of confidence in her own ability to discern the meaning of what she perceived and a submission to others as a result of this loss of confidence.

Joan's description of her voices as minute and multiple reflects more than the separation of her powers of observation from her powers of interpretation. In the earlier interrogations, when Joan spoke of her voices, she had come to stress their identification as Saint Michael, Saint Catherine, and Saint Margaret and to declare, in response to the clerics' questions, that she could tell these saints apart by the greetings they made to her. She had described the visual impression Saint Michael made on her as someone "in the form of a very true worthy man" (165), and the warmth she felt when embracing Saint Catherine and Saint Margaret. She had recounted her conversations with the voices, remembering how they always foretold what would happen to her, how they often comforted and reassured her in her great endeavors, and how they sometimes chastised her when she acted badly. She had dwelled on the emotions she experienced at their meetings, the joy she felt when they were present, and the sorrow she felt when they departed. She had observed, finally, her veneration of these voices, saying she had knelt or bowed when they appeared to her and kissed the ground over which they had passed after they had left. Now, however, when Joan spoke of her voices as "multiple" and "minimal things" or as "very small things," her portrait of these beings has radically changed. Multiplied in number and miniaturized in size, the voices have lost their individuality. They have lost their names and their personal identities, no longer resembling "a very true worthy man" or, indeed, any person at all. Because their bodies no longer mirror human bodies, they can no longer be embraced. They no longer seem to speak with Joan, let alone to comfort or reassure her, and thus no longer seem to inspire the joy and sorrow they once evoked in her. Joan has ceased to have an interpersonal relationship with her voices, a relationship like that which friends might have with each other. If the voices, having become many and small, seem less like people, they have also been stripped of their grandeur and are incapable of being revered. They have diminished figuratively as well as literally. In sum, as Joan's discourse became "objective," as it started to depict empirical phenomena without the meaning or emotion that it had previously attached to them, her voices became objects to be referred to as "things [res]." The information that Joan now provided about the voices reflected not the simple scientific truth of her perceptions, stripped of the interpretations and emotional residue with which this truth was previously obscured (though both the clerics of the fifteenth century and the positivist scientists of the nineteenth and early twentieth centuries took this information in this light), but, rather, her disillusionment with the voices and consequent decathexis from them.

After Joan had answered the clerics' questions, Lavenu confessed her and gave her the Communion she had for so long requested without success.[9] Loiselleur then exhorted Joan to declare to the crowd she would soon face that she had been deceived in placing her faith in her voices and had in turn deceived the people in urging them to place their faith in them as well. He urged her to ask pardon of the crowd for these crimes. Joan replied, according to Loiseleur, "that she would do it willingly, but she did not hope to remember this when it would be necessary to do it, that is, when she would be in public judgment, and she asked her confessor to remind her of it and of other matters concerning her salvation" (422). With this response, Joan admitted not only that she had been tricked by the voices but that she had tricked others as well. She agreed to view herself not merely as another's dupe but as a deceiver in her own right. With this acceptance of her guilt, Joan echoed her words of two days earlier when she had referred to having committed a "great wrong" and an "enormous treason" and when she had stated that she "likes better to do her penance at once, that is in dying, than to support her suffering in prison any longer." With these words, Joan had agreed with the clerics that she had sinned and that she should undergo a penance to expiate that sin. Though she had identified her "great wrong" and "enormous treason" with her repudiation of her voices, instead of with her previous affirmation of them, as the clerics had done, in her allusion to her current sufferings as her "penance," she had conflated her perception of her guilt with the clerics' perception of her blameworthiness. Two days later, when she relapsed from her relapse, rejecting her voices as she had rejected them at Saint-Ouen, she continued to accept her own blameworthiness. Though the nature of the crime for which she was guilty shifted from her onetime belief in her voices to her onetime rejection of them and then to her onetime espousal of them, the guilt remained constant. When she predicted that she would forget to confess her guilt to the people and to ask their pardon, she characterized herself as disconnected in mind and body or intention and act. At this moment of dissociation, she finally alluded to a cleric as "her confessor" and thus recognized these clerics as her spiritual directors, as she had resisted recognizing them until this hour. In this last interview, Joan not only spoke of her voices with scientific detachment and acknowledged that the mystical crown with which she had supposedly persuaded her king of her divine affiliation was nothing more than her promise to him of his coronation, but she submits to the clerics as a penitent submits to a spiritual adviser. Though all along she had resisted the scholastic, inquisitorial, and confessional bases of the clerics' prestige, now she finally bowed to them.

At nine o'clock that morning, Joan was brought forward before the multitudes of people at the Vieux Marché and placed on a platform near the butchers' market hall, across from the platform where the clerics were assembled. Nicolas Midi preached a sermon based on 1 Cor. 12:26, "If one member suffers, the other members suffer with it" (410), in order, as the transcripts relate, to give her salutary advice and to edify the people collected below. Joan was warned to think about the salvation of her soul, to reflect upon her misdeeds, to conceive a true contrition, and to believe in the counsel of the friars and the other clerics who had instructed and advised her. Then, the transcripts relate, because Joan had shown, through her relapse, that she was unworthy of any commutation of her sentence, the clerics proceeded to the condemnation: "Lest you, as a rotten member, infect other members, we proclaim that it is necessary to reject you from the unity of the church, to cut you off from her body, and to abandon you to the secular power, just as we reject you, we cut you off, and we abandon you" (412). The record of the trial ends at this point, with the judges' signatures and the notaries' seals, and does not describe how Joan was then immolated.[10]

Notes

Introduction

1. The original French minutes of interrogation have disappeared, but two partial copies derived from them have come down to us. See the Orléans manuscript, known as "O" and catalogued as ms. 518 (an. 411) in the Bibliothèque Municipale in Orléans, and the Urfé manuscript, known as "U" and catalogued as ms. lat. 8838 in the Bibliothèque Nationale, as well as *La Minute française de l'Interrogatoire de Jeanne la Pucelle, d'après le réquisitoire de Jean d'Estivet et les manuscrits de d'Urfé et d'Orléans,* edited by Paul Doncoeur and Yvonne Lanhers (Melun, France: d'Argences, 1952) and Walter Sidney Scott's *The Trial of Joan of Arc: Being the Verbatim Report of the Proceedings from the Orléans Manuscript* (Westport, Conn.: Associated Booksellers, 1956).

2. Of these five Latin manuscripts, three have survived to this day, all showing a high degree of consistency in their accounts. See ms. 1119 in the Bibliothèque de l'Assemblée Nationale in Paris, identified by the siglum "A," and ms. lat. 5965 and 5966 in the Bibliothèque Nationale in Paris, identified by the sigla "B" and "C." In 1841, Jules-Etienne-Joseph Quicherat produced the first critical edition of the trial transcripts, as well as of the chronicles and other medieval sources on Joan, in the *Procès de condamnation et de réhabilitation de Jeanne d'Arc dite la Pucelle, Publiés pour la première fois d'après les manuscrits de la Bibliothèque Royale suivis de tous les documents historiques qu'on a pu réunir et accompagnés de*

notes et d'eclaircissements, 5 vols. (Paris: Jules Renouard, 1841–49). This edition was succeeded in 1920 by Pierre Champion's *Procès de condamnation de Jeanne d'Arc,* 2 vols. (Paris: Edouard Champion, 1920–21) and in 1960 by Pierre Tisset's and Yvonne Lanhers's *Procès de condamnation de Jeanne d'Arc,* 3 vols. (Paris: Klincksieck, 1960–71). Translations such as Georges and Andrée Duby's *Les Procès de Jeanne d'Arc* (Paris: Gallimard, 1973) have made parts of this trial accessible to French readers, while translations such as Wilfred T. Douglas Murray's *Jeanne d'Arc, Maid of Orleans, Deliverer of France: Being the Story of Her Life, Her Achievements, and Her Death, as Attested on Oath and Set Forth in Original Documents* (New York: McClure, Philipps, 1902) and Wilfred Phillip Barrett's *The Trial of Jeanne d'Arc: Translated into English from the Original Latin and French Documents* (London: Routledge, 1931; reprint, New York: Gotham House, 1932) have made this material available to anglophones. All references in the text will be to Tisset and Lanhers's edition of the trial documents in the first volume of their *Procès de condamnation,* and all translations, from this and from other works, will be my own unless otherwise indicated.

3. On Marguerite Porete, see Paul Fredericq, ed., *Corpus documentorum inquisitionis haeretice pravitatis Neerlandicae,* vol. 1 (Ghent, Belgium: J. Vuylsteke, 1889), 155–60, and vol. 2 (Ghent, Belgium: J. Vuylsteke, 1896), 63–65, and Emilie Zum Brunn and Georgette Epiney-Burgard, *Women Mystics in Medieval Europe,* translated by Sheila Hughes (New York: Paragon House, 1989), 143–50. On the Turlepins, see *Bullaire de l'Inquisition française au XIVe siècle et jusqu'à la fin du Grand Schisme,* ed. J. M. Vidal (Paris: Librairie Letouzey et Ané, 1913), 373 and 393–97, and Robert Lerner, *The Heresy of the Free Spirit in the Later Middle Ages* (Berkeley: University of California Press, 1972), 52–53. On Pierronne of Brittany, see *Procès de condamnation,* ed. Quicherat, 4: 467, 473–74, and 504.

4. On Jean Ségueut, see *Instrument public des sentences portées les 24 et 30 mai 1431 par Pierre Cauchon et Jean Le Maître contre Jeanne la Pucelle,* edited by Paul Doncoeur and Yvonne Lanhers (Melun, France: d'Argences, 1954), 71–30.

5. On Gilles de Rais, see *Le Procès de Gilles de Rais,* edited by Georges Bataille, translated by Pierre Klossowski (Paris: Société Nouvelle des Editions Pauvert, 1965), translated by Richard Robinson as *The Trial of Gilles de Rais* (Los Angeles: Amok Books, 1991). For other printed judicial records of fourteenth- and fifteenth-century heresy cases, see *Le Registre d'Inquisition de Jacques Fournier, Evêque de Pamiers (1318–1325),* 2 vols., edited by Jean Duvernoy (Toulouse, France: Edouard Privat, 1965); *Procès des Templiers,* 2 vols., edited by M. Michelet (Paris: Imprimerie Royale, 1841–51); English Diocese at Westminster, *Heresy Trials in the Diocese of Norwich,* 1428–31 (London: Office of the Royal Historical Society, 1979); and Matthew Spinka, *John Hus at the Council of Constance* (New York: Columbia University Press, 1966). For roughly contemporaneous judicial records in cases not involving heresy, see *Confessions et jugements de criminels au Parlement de Paris (1319–1350),* edited by Monique Langlois and Yvonne Lanhers (Paris: S.E.V.P.E.N., 1970).

6. For the rehabilitation documents, see the *Procès en nullité de la condamnation de Jeanne d'Arc*, 5 vols., edited by Pierre Duparc (Paris: Klincksieck, 1977–89). Duparc has argued for calling this trial not a "rehabilitation" but a *procès en nullité* because it did not so much "rehabilitate" Joan as annul the sentence that had condemned her (5: 11–19). Because of the awkwardness of translating *procès en nullité* into English, because of the tradition of referring to this trial as a "rehabilitation," and because the annulment of Joan's condemnation led, in effect, to her rehabilitation, I have continued to refer to this trial with this older term.

7. For a discussion of the rehabilitation's charges that the judges were biased against Joan for political reasons and that they introduced corrupt English notaries, as well as a refutation of these charges, see *Procès en nullité*, ed. Duparc, 5: 61–64, 83–84.

8. The tasks of the judge in a trial *per inquisitionem* included initiating the procedure, collecting evidence against the accused, and judging this evidence. By the end of the thirteenth century, a *promovens* or *promotor* appears to assist the judge in diocesan trials by developing the case against the accused, so that the judge is left only to pass sentence upon that case. In the fifteenth century, the *promotor* also appears to assist the inquisitor in trials for heretical depravity. Jean d'Estivet served as *promotor* for both of the judges, Bishop Cauchon and Le Maître. See *Procès de condamnation*, ed. Tisset, 3: 59–61.

9. Jules Michelet, "Jeanne d'Arc," in *Histoire de France*, vol. 5 (Paris: Lacroix, 1841), included as "Jeanne d'Arc" in *Oeuvres complètes*, vol. 6, ed. Paul Viallaneix (Paris: Flammarion, 1978) and in *Jeanne d'Arc et autres textes*, ed. Paul Viallaneix (Paris: Gallimard, 1974), trans. Albert Guérard as *Joan of Arc* (Ann Arbor: University of Michigan Press, 1957, reprint, 1967); Anatole France, *Vie de Jeanne d'Arc*, 2 vols. (Paris: Calmann-Lévy, 1908; revised, 1909), trans. Winifred Stephens as *The Life of Joan of Arc*, 2 vols. (New York: John Lane, 1908; revised, 1909); Andrew Lang, *The Maid of France: Being the Story of the Life and Death of Jeanne d'Arc* (London: Longmans, Green, 1908; revised, 1909); and Marina Warner, *Joan of Arc: The Image of Female Heroism* (London: Vintage, Weidenfeld, and Nicolson, 1981). For discussion of Michelet, see Jeanne Calo, *La Création de la femme chez Michelet* (Paris: Nizet, 1975), and Susan Dunn, "Michelet and Lamartine: Making and Unmaking the Nationalist Myth of Jeanne d'Arc," *Romanic Review* 80 (1989): 404–18. France's biography of Joan was extremely controversial for its ultrarationalistic approach to the heroine. For refutations, see Andrew Lang, *La "Jeanne d'Arc" de M. Anatole France* (Paris: Perrin, 1909), and Frantz Funck-Brentano, *Jeanne d'Arc* (Paris: Boivin, 1912; reprint, 1930). For more recent perspectives, see William Searle, *The Saint and the Skeptics: Joan of Arc in the Work of Mark Twain, Anatole France, and Bernard Shaw* (Detroit, Mich.: Wayne State University Press, 1976), and Marie-Claire Bancquart, *Anatole France: Un sceptique passioné* (Paris: Calmann-Lévy, 1984).

10. Pierre Champion, introduction to volume 2 of *Procès de condamnation*, trans. by Coley Taylor and Ruth R. Kerr as "On the Trial of Jeanne d'Arc," in *The Trial of Jeanne d'Arc*, trans. Barrett, 477–539, at 534.

11. Warner, *Joan of Arc*, 5.

12. Willard Trask, *Joan of Arc: Self-Portrait* (New York: Stackpole Sons, 1936), reprint as *Joan of Arc in Her Own Words* (New York: Turtle Point Press, 1996), and Régine Pernoud, *Jeanne d'Arc par elle-même et ses témoins* (Paris: Seuil, 1962), translated by Edward Hyams as *Joan of Arc by Herself and Her Witnesses* (London: Macdonald, 1964).

13. For this genre, see Paul Fournier, *Les Officialités au Moyen Age: Etude sur l'organisation, la compétence, et la procédure des tribunaux ecclésiastiques ordinaires en France de 1180 à 1328* (Paris: Plon, 1880), 41–57.

14. Salomon Reinach, "Observations sur le texte du procès de condamnation de Jeanne d'Arc," *Revue historique* 148 (March/April 1925), 200–23. See also Bernard Gui, *Practica inquisitionis heretice pravitatis*, ed. Célestin Douais (Paris: Picard, 1886), 243–44. For the last two volumes of Gui's work, see Gui, *Manuel de l'inquisiteur*, 2 vols., ed. and trans. Guillaume Mollat (Paris: Champion, 1926–27).

15. Dominick La Capra, *Rethinking Intellectual History: Texts, Contexts, Language* (Ithaca, New York: Cornell University Press, 1983).

16. Ibid., 31.

17. Ibid., 62.

18. Hayden White, "The Value of Narrativity in the Representation of Reality," in his *Content of the Form: Narrative Discourse and Historical Representation* (Baltimore, Md.: Johns Hopkins University Press, 1987), 1–25. See also François Hartog, *Le Miroir d'Hérodote: Essai sur la représentation de l'autre* (Paris: Gallimard, 1980), trans. by Janet Lloyd as *The Mirror of Herodotus: The Representation of the Other in the Writing of History* (Berkeley: University of California Press, 1988), and Annabel M. Patterson, *Reading Holinshed's Chronicles* (Chicago: University of Chicago Press, 1994).

19. See Arsenio Frugoni, *Arnaldo da Brescia nelle fonti del secolo XII* (Turin: Giulio Einaudi Editore, 1954; reprint, 1989); Rita Copeland, "Why Women Can't Read: Medieval Hermeneutics, Statutory Law, and the Lollard Heresy Trials," in *Representing Women: Law, Literature, and Feminism*, ed. Susan Sage Heinzelman and Zipporah Batshaw Wiseman (Durham, N.C.: Duke University Press, 1994), 253–386; and Steven Justice, "Inquisition, Speech, and Writing: A Case from Late-Medieval Norwich," in *Criticism and Dissent in the Middle Ages*, ed. Rita Copeland (Cambridge: Cambridge University Press, 1996), 289–322.

20. Jean-Pierre Barricelli, "Transcript, Legend, and Art: The Thematology of Joan of Arc," *Canadian Review of Comparative Literature/Revue canadienne de littérature comparée*, June 1988: 177–200, at 178. Scholars involved in the Law and Literature movement per se have tended to focus upon modern literary texts, such as the works of Herman Melville, Charles Dickens, Fyodor Dostoyevsky, or Franz Kafka, or upon modern and especially U.S. legal texts, such as the Constitution and statutory law, at the expense of medieval or Continental writings. Numerous medievalists have compensated for the temporal lacuna in the Law and Literature movement by connecting medieval literary works, in which judicial themes,

structures, and vocabulary figure so prominently, with the legal systems behind them. To consider only the French context, in *Medieval French Literature and Law* (Berkeley: University of California Press, 1977), R. Howard Bloch has demonstrated the correspondence between the shift in medieval French law from the trial of God to the inquest and the shift in literature from the chanson de geste to the courtly romance. In *Ravishing Maidens: Sexual Violence in Medieval French Literature and Law* (Philadelphia: University of Pennsylvania Press, 1980), Kathryn Gravdal has compared representations of rape in medieval French literary texts to those in contemporaneous legal documents. In *Rhetoric and the Origins of Medieval Drama* (Ithaca, N.Y.: Cornell University Press, 1992), Jody Enders has brought together the legal aspects of medieval French theater and the theatrical aspects of legal disputes, and in *The Master and Minerva: Disputing Women in French Medieval Culture* (Berkeley: University of California Press, 1995), Helen Solterer has connected the legal concept of defamation to the depiction of women in literary texts such as Jean de Meun's contribution to the *Roman de la rose* and Alain Chartier's *La belle dame sans mercy*. So great has been the interest in the relation between French and Provençal law and literature that John A. Alford and Dennis P. Seniff's bibliography, *Literature and Law in the Middle Ages* (New York: Garland, 1984), already cites, in 1984, 140 entries on this topic.

21. Steven Weiskopf, "Readers of the Lost Arc: Secrecy, Specularity, and Speculation in the Trial of Joan of Arc," in *Fresh Verdicts on Joan of Arc*, ed. Bonnie Wheeler and Charles T. Wood (New York: Garland, 1996), 113–32; and Susan Schibanoff, "True Lies: Transvestism and Idolatry in the Trial of Joan of Arc," in *Fresh Verdicts*, ed. Wheeler and Wood, 31–60. Kelly De Vries has taken a similar approach in "A Woman as Leader of Men: Joan of Arc's Military Career," in *Fresh Verdicts*, ed. Wheeler and Wood, 3–18.

22. Susan Crane, "Clothing and Gender Definition: Joan of Arc," *Journal of Medieval and Early Modern Studies* 26, no. 2 (Spring 1996): 297–320.

23. Barbara A. Hanawalt and Susan Noakes, "Trial Transcript, Romance, Propaganda: Joan of Arc and the French Body Politic," *Modern Language Quarterly* 57, no. 4 (December 1996): 605–31, at 630.

24. Benedict, *Regula Commenta*, in *Patrologiae cursus completus... Series latina*, ed. J.-P. Migne (Paris: Garnier Frères, 1884–1864), 66: 604.

25. See Bernard of Clairvaux, *In Laudibus Virginis matris*, in *Sermones I*, in *Opera*, ed. Jean Leclercq (Rome: Editiones Cistercienses, 1966), 4: 13–58, at 14.

26. Peter Abelard, "Prologue to the *Yes and No*," in *Medieval Literary Theory and Criticism, c. 1100–c. 1375: The Commentary Tradition*, ed. A. J. Minnis and A. B. Smith with David Wallace (Oxford: Clarendon Press, 1988), 87–100, at 87. Peter Abailard, *Sic et non: A Critical Edition*, ed. Blanche E. Boyer and Richard McKeon (Chicago: University of Chicago Press, 1977), 103.

27. Marie-Dominique Chenu, *Introduction à l'étude de Saint Thomas d'Aquin* (Montreal: Institut d'Etudes Médiévales, 1950), trans. A. M. Landry and D. Hughes as *Toward Understanding Saint Thomas* (Chicago: Henry Regnery Com-

pany, 1964), 86. On the *quaestiones*, see also Gérard Marie Paré, Adrien Marie Brunet, Pierre Tremblay, and Gabriel Robert, *La Renaissance du XIIe siècle: Les Ecoles et l'enseignement* (Paris: Vrin; Ottowa: Publications de l'Institut d'Etudes Médiévales d'Ottowa, 1933), esp. 124–25; Martin Grabmann, *Die Geschichte der scholastischen Methode*, 2 vols. (Berlin: Akademie Verlag, 1985–88); Palémon Glorieux, *La Littérature quodlibétique de 1260 à 1320*, 2 vols. (Brussels: Le Saulchoir Kain, 1925); and *Les Genres littéraires dans les sources théologiques et philosophiques médiévales: Définition, critique, et exploitation*, Actes du Colloque International de Louvain-la-Neuve, 25–27 May 1981 (Louvain-la-Neuve, Belgium: Publications de l'Institut d'Etudes Médiévales de l'Université Catholique de Louvain, 1984), esp. Coloman Viola, "Manières personnelles et impersonnelles d'aborder un problème: Saint Augustin et le XIIe siècle. Contribution à l'histoire de la *quaestio*," 11–30; Bernardo C. Bazan, "La *Quaestio disputata*," 31–49; and John F. Wippel, "The Quodlibetal Question as a Distinctive Literary Genre," 67–84.

28. On the *iudicium dei*, see Henry Charles Lea, *Superstition and Force: Essays on the Wager of Law, the Wager of Battle, the Ordeal, Torture*, 3 vols. (Philadelphia: Lea Brothers, 1866), which, despite its age, remains invaluable for the abundance of detail it provides, and Robert Bartlett, *Trial by Fire and Water: The Medieval Judicial Order* (Oxford: Clarendon Press, 1986).

29. On the shift from the trial by God to the trial by inquest, see Adémar Esmain, *Histoire de la procédure criminelle en France et spécialement de la procédure inquisitoire depuis le XIIIe siècle jusqu'à nos jours* (Paris: I. Larose et Forcel, 1882), trans. by John Simpson as *A History of Continental Criminal Procedure with Special Reference to France* (Boston: Little, Brown, 1914; reprint, South Hackensack, N.J.: Rothman Reprints, 1968); Adolphe Tardif, *La Procédure civile et criminelle au XIII–XVe siècles* (Paris: Picard, 1885); Jean-Philippe Lévy, *La Hiérarchie des preuves dans le droit savant du Moyen Age depuis la Renaissance du droit romain jusqu'à la fin du XIVe siècle* (Paris: Librairie de Recueils Sirey, 1939); the collection of articles in *La Preuve: Recueils de la Société Jean Bodin pour l'histoire comparative des institutions*, vol. 2; *Moyen Age et temps modernes* (Brussels: Editions de la Librairie Encyclopédique, 1965), including Jean-Philippe Lévy, "Le Problème de la preuve dans les droits savants du Moyen Age," 137–67; and Marguerite Boulet-Sautel, "Aperçu sur les systèmes des preuves dans la France coutumière du Moyen Age," 275–325; and Bloch, *Medieval French Literature and Law*.

30. See John W. Baldwin, "The Intellectual Preparation of the Canon of 1215 against Ordeals," *Speculum* 36 (1961): 613–36.

31. See *Les Etablissements de S. Louis*, vol. 1, ed. Paul Viollet (Paris: Renouard, 1881), 487–93.

32. On the eliciting of judicial confessions, see Jean-Michel David, "La Faute et l'abandon: Théories et practiques judiciaires à Rome à la fin de la république," in *L'Aveu: Antiquité et Moyen Age*, Actes de la Table Ronde organisée par l'Ecole Française de Rome avec le concours du Centre National de la Recherche Scientifique et l'Université de Trieste, Rome, 28–30 March 1984 (Rome: Ecole Française

de Rome, 1986), 69–87; and Mireille Vincent-Cassy, "Comment obtenir un aveu? Etude des confessions des auteurs d'un meurtre commis à Paris en 1332," in *L'Aveu*, 381–400.

33. On the university's role in prosecuting heresy during this period, see *Bullaire de l'Inquisition française*, ed. Vidal, which provides transcriptions of documents relevant to the Inquisition through 1414; *Chartularium Universitatis Parisiensis*, vol. 4: *1393–1452*, ed. Heinrich Denifle and Emile Châtelain (Paris: Delalain, 1897); and Henry Charles Lea, *A History of the Inquisition of the Middle Ages*, 3 vols. (New York: Harper and Brothers, 1887; reprint, New York: Macmillan Company, 1922), 3: 126–34.

34. See D. W. Robertson Jr., "A Note on the Classical Origins of 'Circumstances' in the Medieval Confessional," *Studies in Philology* 43 (1946): 6–14.

35. *Disciplinary Decrees of the General Councils: Texts, Translation, and Commentary*, ed. H. J. Schroeder (St. Louis, Mo.: Herder, 1937), 260, translation modified. For discussion of this shift, see Pierre-Marie Gy, "Les Définitions de la confession après le quatrième concile du Latran," *L'Aveu*, 283–96 and "Le Précepte de la confession annuelle et la détection des hérétiques," *Revue des sciences philosophiques et théologiques* 58 (1974): 444–50.

36. See John T. McNeill and Helena M. Gamer, eds., *Medieval Handbooks of Penance: A Translation of the Principal "Libri Poenitentiales" and Selections from Related Documents* (New York: Columbia University Press, 1938); Pierre Michaud-Quantin, *Sommes de casuistique et manuels de confession au Moyen Age du XIIe au XVIe siècles* (Louvain, Belgium: Lauwelaerts, 1962); and Leonard E. Boyle, "The Summa for Confessors as a Genre and Its Religious Intent," in *The Pursuit of Holiness in Late Medieval and Renaissance Religion*, ed. Charles Trinkhaus with Heiko A. Oberman (Leiden, Netherlands: E. J. Brill, 1979), 126–30, and "Summae Confessorum," in *Les Genres littéraires*, 227–37.

37. Thomas N. Tentler, *Sin and Confession on the Eve of the Reformation* (Princeton: Princeton University Press, 1977), 88. On confession see also Oscar D. Watkins, *A History of Penance, Being a Study of the Authorities*, 2 vols. (London: Longmans, Green, 1920), and Henry Charles Lea, *A History of Auricular Confession and Indulgences in the Latin Church*, 3 vols. (Philadelphia: Lea Brothers, 1896; reprint, New York: Greenwood Press, 1968).

38. Edward Peters provides useful discussions of the relationship between *inquisitio* and the development of the Inquisition in both *Torture* (New York: Basil Blackwell, 1985; revised, 1996), 40–54, and *Inquisition* (New York: Free Press, 1988; reprint, Berkeley: University of California Press, 1989), 70–71.

39. On the resemblance between judicial and pastoral confessions, see Nicole Bériou, "La Confession dans les écrits théologiques et pastoraux du XIIIe siècle: Médication de l'âme ou démarche judiciaire?" in *L'Aveu*, 261–80; Jacques Chiffoleau, "Sur la practique et la conjoncture de l'aveu judiciaire en France du XIIIe au XVe siècle," in *L'Aveu*, 341–80; and Annie Cazenave, "Aveu et Contrition: Manuels de confession et interrogatoires d'Inquisition en Languedoc et en Cata-

logne (XIIIᵉ–XIVᵉ siècles)," in *La Piété populaire au Moyen Age*, vol. 1, Actes du 99ᵉ Congrès National des Sociétés Savantes, Bescançon (Paris: Bibliothèque Nationale, 1977), 333–52.

40. One might compare the discussion of the *medicus animarum* in the twelfth-century theologian Alain de Lille's *Liber poentitentialis*, ed. Jean Longère, 2 vols. (Louvain, Belgium: Editions Nauwelaerts, 1965), 1: 15, and in the fourteenth-century inquisitor Bernard Gui's *Practica inquisitionis*, 236–37.

1. The Fairy Tree

1. *A Parisian Journal, 1405–1449*, trans. Janet Shirley (Oxford: Clarendon Press, 1968), 233–34. *Procès de condamnation*, ed. Quicherat, 4: 462–63.

2. *A Parisian Journal*, trans. Shirley, 234. *Procès de condamnation*, ed. Quicherat, 4: 463.

3. See Laurence Harf-Lancner, *Les Fées au Moyen Age: Morgane et Mélusine. La naissance des fées* (Geneva: Editions Slatkine, 1984), 7–8, for this distinction.

4. Michel de Montaigne wrote, upon visiting Domrémy in 1580, "Il y a ... un arbre le long d'une vigne qu'on nomme l'Arbre de la Pucelle, qui n'a nulle autre chose à remarquer," *Oeuvres complètes*, ed. Robert Barral and Pierre Michel (Paris: Editions du Seuil, 1967), 457. Edmond Richer, visiting the village in the first quarter of the seventeeth century, was more enthusiastic: "Les branches de ce fau sont toutes rondes et rendent une belle et grande ombre pour s'abriter dessous, comme presque l'on feroit au couvert d'une chambre. Et faut que cet arbre aye pour le moins trois cents ans, qui est une merveille de nature ..." quoted in *Procès de condamnation*, ed. Champion, 2: 369, note 173. The tree was finally destroyed by the Swedes during the wars of the seventeenth century.

5. See Jacques Le Goff, *Les Intellectuels au Moyen Age* (Paris: Editions du Seuil, 1957; reprint, 1985), translated by Teresa Lavender Fagan as *Intellectuals in the Middle Ages* (Cambridge: Basil Blackwell, 1993), 124–29.

6. Jacques Verger, "The University of Paris at the End of the Hundred Years War," in *Universities in Politics: Case Studies from the Late Middle Ages and Early Modern Period*, ed. John W. Baldwin and Richard Goldthwaithe (Baltimore, Md.: Johns Hopkins University Press, 1972), 47–78, at 73.

7. The major source of information about the University of Paris during this period is *Chartularium Universitatis Parisiensis*, ed. Denifle and Chatêlain, vol. 4. For information on study plans and degree requirements, see Hastings Rashdall, *The Universities of Europe in the Middle Ages*, ed. F. M. Powicke and A. B. Emden, vol. 1: *Salerno-Bologna-Paris* (Oxford: Oxford University Press, 1895; reprint 1936), and Gordon Leff, *Paris and Oxford Universities in the Thirteenth and Fourteenth Centuries: An Institutional and Intellectual History* (New York: John Wiley and Sons, 1968). Very little has been written specifically about the University of Paris of the 1420s and 1430s, and what has been written shows more interest in political than in intellectual developments. Though the clerics who participated in Joan's trial are considered to have been prominent persons at the

university in their day, no texts written by them have been edited. For information about professors of theology at the university during this century, see Pierre Feret, *La Faculté de Théologie de Paris et ses docteurs les plus célèbres*, vol. 4: *Moyen Age* (Paris: Alphone Picard et Fils, 1897). See also Jacques Verger, "Les Universités françaises au XVᵉ siècle: Crise et tentatives de réforme," *Cahiers d'histoire* 21 (1976): 43–66; *Les Universités européenes du XIVᵉ au XVIIIᵉ siècle: Aspects et problèmes*, Actes du colloque international à l'occasion du VIᵉ centenaire de l'Université Jagellonne de Cracovie (6–8 May 1964) (Geneva: Slatkine, 1967); Jean Favier, *Paris au XVᵉ siècle, 1380–1500* (Paris: Association d'une Histoire de Paris, 1974); and Simonne Guenée, *Bibliographie de l'histoire des universités françaises des origines à nos jours*, vol. 1: *Généralités: Université de Paris* (Paris: A. et J. Picard, 1981).

8. Charles Robillard de Beaurepaire, *Notes sur les juges et les assesseurs du procès de condamnation de Jeanne d'Arc* (Rouen, France: Espérance Cagniard, 1890). Heinrich Denifle and Emile Châtelain, *Le Procès de Jeanne d'Arc et l'Université de Paris* (Nogent-le-Rotrou, France: Imprimerie Daupeley-Gouverneur, 1897); *Procès de condamnation*, ed. Champion, 2: 324–440; and *Procès de condamnation*, ed. Tisset and Lanhers, 2: 383–425 also give useful information about the clerics involved in the trial.

9. See Feret, *La Faculté de Théologie de Paris*, 46.

10. François Neveux, *L'Evêque Pierre Cauchon* (Paris: Denoël, 1987), esp. chapter 2, "L'Universitaire parisien (c. 1385–1407)," 27–41.

11. *Procès de condamnation*, ed. Champion, 2: lxxiii, no. 1; Denifle and Châtelain, *Le Procès de Jeanne d'Arc*, 10.

12. For the documents of the Council of Basel, see *Monumenta conciliorum generalium seculi XV Concilium Basiliense, Scriptores*, ed. Frantisek Palacky, Ernst Ritter von Birk, Kall Stehlin, and Konrad Wilhelm Hieronimus, 4 vols. (Vienna and Basel, Switzerland: Adolphus Holzausen, 1857–1935). See also Etienne Delaruelle, Edmonde René Labande, and Paul Ourliac, *L'Eglise au temps du grand schisme et de la crise conciliare (1378–1449)*, 2 vols. (Paris: Bloud and Gay, 1962–64).

13. See Antony Black, *Council and Commune: The Conciliar Movement and the Fifteenth-Century Heritage* (London: Burns and Oats, 1979), and "The Universities and the Council of Basle: Collegium and Council," in *The Universities in the Late Middle Ages*, ed. Jozef Ijsewijn and Jacques Paquet (Leuven, Belgium: Leuven University Press, 1978), 511–23, at 511.

14. Quoted in Jean-Baptise-Joseph Ayroles, *L'Université de Paris au temps de Jeanne d'Arc et la cause de sa haine contre la libératrice* (Paris: X. Rondelet et Cie., 1902), 13.

15. See Black, *Council and Commune*, 55.

16. Quoted in Ayroles, *L'Université de Paris*, 12.

17. Ibid.

18. See Anders Piltz, *The World of Medieval Learning*, trans. David Jones (Oxford: Basil Blackwell, 1981; translation of *Medeltidens lärda vörla* [Stockholm: Bokförlaget, 1978]); 65.

19. Ibid.

20. Donald Weinstein and Rudolph M. Bell, *Saints and Society: The Two Worlds of Western Christendom, 1000–1700* (Chicago: University of Chicago Press, 1982), 67.

21. For the fullest discussion of Domrémy at this time, see Siméon Luce, *Jeanne d'Arc à Domrémy: Recherches critiques sur les origines de la mission de la Pucelle* (Paris: Champion, 1886); and, more recently, Pierre Duparc, "Une Jeanne historique," in *Procès en nullité*, ed. Duparc, 5: esp. 139–41.

22. See Johan Huizinga, *The Autumn of the Middle Ages*, trans. Rodney J. Payton and Lurich Mammitzsch (Chicago: University of Chicago Press, 1996; translation of *Herfsttij der Middeleeuwen: Studie over levens- en gedachten-vormen der viertiende en vijftiende eeuw in Frankrijk en de Nederlanden* [Haarlem, Netherlands: H. D. Tjeenk, Willink, 1919]); and Richard Kieckhefer, *Unquiet Souls: Fourteenth-Century Saints and Their Religious Milieu* (Chicago: University of Chicago Press, 1984).

23. Francis Rapp, "Jeanne d'Arc, témoin de la vie religieuse en France au XVᵉ siècle," in *Jeanne d'Arc: Une Epoque, un rayonnement*, Colloque d'Histoire Médiévale, Orléans, October 1979 (Paris: Editions du Centre National de la Recherche Scientifique, 1982), 169–79, esp. 172–73.

24. See Maximus Tyrius, *Dissertationes*, ed. Michael B. Trapp (Stuttgart: B. G. Teubner, 1994), viii, 8; and Pliny, *Natural History*, trans. H. Rackham, vol. 4 (Cambridge, Mass.: Harvard University Press, 1945), 549. For discussion, see Paul Sébillot, *Le Folk-lore de France*, vol. 6: *La Flore* (Paris: Librairie orientale et américaine, 1906; reprint, Paris: Editions Imago, 1985), esp. the section on "Culte des Arbres," 77–84; and James George Frazer, *The Golden Bough: A Study in Magic and Religion*, part 1: *The Magic Art and the Evolution of Kings*, vol. 2 (London: Macmillan, 1890; reprint, New York: Saint Martin's Press, 1990), esp. ch. 9, "The Worship of Trees," 7–58, and ch. 20, "The Worship of the Oak," 439–75.

25. Cited in *Procès en nullité*, ed. Duparc, 2: 412. Christine de Pizan, in her *Ditié de Jehanne d'Arc*, ed. Angus J. Kennedy and Kenneth Varty (Oxford: Society for the Study of Mediaeval Languages and Literature, 1977); Mathieu Thomassin, in his *Registre delphinal*, in *Procès de condamnation*, ed. Quicherat, 4: 305; and Walter Bower, in his *Scotichronicon*, in *Procès de condamnation*, ed. Quicherat, 4: 480 also refer to this prophecy. For discussion of the prediction, see Olivier Bouzy, "Prédication ou récupération: Les prophéties autour de Jeanne d'Arc dans les premiers mois de l'année 1429," *Bulletin de l'Association des Amis du Centre Jeanne d'Arc* 14 (1990): 39–55.

26. See Louis Carolus-Barré, " 'Jeanne, êtes-vous en état de grace?' et les prières du prône au XVᵉ siècle," *Bulletin de la Société des Antiquaires de France*, 1958: 204–8.

27. *Procès en nullité*, ed. Duparc, 1: 368. For discussion of Joan's education, see Duparc, *Procès en nullité*, 5: 144–48.

28. Weinstein and Bell, *Saints and Society,* 29. André Vauchez discusses the phenomenon of the "puer cor senile gerens" in *La Sainteté en occident aux derniers siècles du Moyen Age d'après les procès de canonisation et les documents hagiographiques* (Rome: Ecole Française de Rome, 1981), 596ff.

29. Caroline Walker Bynum, "Women's Stories, Women's Symbols: A Critique of Victor Turner's Theory of Liminality," in *Anthropology and the Study of Religion,* ed. Frank Reynolds and Robert Moore (Chicago: Center for the Scientific Study of Religion, 1984), 105–25, (reprint in *Fragmentation and Redemption: Essays on Gender and the Human Body in Medieval Religion* [New York: Zone Books, 1991], 27–51). For Weinstein and Bell, the major conflicts between holy girls and their parents occurred over the prospect of the girls' marriages. Like the parents in their study, Joan's mother and father seem to have supported the case of a man from nearby Toul, who sued Joan for reneging upon a promise to marry him but lost in court. Of this clash between her parents and herself, Joan stated, "ipsa obediebat in omnibus, preterquam in processu quem habuit in civitate Tullensi pro causa matromonii" (127), even here stressing the rarity of such moments of dissension.

30. *Procès en nullité,* ed. Duparc, 1: 281.

31. See Madeleine Jeay, "Clercs et paysans au XVᵉ siècle: Une relecture de l'épisode de l'arbre aux fées dans le procès de Jeanne d'Arc," in *Normes et pouvoir à la fin du Moyen Age,* ed. Marie-Claude Déprez-Masson, Actes du Colloque La Recherche en Etudes Médiévales au Québec et en Ontario, Montreal, 16–17 May 1987 (Montreal: Editions CERES, 1989), 145–63.

32. *Procès en nullité,* ed. Duparc, 1: 254, 262, and 283.

33. Ibid., 256–57. Beatrice Estellin likewise related that people went to walk near this tree "propter pulchritudinem arboris," ibid., 258.

34. Ibid., 276.

35. Ibid., 277.

36. Ibid., 258.

37. Nicole Belmont, in "Folk Beliefs and Legends about Fairies in France," in *Mythologies,* ed. Yves Bonnefoy and Wendy Doniger, trans. David White (Chicago: University of Chicago Press, 1991), 2: 743–46, explains these accounts of marriages broken by disappearing fairies as versions of myths of the golden age, in which man's connection to divine beings is lost through his misdeeds. She writes, "These legends also manifest, more or less explicitly, a symbolic teaching: the world of fairies and sprites disappeared in the face of Christianity because they belonged to paganism. Once again the ideology of survival is at work: legends about fairies and their relations with humans are very much of the present, but they tell of a past regarded as finished. The past nevertheless remains inscribed in various places which thus serve as the basis for remembering it" (746). Laurence Harf-Lancner interprets the double face of fairies in these legends as a reflection of men's perception of the double face of women in love relationships. Like Mélusine, women submit to men or, like Morgan, they make men submit to them, yet they never

cease to retain a mysterious alterity symbolized by the other world from which fairies come and to which they return but of which men forever remain ignorant (*Les Feés,* 45). Pierre Gallais, in *La Fée à la fontaine et à l'arbre: Un archetype du conte merveilleux et du récit courtois* (Amsterdam and Atlanta, Ga.: Rodolpi, 1992), has approached these fairy tales from a Jungian perspective, stressing the universal archetypes of the water, the tree, and the woman associated with them.

38. *Procès en nullité,* ed. Duparc, 1: 264–65.

39. *The Lais of Marie de France,* trans. Glyn S. Burgess and Keith Busby (Harmondsworth, England: Penguin, 1986), 87. *Les Lais de Marie de France,* ed. Jean Rychner (Paris: Honoré Champion, 1969), 105, lines 91–98.

40. See Perceval de Boulainvilliers's letter to the duke of Milan in *Procès de condamnation,* ed. Quicherat, 5: 116.

41. Margaret Alice Murray, "Joan of Arc and Gilles de Rais," Appendix IV, in *The Witch-Cult in Western Europe* (Oxford: Clarendon Press, 1921; reprint, 1962), 270–79, at 272.

42. Norman Cohn, *Europe's Inner Demons: An Enquiry Inspired by the Great Witch-Hunt* (New York: Basic Books, 1975); and Jeffrey Burton Russell, *Witch-craft in the Middle Ages* (Ithaca, N.Y.: Cornell University Press, 1972).

43. Carlo Ginzburg, *Night Battles: Witchcraft and Agrarian Cults in the Six-teenth and Seventeenth Centuries,* trans. John and Anne C. Tedeschi (Harmonds-worth, England: Penguin Books, 1985; translation of *I Benandanti: Richerche sulle stregoneria e sui culti agravi tra cinquecento e seicento.* [Turin: Guilio Einaudi, 1966]), xiii.

44. See Jeay, "Clercs et paysans au XVᵉ siècle."

2. The Voices from God

1. For introductions to these women's works, see *Medieval Women's Vi-sionary Literature,* ed. Elizabeth Alvida Petroff (Oxford: Oxford University Press, 1986); Zum Brun and Epiney-Burgard, eds., *Women Mystics*; Valerie M. Lagorio, "The Medieval Continental Women Mystics: An Introduction," in *An Introduction to the Medieval Mystics of Europe,* ed. Paul E. Szarmach (Albany: SUNY Press, 1984), 161–93; Peter Dinzelbacher and Dieter R. Bauer, eds., *Frauenmystik im Mittelalter* (Ostfildern bei Stuttgart: Schwabenverlag, 1983); and André Vauchez, "Female Prophets, Visionaries, and Mystics in Medieval Europe, in his *The Laity in the Middle Ages: Religious Beliefs and Devotional Practices,* ed. Daniel E. Born-stein, trans. Margery J. Schneider (Notre Dame, Ind.: University of Notre Dame Press, 1993), 219–29. For a general treatment of medieval visionaries of both sexes, thematically rather than historically organized, see Peter Dinzelbacher, *Vision und Visionliteratur im Mittelalter* (Stuttgart: Anton Hiersemank, 1981).

2. For these statistics, see Weinstein and Bell, *Saints and Society,* 228.

3. On the beguines, see Lerner, *The Heresy of the Free Spirit*; Ernest W. McDonnell, *The Beguines and the Beghards in Medieval Culture* (New Brunswick, N.J.: Rutgers University Press, 1953; New York: Octagon, 1969); Fiona Bowie, ed.,

Béguine Spirituality: Mystical Writings of Mechthild of Magdeburg, Beatrijs of Nazareth, and Hadewijch of Brabant, trans. Oliver Davis (New York: Crossroad Books, 1989); and Elizabeth Alvilda Petroff, "A New Feminine Spirituality: The Beguines and Their Writings in Medieval Europe," in her *Body and Soul: Essays on Medieval Women and Mysticism* (Oxford: Oxford University Press, 1994), 51–65.

4. André Vauchez, "Joan of Arc and Female Prophecy in the Fourteenth and Fifteenth Centuries," in his *The Laity in the Middle Ages,* 255–64, and "Mystical Sanctity at the Time of the Avignon Papacy and the Great Schism," in the same volume, 231–36. See also Anne Llewellyn Barstow, *Joan of Arc: Heretic, Mystic, Shaman* (Lewiston, Maine: Edwin Mellen Press, 1986), for information about women visionaries contemporaneous to Joan.

5. For this prophecy, not recorded in any surviving accounts of Marie's pronouncements, see *Procès en nullité,* ed. Duparc, 1: 375.

6. Caroline Walker Bynum, "Religious Women in the Later Middle Ages," in *Christian Spirituality: High Middle Ages and Reformation,* ed. Jill Raitt (New York: Crossroad Books, 1985), 121–39, at 129.

7. Both Weinstein and Bell, in *Saints and Sanctity,* 220–38, and Bynum, in "Religious Women in the Later Middle Ages," 120, pursue these analogies.

8. On these cases, see André Vauchez, "The Reaction of the Church to Late-Medieval Mysticism and Prophecy," in his *The Laity in the Middle Ages,* 243–53.

9. Grace M. Jantzen, in *Power, Gender, and Christian Mysticism* (Cambridge: Cambridge University Press, 1995), explores the relationship between women mystics and their male companions. See also John Coakley, "Friars as Confidants of Holy Women in Medieval Dominican Hagiography," in *Images of Sainthood in Medieval Europe,* ed. Renate Blumenfeld-Kosinski and Timea Szell (Ithaca, N.Y.: Cornell University Press, 1991), 222–46; and Elizabeth Alvilda Petroff, "Male Confessors and Female Penitents: Possibilities for Dialogue," in her *Body and Soul,* 139–60. Whereas Bynum perceives the women as dependent upon the men and, therefore, as losing their onetime spiritual independence, Vauchez perceives the men as dependent upon the women and, hence, as falling under their power; see Bynum, "Religious Women in the Later Middle Ages"; and Vauchez, "The Reaction of the Church."

10. The studies offering explanations for Joan's voices fall, in general, into three categories. First, a large number of critics — from Monsignor Félix Dupanloup, the bishop of Orléans instrumental in Joan's canonization, to Régine Pernoud, the author of numerous popular works on Joan and founder of the Centre Jeanne d'Arc in Orléans — maintain that Joan's voices did in fact derive from God. Philippe-Hector Dunand's *Etude historique sur les voix et visions de Jeanne d'Arc,* 2 vols. (Paris: Charles Poussielgue, 1903), provides the most exhaustive exposition of this thesis. In the first part of this work, Dunand, a self-proclaimed follower of the "critical-historical school," argues that Joan's knowledge of a secret the dauphin had shared only with God, her retrieval of a mysterious sword buried in the church of Saint Catherine de Fierbois, and her predictions of the relief of Or-

léans, the victory at Patay, the king's coronation, the conquest of Paris, and the expulsion of the English from France are as well documented as any events of the late Middle Ages and that to doubt the occurrence of these miracles is to doubt the very existence of Joan of Arc. In the second part of this work, Dunand speaks openly as a Catholic, demonstrating that Joan satisfied the criteria of *persona, modus,* and *effectus* through which the church approves revelations. Such a mystical interpretation of Joan's voices poses self-evident problems for non-Christians. But in addition, such a reading is also complicated by the church's removal of Saint Catherine and Saint Margaret (the figures with whom Joan eventually identified her voices) from the calendar as apocryphal. Indeed, when the Office for the Congregation of Saints finally approved Joan's canonization in 1920, it identified her not as a martyr who died in defense of her legitimately holy voices but as a virgin of exemplary life.

Six years after the appearance of Dunand's work, Anatole France produced his own two-volume *Vie de Jeanne d'Arc,* in which he dismisses Joan's voices as hallucinations and includes in an appendix a letter by a Sorbonne neuropathologist, Georges Dumas, that attributes these hallucinations to hysteria. Endless specialists in medicine and psychology have joined Dumas in diagnosing the illnesses that caused Joan's revelations. Whereas the physicians largely base their interpretations upon Jean d'Aulon's observation that she did not suffer from "la secrete maladie des femmes" (*Procès en nullité,* ed. Duparc, 1: 496), the psychiatrists ground their verdicts upon Joan's recollection of her father's declaration that he would prefer to see her drowned than become a camp follower. See, for example, Roger Money-Kyrle, "A Psycho-Analytic Study of the Voices of Joan of Arc," *British Journal of Medical Psychology* 13 (1933): 63–81; and F. E. Kenyon, "The Life and Health of Joan of Arc," *Practicioner* 207, no. 1242 (December 1971): 835–42.

Spiritualists provide the third branch of interpretation of Joan's voices. Andrew Lang depicts the voices as a primarily subjective phenomenon in *The Maid of France,* especially appendix D, "The Voices and Visions of Jeanne d'Arc," 327–30, and in "The Voices of Jeanne d'Arc" in his *The Valet's Tragedy and Other Studies* (London: Longmans, Green, 1903), 193–227. Léon Denis provides a more radical spiritualist reading of Joan's voices in his *Jeanne d'Arc Médium* (Paris: Librairie des Sciences Psychiques, 1910), trans. by Arthur Conan Doyle as *The Mystery of Joan of Arc* (London: J. Murray, 1934). Denis asserts that Joan, like other sensitive souls throughout history, detected objective, occult forces that pervade the universe and that she identified these forces according to the religious idiom available to her.

Even before the turn of the twentieth century, Pierre Lanéry d'Arc's *Le Livre d'or de Jeanne d'Arc: Bibliographie raisonnée et analytique des ouvrages relatifs à Jeanne d'Arc* (Paris: Librairie Techener, 1894) provided annotated references to forty works addressing the debate "Inspiration or hallucination?" (699–739). All of these authors, whether Catholic, rationalist, or spiritualist, perceive the trial transcripts as a means of gaining access to a reality external to the text and thus differ from what I am attempting to achieve in this chapter.

11. *Procès en nullité*, ed. Duparc, 1: 326.

12. Ibid., 381.

13. Ibid., 471.

14. Ibid., 323.

15. Ibid.

16. Ibid., 486.

17. *A Parisian Journal*, trans. Shirley, 255. *Procès de condamnation*, ed. Quicherat, 4: 478.

18. *Procès en nullité*, ed. Duparc, 5: 167.

19. Henri Wallon, in *Jeanne d'Arc*, 2 vols. (Paris: Firmin-Didot, 1860; reprint, 1876), and Johan Huizinga, in "Mr. Shaw's Saint Joan," in *Men and Ideas: History, the Middle Ages, and the Renaissance*, trans. James S. Holmes and Hans von Marle (New York: Meridian Books, 1959), 207–39 at 223, also suggest that Joan only began at Rouen to identify her voices with these saints. Luce, in *Jeanne d'Arc à Domrémy*, (cxxxv), refutes Wallon's argument by citing Joan's allusion to having previously identified her voices at Poitiers. Yet the minutes from Poitiers have disappeared and cannot be called on to verify this claim, no witnesses at the rehabilitation recalled any such testimony, and, as we have seen, Joan's claim to have identified the voices at Rouen was made amid a series of self-contradictory statements, the referentiality of which remains suspect. Luce considers Joan's responses in the transcripts from Rouen as a repository of facts about her and gives no attention to the interplay between the questions and these responses.

20. Saint Catherine and Saint Margaret, it should be noted, were among the most popular saints of the Middle Ages and were often paired together. Pierre Duparc points out that Saint Catherine was considered, as of the fourteenth century, the most powerful intercessor before God after the Virgin Mary and, along with Saint John the Baptist, was one of the most popular subjects of religious statues. Joan's connections with this saint, from her village life, have often been observed. There was a church dedicated to Saint Catherine in Maxey, across the river from Domrémy. Anatole France writes of Saint Catherine, "On lui faisait dans la vallée de la Meuse des oraisons en rimes, comme celle-ci: 'Ave, très sainte Catherine, / Vièrge pucelle nette et fine,'" *Vie de Jeanne d'Arc*, 1: 111. Joan's older sister was named Catherine; she died before 1429 and remained so dear to Joan that Joan asked her pregnant aunt Aveline, if her child was a girl, to name her after her late sister.

It has often been noted that a statue of Saint Margaret, existent today, was probably in the church in Domrémy during Joan's lifetime. According to France, "Madame sainte Marguerite était grandement honorée dans le royaume de France et elle y faisait beaucoup de grâces. Elle assistait les femmes en couches et protégeait les paysans au labour. Elle était la patronne des liniers, des recommanderesses, des mégissiers et des blanchisseurs de laine. On lui était dévot en Champagne et en Lorraine autant qu'en aucun pays chrétien" (ibid., 108).

21. On the gender of angels, see Stuart Schneiderman, *An Angel Passes: How the Sexes Became Undivided* (New York: New York University Press, 1988).

22. For the image of Saint Michael at this point in history, see Siméon Luce, "Le Culte de saint Michel au XVᵉ siècle et la victoire du Mont Saint-Michel," in his *Jeanne d'Arc à Domrémy*, lxxxix–cxx; Etienne Delaruelle, "L'Archange Saint Michel dans la spiritualité de Jeanne d'Arc," in his *La Piété populaire au Moyen Age* (Turin: Bottega d'Erasmo, 1975), 389–400; Colette Beaune, *Naissance de la nation France* (Paris: Gallimard, 1982), ed. Frederic L. Cheyette and trans. Susan Ross Huston as *The Birth of an Ideology: Myths and Symbols of Power in Late-Medieval France* (Berkeley: University of California Press, 1991); and François-Marie Lethel, "Jeanne d'Arc et l'ange," in *Colloque sur l'ange*, Centre européen d'art sacré, Pont-à-Mouson, Meurthe-et-Moselle, 26–28 June 1981, Abbaye des Prémontrés (Pont-à-Mouson, France: Imprimerie du Centre Culturel des Prémontrés, 1982), 55–70. Pierre Duparc has suggested, interestingly, that it was no accident that Joan named as one of her voices the archangel who expelled the wicked angels from Paradise and conducted worthy human souls to heaven after their deaths. Duparc proposes that "en 1429 l'idée d'une guerre juste menée contre l'envahisseur, d'une lutte contre les méchants, ainsi que l'aide aux combattants trépassés, pouvaient se conjuguer pour faire de saint Michel l'inspirateur indirect de Jeanne, le symbole de la résistance à l'ennemi" (*Procès en nullité*, ed. Duparc, 5: 169). It has been observed, in addition, that Joan was no doubt familiar with Saint-Mihiel, the capital of the duchy of Bar, and Saint-Michel-sur-Meurthe in the canton of Saint-Dié.

23. *Biblia sacra iuxta vulgatam versionem*, ed. Bonifactius Fischer and Robert Weber (Stuttgart: Deutsche Bibelgesellschaft, 1983), 1 Cor. 12:10.

24. For discussion of this context, see Thomas Hohmann, ed. and trans., *Heinrich von Langenstein "Unterschiedung der Geister": Lateinische und deutsche. Texte und Untersuchungen zu Ubersetzungsliteratur aus der Wiener Schule* (Munich: Artemis Verlag, 1977), 33–50.

25. Gerson's writings are available in the ten volumes of his *Oeuvres complètes*, ed. Palémon Glorieux (Paris: Desclée, 1960–73). Secondary materials on Gerson are not prodigious. See James Louis Connally, *Jean Gerson: Reformer and Mystic* (Dubuque, Iowa: William C. Brown, 1928; reprint, 1964); Marie-Joseph Pinel, *La Vie ardente de Gerson* (Paris: Bloud and Gay, 1929); and André Combes, *La Théologie mystique de Gerson*, 2 vols. (Rome: Desclée, 1963; reprint, 1964).

26. "De distinctione verarum visionum a falsis" is available in Gerson, *Oeuvres complètes*, 3: 36–56; "De probatione spirituum" in 9: 177–184; "De examinatione doctrinarum" in 9: 458–76. The first two treatises have been translated and commented upon by Paschal Boland, *The Concept of "Discretio Spirituum" in John Gerson's "De Probatione Spirituum" and "De Distinctione Verarum Visionum a Falsis"* (Washington, D.C.: Catholic University of America Press, 1959). Boland argues that Gerson was the first to develop guidelines for telling true visions from false ones, though Hugh of Saint-Victor did precede Gerson in requiring visionaries to display humility, a willingness to accept counsel, patience, truthfulness, and charity, the five qualities displayed by the Virgin Mary at the Annunciation.

For the Augustinian origins of *discretio spirituum*, see Frank Tobin, "Medieval Thought on Visions and Its Resonance in Mechthild von Magdeburg's Flowing Light of the Godhead," in *Vox Mystica: Essays on Medieval Mysticism in Honor of Professor Valerie M. Lagorio*, ed. Anne Clark Barlett and Valerie Marie Lagorio (Cambridge: D. S. Brewer, 1995), 41–53.

27. For the Latin originals of the two treatises, see Dorothy G. Wayman, "The Chancellor and Jeanne D'Arc, February–July, A.D. 1429," *Franciscan Studies* 17, nos. 2–3 (June–September 1957): 273–305. "De mirabili victoria" can also be found in Gerson, *Oeuvres complètes*, 9: 661–65, and *Procès en nullité*, ed. Duparc, 2: 33–39. For English translations of the treatises, see H. G. Francq, "Jean Gerson's Theological Treatise and Other Memoirs in Defence of Joan of Arc," *Revue de l'Université d'Ottawa* 41, no. 1 (January–March 1971): 58–80. Georges Peyronnet discusses the complexities of this problem of attribution again in "Gerson, Charles VII, et Jeanne d'Arc," *Revue d'Histoire Ecclésiastique* 84, no. 2 (March–June 1989): 334–70. See also Gertrude H. Merkle, "Martin Le Franc's Commentary on Jean Gerson's Treatise on Joan of Arc," in *Fresh Verdicts*, eds. Wheeler and Wood, 177–88.

28. William A. Christian has already examined the relation between Gerson's treatise on true and false revelations and Joan's trial; see his *Apparitions in Late Medieval and Renaissance Spain* (Princeton: Princeton University Press, 1981), 188–94 et passim.

29. "Translation of *De distinctione*," in Boland, *The Concept*, 83. Gerson, "De distinctione," 3:40. (Luke 2:19).

30. "Translation of *De distinctione*," in Boland, *The Concept*, 82. Gerson, "De distinctione," 3:39.

31. "Translation of *De probatione spirituum*," in Boland, *The Concept*, 29. Gerson, "De probatione spirituum," 9: 180.

32. Thomas Aquinas, *Summa theologiae*, vol. 9: *Angels*, 1a. 50–64, (Cambridge: Blackfriars, 1964–1968), 4.

33. Ibid., 30.

34. Ibid., vol. 8: *Creation, Variety, and Evil*, 1a., 44–49, Qu. 45, art. 4.

35. The clerics, of course, were trying to trap Joan by encouraging her to speak of her voices in such a corporeal manner. As Gerson wrote in "La Montaigne de contemplation" in *Oeuvres complètes*, 7: 16–55, the contemplative should apprehend not an external object but, rather, internal emotions. She should experience God not as a physical being of definite size and color but as "a sweetness, a plenitude, a taste, a melody, and such feelings that we cannot recount by comparing them to any similar thing" (54). "God is neither large corporally, nor white, nor red, nor clear, nor colored," he warned (54).

36. Etienne Delaruelle maintains that the term *preudomne* in this sentence evokes a man who would escort a young woman during her travels, as Saint Michael might be thought to escort Joan during her wanderings throughout France, and with a chaste man, just as the term *preud'femme* (which would eventually lead to

the term "prude") suggested a chaste woman. See his "L'Archange Saint Michel dans la spiritualité de Jeanne d'Arc" in *La Piété populaire*.

3. The Departure for France

1. On cross-dressing in general, see Margery Garber, *Vested Interests: Cross-Dressing and Cultural Anxiety* (New York: Routledge, 1992); Vern L. Bullough and Bonnie Bullough, *Cross Dressing, Sex, and Gender* (Philadelphia: University of Pennsylvania Press, 1993); and Leslie Feinberg, *Transgender Warriors: Making History from Joan of Arc to RuPaul* (Boston: Beacon Press, 1996). As Bullough and Bullough write, in the Middle Ages, men who assumed feminine disguise and feminine roles were regarded harshly, as striving to lower their condition, but women who assumed masculine disguise and masculine roles were usually regarded sympathetically, as attempting to raise their status. Whereas men who disguised themselves as women were seen as making themselves more sexual — whether by seeking opportunities for seduction in closed, all-female communities or by implicitly making themselves available as the passive, feminine partner in a homosexual liaison — women who disguised themselves as men were usually seen as making themselves less sexual, since they thus exposed themselves to women's desires but did not themselves desire. See also Valerie R. Hotchkiss, *Clothes Make the Man: Female Cross Dressing in Medieval Europe* (New York: Garland, 1996) and Caroline Walker Bynum's writings, including "Women's Stories, Women's Symbols," in *Fragmentation and Redemption*, at 38; "... and Woman His Humanity: Female Imagery in the Religious Writing of the Later Middle Ages," in *Gender and Religion: On the Complexity of Symbols*, ed. Caroline Walker Bynum, Steve Harrell, and Paula Richman (Boston: Beacon Press, 1986), 257–88, reprint in *Fragmentation and Redemption*, 151–79, at 170–71; and *Holy Feast and Holy Fast: The Religious Significance of Food to Medieval Women* (Berkeley: University of California Press, 1987), at 290–91.

2. *Biblia sacra*, Deut. 22:5.

3. See *Decretum Gratiani emendatum et notationibus ... Gregorii XIII*, ed. Justus Henning Boehmer, in *Patrologiae Cursus Completus ... Series Latina*, 187: 165.

4. Aquinas, *Summa theologiae*, vol. 44: *Well-Tempered Passion* (2a2ae. 155–70), qu. 169, art. 2, 238.

5. On the Canaanites' idolatry, see S. R. Driver, *A Critical and Exegetical Commentary on Deuteronomy*, 3rd ed. (Edinburgh: T. and T. Clark, 1902; reprint, 1986), and Schibanoff, "True Lies."

6. Aquinas, *Summa theologiae*, vol. 44: *Well-Tempered Passion*, qu. 169, art. 2, 238.

7. On women monks, see Marie Delcourt, "Le Complexe de Diane dans l'hagiographie chrétienne," *Revue de l'Histoire des Religions* 153 (1958): 1–33; John Anson, "The Female Transvestite in Early Monasticism: The Origin and Development of a Motif," *Viator* 5 (1974): 1–30; and Evelyne Patlagean, "L'Histoire de la

femme déguisée en moine et l'évolution de la sainteté féminine à Byzance," *Studi Medievali,* 3rd series, 17 (1976): 597–623. See also Hotchkiss, "'Female Men of God': Cross Dressing in Medieval Hagiography," chapter 2 in *Clothes Make the Man,* 13–31. As Hotchkiss suggests, the women monks were admired because they were seen as rejecting not only the world and its sins but femininity and its worldly associations; they were perceived as doing penance for their feminine weakness as well as for their human sinfulness.

8. See Hotchkiss, "The Lives and Death of Hildegund von Schönau," chapter 3 in *Clothes Make the Man,* 33–47.

9. See Michel Salvat, "Amazonia: Le Royaume de Femmenie," in *La Représentation de l'antiquité au Moyen Age,* Actes du Colloque, March 26, 27, and 28, 1981, Université de Picardie (Vienna: Verlag Karl M. Halosar, 1982), 229–41, and Abby Wettan Kleinbaum, *The War against the Amazons* (New York: New Press, 1983). Pierre Samuel's *Amazones, guerrières et gaillardes* (Brussels: Editions Complexe, 1975) provides information about medieval women warriors who could serve as points of comparison for Joan, such as Scatach, Queen Maeve, Ruadh, Ailne, and Morrigu of Irish legend; Swanhild, Rinda, Sela, Rusilla, Gurid, Gudrun, and Brunhilde of Scandinavian eddas and sagas; Maruelle of Stilimen, a Greek girl who led a combat against the Turks in 1307; Jeanne of Flanders, who led her troops in battle in the 1340s after the capture of her husband; Jeanne of Penthièvre, who fought against Jeanne of Flanders; Maria of Puzzuoli, who fought in Italy in the 1340s and who is described in a letter by Petrarch (see *Letters from Petrarch,* trans. Morris Bishop [Bloomington: Indiana University Press, 1966]); and, of course, Jeanne Hachette, who defended Beauvais against attack by the duke of Burgundy in 1472. See also Megan McLaughlin, "The Woman Warrior: Gender, Warfare, and Society in Medieval Europe," *Women's Studies* 17 (1990): 193–209.

10. Deborah Fraioli, "Why Joan of Arc Never Became an Amazon," in Wheeler and Wood, eds., *Fresh Verdicts,* 189–204, at 190.

11. Giovanni Boccaccio, *De mulieribus claris,* ed. Vittorio Zaccaria (Milan: A. Mondadori, 1967), translated by Guido A. Guarino as *Concerning Famous Women* (New Brunswick, N.J.: Rutgers University Press, 1963), xxxviii–xxxix.

12. Christine de Pizan, "The *Livre de la cité des dames* of Christine de Pisan: A Critical Edition," 2 vols., edited by Maureen C. Curnow (Ph.D. diss., Vanderbilt University, 1975), and *The Book of the City of Ladies,* translated by Earl Jeffrey Richards (New York: Persea Press, 1982). See Maureen Quilligan, *The Allegory of Female Authority: Christine de Pizan's "Cité des Dames"* (Ithaca, N.Y.: Cornell University Press, 1991), 87–92 for discussion of Amazons in this work.

13. See Michèle Perret, "Travesties et transexuelles: Yde, Silence, Grisandole, Blanchandine," *Romance Notes* 25, no. 3 (Spring 1985): 328–40, and Hotchkiss, "Cross Dressing and Sexuality," chapter 7 in *Clothes Make the Man,* 105–24.

14. See *Procès en nullité,* ed. Duparc, 2: 206–8, 248–49, 262–63, 327–28, and 457–75. See also Jane Marie Pinzino, "Devil or Angel: Fifteenth-Century Verdicts on Joan of Arc" (Ph.D. diss., University of Pennsylvania, 1996).

15. Adrien Harmand, *Jeanne d'Arc: Ses costumes, son armure. Essai de re-constitution* (Paris: Librairie Ernest LeRoux, 1929).

16. See Schibanoff, "True Lies," 47.

17. Tisset and Lanhers translate this passage into French as "ayant aban-donné l'habit de femme, elle a imité le comportment des hommes," in *Procès de condamnation*, 2: 316, yet Barrett renders this line as "this woman... has re-jected woman's dress and imitated the costume of men" in *The Trial of Jeanne d'Arc*, 292. It is not entirely clear whether the second occurrence of *habitus* is to be translated as "comportment" or "costume," yet the transcripts normally speak of Joan as "assuming [*assumendo*]," "using [*utendo*]," or having "put on [*induta*]" men's clothes (205, 207, for example), instead of having "imitated [*imi-tata*]" men's *habitus*: they usually depict her as wearing men's clothes rather than merely pretending to wear them. Also, the canonists begin this brief charge by censuring Joan for having cut her hair "quam sibi Dedit ad velamen" (363) and thus, by echoing 1 Cor. 11.4–15, again connect Joan's rejection of women's tradi-tional appearance with her rejection of women's traditional submissiveness to men.

18. *Procès de condamnation*, ed. Quicherat, 4: 446.

19. Ibid., 446–47.

20. On the history of *curiositas*, see André Labhardt, "Curiositas: Notes sur l'histoire d'un mot et d'une notion," *Museum Helveticum*, 1960: 206–24; Nicole Czechowski, ed., *La Curiosité: Les vertiges du savoir* (Paris: Editions Autrement, 1993); Gunther Bös, *Curiositas: Die Rezeption eines antiken Begriffes durch christliche Autoren bis Thomas von Aquin* (Paderborn: Schöningen, 1993); and Edward M. Peters, "Transgressing the Limits Set by the Fathers: Authority and Impious Exe-gesis in Medieval Thought," in *Christendom and Its Discontents: Exclusion, Persecu-tion, and Rebellion, 1000–1500*, ed. Scott L. Waugh and Peter D. Diehl (Cambridge: Cambridge University Press, 1996), 338–62.

21. *The Oxford English Dictionary*, 2nd ed., ed. J. A. Simpson and E. S. C. Weiner (Oxford: Clarendon Press, 1989), 4: 144. I am grateful to Mark Lambert for his help with this point.

22. *Procès de condamnation*, ed. Tisset and Lanhers, 2: 294.

23. *Selections from "A deo exivit," "Contra curiositatem studentium," and "De mystica theologia speculativa,"* ed. and trans. Steven E. Ozment (Leiden: E. J. Brill, 1969), 29. Gerson, "Contra curiositatem studentium," in *Oeuvres complètes*, 3: 224–49, at 230.

24. Shakespeare, *Henry VI, Part One*, 5.4.7.

4. The Sign for the King

1. Christian, *Apparitions in Late Medieval and Renaissance Spain*, 139.

2. Ibid., 62.

3. Ibid., 8.

4. Ibid., 189.

5. *Procès en nullité*, ed. Duparc, 1: 326 and 328.

6. Ibid., 472.

7. *Biblia sacra*, Isa. 60:3.

8. *Procès en nullité*, ed. Duparc, 1: 400.

9. *Procès de condamnation*, ed. Quicherat, 4: 52–53.

10. Ibid., 53.

11. *Procès en nullité*, ed. Duparc, 1: 462.

12. Wallon, *Jeanne d'Arc*, and Claude Desama, "La Première Entrevue de Jeanne d'Arc et de Charles VII à Chinon (mars 1429)," *Analecta Bollandiana* 84, nos. 1–2 (1966): 113–26.

13. Desama, "La Première Entrevue," 120.

14. *Procès en nullité*, ed. Duparc, 1: 400.

15. *Procès de condamnation*, ed. Quicherat, 4: 270–71.

16. *Procès en nullité*, ed. Duparc, 1: 475.

17. Ibid., 381.

18. Ibid., 390.

19. Thomas Basin, *Histoire de Charles VII*, ed. and trans. Charles Samaran (Paris: Société d'Edition "Les Belles Lettres," 1933; revised, 1964), 132.

20. The "abbreviator of the trial," who compiled an account of Joan around 1500, and the *Miroir des femmes vertueuses* dramatized this exchange between Joan and the king, though they provided no source for the information, as did Sala. In the former text, Joan reminded the king of his request of God that "se vous n'estiez vray héritier du royaume de France, que ce fust son plaisir vous oster le courage de le poursuivre, affin que vous ne fussiez plus cause de faire et soustenir la guerre dont procède tant de maulx, pour recouvrir ledit royaulme,' " *Procès de condamnation*, ed. Quicherat, 4: 258. In the latter text, the author related that the king revealed that a few days before she had first come to him, he had risen from his bed at night in his chemise, knelt down next to his bed, and begged the Virgin Mary that "s'il estoit vray filz du roy de France et héritier de sa couronne, il pleust à la dame suplier son filz que il luy donnast ayde et secours contre ses ennemys mortelz et adversaires en manière que il les peust chasser hors de son royaulme et icelluy gouverner en paix; et s'il n'estoit filz du roy et le royaulme ne luy appartenist, que le bon plaisir de Dieu fut luy donner patience et quelques possessions temporelles pour vivre honnorablement en ce monde" (271). When Joan spoke to him, the king realized that God had revealed this "mistere" to her. It was she who convinced him that he was the true heir and who brought him the help he needed to overcome his enemies.

21. See Jules-Etienne-Joseph Quicherat, *Aperçus nouveaux sur l'histoire de Jeanne d'Arc* (Paris: Jules Renouard, 1850; translated by H. G. Francq as *New Aspects of the Case History of Jeanne d'Arc* [Brandon, Manitoba: Brandon University Press, 1971]), 66; Pernoud and Clin, *Jeanne d'Arc*, 41–42; and *Procès en nullité*, ed. Duparc, 5: 188–92.

22. *Procès en nullité*, ed. Duparc, 1: 390.

23. As the record of this last interview with Joan is inserted after the conclusion of the trial and after the notaries' signatures, seals, and affirmations of the document's authenticity, there is considerable debate about its reliability. For a summary of this discussion, see *Procès de condamnation,* ed. Tisset and Lanhers, 3: 41–45. Again, as I am focusing upon the transcripts as a text and not as a representation of historical reality, this discussion does not impinge upon my reading of these final testimonies.

24. Though Joan's last words passed without comment by the clerics at Rouen, spoken as they were after the sentence of her condemnation as a relapsed heretic had been written, they were glossed by the clerics who contributed briefs to the rehabilitation. Jean Bréhal described Joan as speaking through "figura veritatis," *Procès en nullité,* ed. Duparc, 2: 481. Thomas Basin similarly commented, "respondit eis quantum potuit signum illud occultando, quasi parabolice seu metaphorice respondendo" (2: 203). Elie Bordeilles and Guillaume Bouillé similarly described Joan as having spoken "metaphorice" (2: 124, 339, 341). Though it may well be tempting to try to connect Joan's depiction of the angel and the sign with medieval theories of figures, parables, or metaphors, as the clerics at the rehabilitation did, it is worth remembering that all four of the clerics who cited Joan's words on the morning of her execution cited her as using no such literary or judicial terms to describe her speech act and that Toutmouillé, who did quote her using a literary term, stated that she spoke of a simple "ficcio." As fascinating as it might be to connect Joan's language to a medieval literary or judicial trope, there is no reason to assume that Joan would have been familiar with the written texts, mostly of learned rather than popular origin, that constituted the medieval allegorical tradition and there is no evidence in records of her speech to suggest that this tradition had any influence upon her discourse. On allegory, see, for example, Angus Fletcher, *Allegory: The Theory of a Symbolic Mode* (Ithaca, N.Y.: Cornell University Press, 1964); Maureen Quilligan, *The Language of Allegory* (Ithaca, N.Y.: Cornell University Press, 1979); and Stephen J. Greenblatt, ed., *Allegory and Representation: Selected Papers from the English Institute, 1979–80* (Baltimore, Md.: Johns Hopkins University Press, 1981). On legal fictions, see Kathy Eden, *Poetic and Legal Fictions in the Aristotelian Tradition* (Princeton: Princeton University Press, 1986); and Owen Barfield, "Poetic and Legal Fiction," in his *Essays Presented to Charles Williams* (Oxford: Oxford University Press, 1947), 106–27. The most relevant discussion of the "figure of truth" like that which Joan employs is still to be found in the commentaries in the rehabilitation documents.

25. Wayman, "The Chancellor and Jeanne d'Arc," 298. Translation is my own.

26. Jean Rogier recalled a letter from Regnault to the people of Reims stating that "Dieu avoit souffert prendre Jehanne la Pucelle pour ce qu'el s'estoit constitué en orgueil, et pour les riches habitz qu'el avoit pris; et qu'el n'avoit faict ce que Dieu luy avoid commandé, ains avoit faict sa volonté," *Procès de condamnation,* ed. Quicherat, 4: 168–69.

27. *Procès en nullité*, ed. Duparc, 2: 139–40.

28. Ibid., 1: 331.

29. John Freccero, "Medusa: The Letter and the Spirit," in *Dante: The Poetics of Conversion* (Cambridge: Harvard University Press, 1986), 119–35, at 130.

30. See Edouard Perroy, *La Guerre de cent ans* (Paris: Gallimard, 1945; translated by W. B. Wells as *The Hundred Years War* [London: Eyre and Spottiswoode, 1951; reprint, New York: Capricorn, 1965]). See also Desmond Seward, *The Hundred Years' War: The English in France, 1337–1453* (New York: Atheneum, 1978).

31. *Procès de condamnation*, ed. Quicherat, 4: 31.

32. Ibid., 472.

33. Ibid., 326 and 328.

34. *Procès en nullité*, ed. Duparc, 2: 33–34

35. Ibid., 203. See also 2: 196–97, 286, 323–26, and 443.

36. Ibid., 5: 158.

37. *Procès de condamnation*, ed. Quicherat, 4: 282.

38. Ibid., 309.

39. Christine de Pizan, *Ditié de Jehanne d'Arc*.

5. The Inquiry at Rouen

1. In this chapter, all page numbers in the text refer to *Procès en nullité*, ed. Duparc, vol. 1.

2. *Procès de condamnation*, ed. Tisset and Lanhers, 1: 74 and 92.

3. Michelet, *Joan of Arc*, 76, 78, 78.

4. Ibid., 77.

5. Ibid., 84.

6. Thomas de Quincey, "Joan of Arc," in *The Collected Writings of Thomas De Quincey*, vol. 5, ed. David Masson (Edinburgh: Adam and Charles Black, 1890), 384–416, at 404.

7. Vita Sackville-West, *Saint Joan of Arc* (New York: Literary Guild, 1936).

8. Warner, *Joan of Arc*, 117.

9. See David von Augsburg [pseudo.], "Der Tractat des David von Augsberg über die Waldesier," ed. W. Preger, *Abhandlungen der bayerischen Akademie der Wissenschaften*, 14, no. 2 (1878): 205–35; Passau Anonymous, in *Quellen zur Geschichte der Waldenser*, ed. Alexander Patschovsky and Kurt-Victor Selge (Gütersloh: Gerd Mohn, 1973), 70–103 (translated by Edward Peters as "The Passau Anonymous: On the Origins of Heresy and the Sect of the Waldensians," in *Heresy and Authority in Medieval Europe: Documents in Translation*, ed. Edward Peters [Philadelphia: University of Pennsylvania Press, 1980], 150–63); Gui, *Practica inquisitionis*, as well as "Bernard Gui's Description of Heresies" in *Heresies of the High Middle Ages: Selected Sources Translated and Annotated*, ed. and trans. Walter L. Wakefield and Austin P. Evans (New York: Columbia University Press, 1969; reprint, 1991), 373–445; Nicholas Eymerich, *Directorium inquisitorum* (Rome:

Ferrarium, 1587; translated by Louis Sala-Molins as *Le Manuel des inquisiteurs* [Paris: Mouton, 1973]). See also Antoine Dondoine, "Le Manuel de l'inquisiteur (1230–1330)," *Archivum Fratrum Praedicatorum* 17 (1947): 85–194, reprint in *Les Hérésies et l'Inquisition, XIIᵉ–XIIIᵉ siècles: Documents et études,* ed. Yves Dossat (Aldershot, England: Variorum, 1990), 84–194; and Wakefield and Evans, "A List of Polemical Sources," in *Heresies of the High Middle Ages,* 633–38.

10. Louis Lambert, *Traité théorique et practique de police judiciaire à l'usage des commissaires de police ainsi que des procureurs de la République, des juges d'instructions, et des autres officiers de police judiciaire,* 2nd and 3rd eds. (Lyons, France: Johannès Desvigne, 1947; reprint 1955), and Robert Borel, *Traité des practiques policières* (Lyons, France: Johannès Desvigne, 1946).

11. Arthur S. Aubry Jr. and Rudolph R. Caputo, *Criminal Interrogation* (Springfield, Ill.: Charles C Thomas, 1965; reprint, 1980); Fred E. Inbau and John E. Reid, *Criminal Interrogation and Confessions* (Baltimore, Md.: Williams and Wilkins, 1962); Charles E. O'Hara and Gregory L. O'Hara, *Fundamentals of Criminal Investigation,* 6th ed. (Springfield, Ill.: Charles C Thomas, 1956; reprint, 1994); and Robert F. Royal and Steven R. Schutt, *The Gentle Art of Interviewing and Interrogation* (Englewood Cliffs, N.J.: Prenctice-Hall, 1976). John Walkley, in *Police Interrogation: A Handbook for Investigation* (Cambridge: Black Bear Press, 1987; reprint, 1990), identifies these four manuals as the most important in the United States, as does Robert Bruce Leibowitz in "The Psychology of Police Confession and the Impact of 'Miranda': A Study of the Interrogative Methods over a Fifty-Year Period," Ph.D. diss., University of California at Santa Cruz, 1991. Justice Earl Warren's opinion on the *Miranda* case, reproduced in Richard J. Medalie, *"Escobedo" to "Miranda": The Anatomy of a Supreme Court Decision* (Washington, D.C.: Lerner Law Book Co., 1966), is particularly illuminating of the contradiction inherent in modern interrogation. On the one hand, Warren criticized interrogation for pressuring the defendant to bear witness against himself despite the U.S. Constitution's Fifth Amendement barring self-incrimination. He complained that "it is obvious that such an interrogation environment is created for no purpose other than to subjugate the individual to the will of his examiner. This atmosphere carries its own badge of intimidation. To be sure, this is not physical intimidation, but it is equally destructive of human dignity" (210). On the other hand, the justice argued that by instituting the *Miranda* warnings, the Court provided "safeguards" that counterweighed the inherently coercive nature of custodial interrogation. Though Warren would have preferred all confessions to result not from police pressures but from the suspect's "free and rational choice," he acknowledged the frequent necessity of police pressure to induce confessions and to solve crimes.

12. Headquarters Department of the Army, *Intelligence Interrogation Field Manual 30–15* (Fort Huachuca, Ariz.: U.S. Army Intelligence Center and School, 1978).

13. Eymerich, *Directorium inquisitorium,* 433b.

14. Ibid., 434a.

15. Ibid.

16. Ibid.

17. Inbau and Reid, *Criminal Interrogation and Confessions*, 80. The army manual likewise proposes what its anonymous authors call the "file and dossier" technique, in which the interrogator confronts the source with a folder, padded with extra paper and festooned with index tabs labeled "education," "employment," "criminal record," "military service," and other categories, and that he read selected known information about the source from this seemingly bulky file. "If the technique is successful," predict the authors of this manual, "the source will be impressed with the 'voluminous' file, conclude that everything is known, and resign himself to complete cooperation during the interrogation" (Department of the Army, *Intelligence Interrogation*, 2–9). Lambert similarly advises, "Even when there is nothing serious in our file (and this is the most frequent occurrence), the man's total ignorance of the state of our inquest and of the degree of our conviction permits us to let him believe in an already persuasive case and an established conviction" (Lambert, *Traité théorique*, 2nd ed., 701–2). He concludes, "A few adroit words tossed negligently on whatever two or three insignificant points of truth which we possess will persuade him that we know all and that it is thus preferable, for him, to move to a confession."

18. Inbau and Reid, *Criminal Interrogation and Confessions*, 80.

19. Eymerich, *Directorium inquisitorum*, 433b. Literally, the inquisitors must "blunt a nail with a nail."

20. Ibid., 433b. To compare, see "*dolo vos cepi*," *Biblia sacra*, 2 Cor. 12:16.

21. Department of the Army, *Intelligence Interrogation*, 1–5.

22. Lambert, *Traité théorique*, 3rd ed., 702, 717.

23. Inbau and Reid, *Criminal Interrogation and Confessions*, 207.

24. Ibid., 208.

25. Lambert, *Traité théorique*, 2nd ed., 698.

26. Eymerich, *Directorium inquisitorum*, 434a.

27. Ibid., 434a.

28. Department of the Army, *Intelligence Interrogation*, 2–11.

29. Ibid.

30. Ibid.

31. Ibid., 2–22.

32. Aubry and Caputo, *Criminal Interrogation*, 240.

33. Ibid., 698–99.

34. Lambert, *Traité théorique*, 3rd ed., 709. Lambert explains, "La tension dont nous parlons ne tient qu'au surmenage de l'intelligence et du système nerveux d'un homme qui, par son crime, a abdiqué cette enviable quiétude de ceux qui n'ont rien fait de contraire aux lois. Ce hors-la-loi qui se cache chez les honnêtes gens et qui même leur jeu, s'épuise à ce double jeu; il craint sans cesse d'avoir commis une maladresse, une imprudence qui le fera prendre. Grande est son anx-

iété lorsqu'il sent l'enquête se dérouler près de lui, alors même qu'elle semble ne pas devoir le toucher.... On conçoit dès lors comme il sera pertinent, à l'égard de cet homme, et de *jouer la conviction, et de prolonger le plus longtemps possible l'interrogatoire,* plus exactement cette scène au cours de laquelle nous le laisserons s'épuiser en de vaines dénégations," ibid., 708.

35. Borel, *Traité des practiques policières,* 180.

36. Department of the Army, *Intelligence Interrogation,* 2–13.

37. Ibid., 2–22.

38. *Biblia sacra,* 1 Cor. 1:22–23, 3:18–19.

39. *Procès de condamnation,* ed. Tisset and Lanhers, 1: 137, 139, and 118.

40. Ibid., 117.

41. Ibid., 73.

42. Ibid., 147.

43. Michelet, *Jeanne d'Arc,* 38. (The introduction to this work is omitted from the translation.)

44. Champion, "On the Trial of Jeanne d'Arc," 534.

45. Warner, *Joan of Arc,* 5.

6. The Confession of Conscience

1. As before, all references in the text will be to Tisset and Lanhers's edition of the trial documents in the first volume of their *Procès de condamnation.*

2. See Bériou, "La Confession dans les écrits théologiques et pastoraux."

3. Michel Foucault, *L'Histoire de la sexualité* (Paris: Gallimard, 1976; reprint, 1997), translated by Robert Hurley as *The History of Sexuality,* vol. 1: *An Introduction* (New York: Vintage Books, 1990), 58–65.

4. *The Tree of Battles of Honoré Bonet,* translated by G. W. Coopland (Liverpool: University Press, 1949), 158–59.

5. See Pierre Rocolle, *Un Prisonnier de guerre nommé Jeanne d'Arc* (Paris: S. O. S., 1982).

7. The Prison Cell

1. This appeal to the pope, and the clerics' dismissal of it, would provide much grounds for discussion at the rehabilitation trial. According to the transcripts of the condemnation trial, the clerics told Joan that it was impossible to seek out the pope because he was too far away and because the clerics at Rouen were authorized to judge her.

2. *Procès en nullité,* ed. Duparc, 1: 225.

3. At the rehabilitation trial, the clerics testified that there had been some confusion on their platform after Joan interrupted Cauchon. Jean Monnet stated that the bishop turned to Henry Beaufort, the cardinal of England and a great-uncle to King Henry VI, to ask him what he should do at this point and that Beaufort instructed him to accept Joan's repentance. Others, however, said that the English protested the Burgundians' acceptance of Joan's abjuration and that

Cauchon overrode their objections. According to Pierre Bouchier, André Marguerie, and Pierre Miget, the English chaplain of the cardinal opposed admitting Joan's abjuration on the grounds that the Burgundians were being too favorable to her (*Procès en nullité*, ed. Duparc, 1: 200, 227, 231). According to Guillaume Du Désert, the chaplain opposed admitting the statement on the grounds that Joan laughed while signing it and thus showed that it was nothing but "una derisio" (213). Jean de Mailly, Guillaume Manchon, and others agreed with Du Désert that Joan was laughing or smiling at this time and did not appear to be taking the abjuration seriously. Bouchier, Du Désert, and Miget stated that Cauchon answered the chaplain angrily, informing him that he was bound to seek Joan's salvation rather than her death and that he would act in accordance with his conscience.

4. The phrase "et qu'elle eust une femme" appears in the French minutes.

5. The Dominican friars Isembard de La Pierre and Martin Lavenu testified at the rehabilitation that Joan had informed them that after her abjuration, "a great English lord" or "a personage having great authority" had entered her cell and had tried to rape her and that she had resumed wearing men's clothes in order to be more capable of resisting such attempts. Guillaume Manchon stated similarly that Joan told them she had resumed wearing men's clothes "ad sue pudicitie defensionem, quia non erat tuta in habitu muliebri cum suis custodibus, qui voluerant attemptare sue pudicitie" and added that all this was contained in the trial (*Procès en nullité*, ed. Duparc, 1: 427). Indeed, according to Manchon and others, Joan had earlier defended her preference for men's clothing by reminding her interrogators of the attempts her guards had made to rape her and that, in one such instance, if Richard of Beauchamp, the earl of Warwick, had not come in response to her cries, they would have succeeded. Jean Massieu, however, testified that Joan had returned to masculine clothes because her feminine dress was taken away from her while she lay asleep. Many witnesses affirmed that after the abjuration, the English cursed and threatened the Burgundians for not having delivered Joan to the secular arm for punishment and that by leaving her vulnerable to sexual assault or by the theft of her clothes, the Burgundians incited Joan to act in a way that would enable them to condemn her as a relapsed heretic. If Joan's return to these clothes was the result not merely of Joan's own initiative but of the clerics' conspiracy with the English against her, then their refusal, recorded in the transcripts from the condemnation trial, to respond to her insinuations of sexual violence or to assume responsibility for promises they allegedly made reflects not simply their conviction that they were not accountable to an accused heretic but a cover-up of their role in bringing her to change her clothes. If they were indeed culpable, then their refusal to respond to Joan or to assume responsibility toward her complemented the Englishmen's violence, and they perpetrated a symbolic violence analogous to the physical violence allegedly perpetrated by the English, a symbolic violence that at once mirrors and exonerates the physical violence perpetrated by their allies. It is this role in bringing about her change of

clothes and her downfall that, according to Lavenu, Joan evoked during her execution: when Joan caught sight of Cauchon, Lavenu related, "eidem dixit quod ipse erat causa sua mortis, et quod sibi promiserat quod eam poneret in manibus Ecclesie, et ipse eam dimiserat in manibus suorum inimicorum capitalium" (*Procès en nullité*, ed. Duparc, 1: 443).

6. Great attention has been paid to the fact that the abjuration included in the trial transcripts does not appear to have been the same as the one Joan signed. The abjuration formulas included in the transcripts, one in French, the other in Latin, are both lengthy and begin with the lines "Toute personne qui a erré" or "Quociens humane mentis oculus," yet the clerics who testified at the rehabilitation, Pierre Miget, Jean Monnet, Guillaume de La Chambre, Nicolas Taquel, Jean Massieu, and Thomas de Courcelles, recalled that Joan had signed a brief document, no more than six to eight lines in length, that began with the words "Je Jehanne." Though some historians have taken this discrepancy as proof that Joan never abjured, Pierre Tisset argues convincingly that "l'abjuration en elle-même, si sa teneur est incertaine, n'est pas discutable (*Procès de condamnation*, ed. Tisset and Lanhers, 3: 135). Tisset has suggested, in order to explain why the short, signed abjuration may have been replaced by a longer, unsigned version in the transcripts, that "pour un esprit du XVe siècle, étant donné que Jeanne a souscrit effectivement une abjuration, ces formules longues qui avec certes plus de véhémence, d'ampleur et de formalisme, articulaient au fond les mêmes choses que la formule de Saint-Ouen, présentatient des garanties de sincérité, voire d'authenticité, comparables à celles de la cédule même souscrite par Jeanne" (141).

7. Aquinas, *Summa Theologiae*, vol. 25, *Sin* (1a2ae, qu. 71–80), Qu. 76, Art. 1, 144.

8. Tisset comments, "Jeanne aimait le son des cloches. Ses compagnons de jeunesse ont rapporté qu'elle s'agenouillait aux champs en les entendant (Jean Watrin, Simonin Musnier); l'ancien marguillier Perrin Drappier se rappelle qu'elle le réprimandait lorsqu'il ne les sonnait point à complies; Dunois dit qu'elle aimait se recueillir le soir à l'église et qu'elle faisait sonner les cloches presque pendant une demi-heure," *Procès de condamnation*, ed. Tisset and Lanhers, 2: 364.

9. Jean Massieu related that the celebration of Holy Communion in which Joan participated was highly irregular. He testified at the rehabilitation that a certain Pierre brought the host on the paten of a chalice, covered by the chalice's linen corporal, without light, assistant, surplice, or stole. Indeed, the judges' decision to allow Joan Communion before her execution has puzzled readers of the trial transcripts since the time of the rehabilitation. It is not clear how they could have administered to Joan a sacrament that tied the individual to the church immediately before pronouncing her excommunication from the church. One explanation is that though the judges felt that Joan still needed to pay her debt to the external tribunal by dying at the stake, they were satisfied, after her second renouncement of her voices and submission to the clerics, that she had paid her debt to the internal tribunal and was thus worthy of Communion. This interpre-

tation requires the reader to accept the authenticity of this second repentance, as depicted in the posthumous documents of the trial and as announced in Henry VI's letters to prelates and potentates, despite the insistence of the final sentence that Joan's persevered in her error. Jean Bréhal at the rehabilitation assumed what would be the prototypical ambivalent stance toward these documents, unsigned by the notaries, when he at once rejected their the validity and excused Joan's behavior as they represented it. As most readers are prepared to believe the authenticity of these documents' depiction of a final interview between the clerics and Joan, of Joan's final illuminations about the sign that was given to her king to persuade him of her mission, and of the penance and Communion that was so well substantiated by the rehabilitation testimony, there seems to be little justification for rejecting Joan's final demeanor.

10. Though the church merely abandoned the relapsed heretic to the secular arm and though it was the secular arm that took upon itself the task of burning him or her at the stake, Joan's execution was unusual in that there was no separate, secular sentence. After Cauchon read the sentence, the bailiff seems to have merely instructed the soldiers to bring Joan to the stake with the words "ducite, ducite" (*Procès en nullité*, ed. Duparc, 1: 427).

Selected Bibliography

Bibliographies

Lanéry d'Arc, Pierre. *Le Livre d'Or de Jeanne d'Arc: Bibliographie raisonée et analytique des ouvrages relatifs à Jeanne d'Arc. Catalogue méthodique, descriptif, et critique des principales études historiques, littéraires, et artistiques, consacrées à la Pucelle d'Orléans depuis le XVe siècle jusqu'à nos jours*. Paris: Techener, 1894. Reprint, Amsterdam: B. R. Grüner, 1970.

Margolis, Nadia. *Joan of Arc in History, Literature, and Film: A Select Annotated Bibliography*. New York: Garland, 1990.

Medieval Texts

Aquinas, Thomas. *Summa theologiae*. 60 vols. Cambridge: Blackfriars, 1964–68.

Basin, Thomas. *Histoire de Charles VII*. Vol. 1: *1407–44*. Edited and translated by Charles Samaran. Paris: Société d'Edition "Les Belles Lettres," 1933. Revised, 1964.

Biblia sacra iuxta vulgatam versionem. Edited by Bonifactius Fischer and Robert Weber. Stuttgart: Deutsche Bibelgesellschaft, 1983.

Boccaccio, Giovanni. *De mulieribus claris*. Edited by Vittorio Zaccaria. Milan: A. Mondadori, 1967. Translated by Guido A. Guarino as *Concerning Famous Women*. New Brunswick, N.J.: Rutgers University Press, 1963.

Bullaire de l'Inquisition française au XIVe siècle et jusqu'à la fin du Grand Schisme. Edited by J. M. Vidal. Paris: Librairie Letouzey et Ané, 1913.

de Cagny, Perceval. *Chronique des ducs d'Alençon.* Edited by Henri Moranvillé. Paris: Librairie C. Klincksieck, 1902.

Chartier, Alain. *Epistola de Puella.* In *Oeuvres latines,* edited by Pascale Bourgain-Hemeryck, 44–53. Paris: Centre National de la Recherche Scientifique, 1977.

Chartier, Jean. *Chronique de Charles VII.* 3 vols. Edited by Auguste Vallet de Viriville. Paris: Pierre Jannet, 1858.

Chartularium Universitatis Parisiensis. Vol. 4: *1393–1452.* Edited by Heinrich Denifle and Emile Châtelain. Paris: Delalain, 1897.

Chastellain, Georges. *Chronique des ducs de Bourgogne.* Vols. 1–5 of *Oeuvres.* Edited by Joseph Kervyn de Lettenhove. Brussels: Académie Royale de Belgique, 1863–66. Reprint, Geneva: Slatkine, 1971.

Christine de Pizan. *Ditié de Jehanne d'Arc.* Edited by Angus J. Kennedy and Kenneth Varty. Oxford: Society for the Study of Medieval Languages and Literatures, 1977.

———. "The *Livre de la cité des dames* of Christine de Pizan: A Critical Edition." 2 vols. Edited by Maureen C. Curnow. Ph.D. diss., Vanderbilt University, 1975. Also in English as *The Book of the City of Ladies,* translated by Earl Jeffrey Richards. New York: Persea Press, 1982.

Chronique de la Pucelle, ou Chronique de Cousinot. Edited by Auguste Vallet de Viriville. Paris: Auguste Delahays, 1859. Reprint, Paris: Garnier, 1888.

Chronique du Mont-Saint-Michel (1343–1468). 2 vols. Edited by Siméon Luce. Paris: Firmin Didot, 1879–83.

Confessions et jugements de criminels au Parlement de Paris (1319–1350). Edited by Monique Langlois and Yvonne Lanhers. Paris: S.E.V.P.E.N., 1971.

Eymerich, Nicholas. *Directorium inquisitorum.* Rome: Ferrarium, 1587. Translated by Louis Sala-Molins as *Le Manuel des inquisiteurs.* Paris: Mouton, 1973.

de Fauquembergue, Clément. *Journal.* 3 vols. Edited by Alexandre Tuetey and Henri Lacaille. Paris: Renouard, 1903–15.

Le Franc, Martin. *Le Champion des Dames.* Edited by Arthur Piaget. Lausanne: Payot, 1968.

Gerson, Jean. *Oeuvres complètes,* 10 vols. Edited by Palémon Glorieux. Paris: Desclée, 1960–73.

———. "De mirabili victoria." In *Procès en nullité de la condamnation de Jeanne d'Arc,* 5 vols., edited by Pierre Duparc, 2: 33–39. Paris: Klinksieck, 1977–89.

————. "De quadam puella." In "The Chancellor and Jeanne d'Arc," by Dorothy G. Wayman, 296–303. *Franciscan Studies* 17 (1957): 273–303.

Gui, Bernard. *Practica inquisitionis heretice pravitatis.* Edited by Célestin Douais. Paris: Picard, 1886.

————. *Manuel de l'inquisiteur.* 2 vols. Edited and translated by Guillaume Mollat. Paris: Champion, 1926–27.

Hohmann, Thomas, ed. and trans. *Heinrich von Langenstein "Unterschiedung der Geister": Lateinische und deutsche Texte und Untersuchungen zu Ubersetzungsliteratur aus der Wiener Schule.* Munich: Artemis Verlag, 1977.

Instrument public des sentences portées les 24 et 30 mai 1431 par Pierre Cauchon et Jean Le Maître contre Jeanne la Pucelle. Edited by Paul Doncoeur and Yvonne Lanhers. Melun, France: d'Argences, 1954.

Journal d'un Bourgeois de Paris. Edited by Colette Beaune. Paris: Lettres Gothiques, 1991.

Kramer, Heinrich, and James Sprenger. *The Malleus Maleficarum.* Translated by Montague Summers. New York: Dover, 1971.

Lefèvre de Saint-Remy, Jean. *Chronique.* 2 vols. Edited by François Morand. Paris: Jules Renouard, 1876–81.

McNeill, John T., and Helena M. Gamer, eds. *Medieval Handbooks of Penance: A Translation of the Principal "Libri Poenitentiales" and Selections from Related Documents.* New York: Columbia University Press, 1938.

La Minute française de l'Interrogatoire de Jeanne la Pucelle, d'après le réquisitoire de Jean d'Estivet et les manuscrits d'Urfé et d'Orléans. Edited by Paul Doncoeur and Yvonne Lanhers. Melun, France: d'Argences, 1952.

de Monstrelet, Enguerrand. *Chroniques: 1400–1444.* 6 vols. Edited by Louis Claude Douët d'Arcq. Paris: Jules Renouard, 1857–62.

Monumenta conciliorum generalium seculi XV Concilium Basiliense, Scriptores. 4 vols. Edited by Frantisek Palacky, Ernst Ritter von Birk, Karl Stehlin, Konrad Wilhelm Hieronimus. Vienna and Basel, Switzerland: Adolphus Holzausen, 1857–1935.

Morosini, Antonio. *Chronique: Extraits relatifs à l'histoire de France.* 4 vols. Translated and edited by Léon Dorez. Paris: Renouard, 1892–1902.

A Parisian Journal, 1405–1449. Edited by Janet Shirley. Oxford: Clarendon Press, 1968.

Patrologiae cursus completus . . . Series latina. Edited by J.-P. Migne. Paris: Garnier Frères, 1844–64.

Petroff, Elizabeth Alvida, ed. *Medieval Women's Visionary Literature.* Oxford: Oxford University Press, 1986.

Le Procès de condamnation de Jeanne d'Arc. 2 vols. Edited by Pierre Champion. Paris: Edouard Champion, 1920–21.

Procès de condamnation de Jeanne d'Arc. 3 vols. Edited by Pierre Tisset and Yvonne Lanhers. Paris: Klinksieck, 1960–71.

Le Procès de condamnation de Jeanne d'Arc: Reproduction en fac-simile du manuscrit authentique. Edited by Jean Marchand. Paris: Plon, 1955.

Procès de condamnation et de réhabilitation de Jeanne d'Arc dite la Pucelle. Publiés pour la première fois d'après les manuscrits de la Bibliothèque Royale, suivis de tous les documents historiques qu'on a pu réunir et accompagnés de notes et d'éclaircissements. 5 vols. Edited by Jules-Etienne-Joseph Quicherat. Paris: Jules Renouard, 1841–49.

Le Procès de Gilles de Rais. Edited by Georges Bataille. Translated by Pierre Klossowski. Paris: Société Nouvelle des Editions Pauvert, 1965. Translated by Richard Robinson as *The Trial of Gilles de Rais* (Los Angeles: Amok Books, 1991).

Procès en nullité de la condamnation de Jeanne d'Arc. 5 vols. Edited by Pierre Duparc. Paris: Klinksieck, 1977–89.

Critical Texts

Anson, John. "The Female Transvestite in Early Monasticism: The Origin and Development of a Motif." *Viator* 5 (1974): 1–30.

L'Aveu: Antiquité et Moyen Age. Actes de la Table Ronde organisée par l'Ecole Française de Rome avec le concours du Centre National de la Recherche Scientifique et l'Université de Trieste, Rome, 28–30 March 1984. Rome: Ecole Française de Rome, 1986.

Ayroles, Jean-Baptiste-Joseph. *Les Iniquités du procès de condamnation de la Vénérable Jeanne la Pucelle.* Lyons, France: Imprimerie X. Jevain, 1904.

———. *L'Université de Paris au temps de Jeanne d'Arc et la cause de sa haine contre la Libératrice.* Paris: X. Rondelet et Cie, 1902.

Baldwin, John W. "The Intellectual Preparation of the Canon of 1215 against Ordeals." *Speculum* 36 (1961): 613–36.

Barricelli, Jean-Pierre. "Transcript, Legend, and Art: The Thematology of Joan of Arc." *Canadian Review of Comparative Literature/Revue candadienne de littérature comparée,* June 1988: 177–200.

Barstow, Anne Llewellyn. *Joan of Arc: Heretic, Mystic, Shaman.* Lewiston, Maine: Edwin Mellen Press, 1986.

Bartlett, Robert. *Trial by Fire and Water: The Medieval Judicial Order.* Oxford: Clarendon Press, 1986.

Bazan, Bernardo C. "La *Quaestio Disputata*." In *Les Genres littéraires dans les sources théologiques et philosophiques médiévales: Définition, critique, et exploitation,* 31–49. Actes du Colloque international de Louvain-la-Neuve, 25–27 May 1981. Louvain-la-Neuve, Belgium: Publications de l'Institut d'Etudes Médiévales de l'Université Catholique de Louvain, 1984.

Beaune, Colette. *Naissance de la nation France.* Paris: Gallimard, 1985. Edited by Frederic L. Cheyette. Translated by Susan Ross Huston as *The Birth of an Ideology: Myths and Symbols of Power in Late-Medieval France.* Berkeley: University of California Press, 1991.

de Beaurepaire, Charles Robillard. *Notes sur les juges et les assesseurs du procès de condamnation de Jeanne d'Arc.* Rouen, France: Espérance Cagniard, 1890.

———. *Recherches sur le procès de condamnation de Jeanne d'Arc.* Rouen, France: Lebrument, 1869.

Belmont, Nicole. "Folk Beliefs and Legends about Fairies in France." In *Mythologies,* edited by Yves Bonnefoy and Wendy Doniger, translated by David White, 2: 743–46. Chicago: University of Chicago Press, 1991.

Bériou, Nicole. "La Confession dans les écrits théologiques et pastoraux du XIIIᵉ siècle: Médication de l'âme ou démarche judicaire?" In *L'Aveu: Antiquité et Moyen Age,* 261–80. Actes de la Table Ronde organisée par l'Ecole Française de Rome avec le concours du Centre National de la Recherche Scientifique et l'Université de Trieste, Rome, 28–30 March 1984. Rome: Ecole Française de Rome, 1986.

Billard, André. *Jehanne d'Arc et ses juges.* Paris: Editions Auguste Picard, 1933.

Black, Antony. *Council and Commune: The Conciliar Movement and the Fifteenth-Century Heritage.* London: Burns and Oats, 1979.

———. "The Universities and the Council of Basle: Collegium and Council." In *The Universities in the Late Middle Ages,* edited by Jozef Ijsewijn and Jacques Paquet, 511–23. Leuven, Belgium: Leuven University Press, 1978.

Bloch, R. Howard. *Medieval French Literature and Law.* Berkeley: University of California Press, 1977.

Boissonnade, Prosper. "Une Etape capitale dans la mission de Jeanne d'Arc: Le Séjour de la Pucelle à Poitiers, la quadruple enquête et ses résultats (1ᵉʳ mars–10 avril 1429)." *Revue des questions historiques* 113 (1930): 12–67.

Boland, Paschal. *The Concept of "Discretio Spirituum" in John Gerson's "De Probatione Spirituum" and "De Distinctione Verarum Visionum a Falsis."* Washington, D.C.: Catholic University of America Press, 1959.

Boulet-Sautel, Marguerite. "Aperçu sur les systèmes des preuves dans la France coutumière du Moyen Age." In *La Preuve: Recueils de la Société Jean Bodin pour l'Histoire Comparative des Institutions.* Vol. 2: *Moyen Age et temps modernes,* 275–325. Brussels: Editions de la Librarie Encyclopédique, 1965.

Bouzy, Olivier. "Prédication ou récupération: Les prophéties autour de Jeanne d'Arc dans les premiers mois de l'année 1429." *Bulletin de l'Association des Amis du Centre Jeanne d'Arc* 14 (1990): 39–55.

———. "Transcription Errors in Texts of Joan of Arc's History." In *Fresh Verdicts on Joan of Arc,* edited by Bonnie Wheeler and Charles T. Wood, 73–83. New York: Garland, 1996.

Boyle, Leonard E. "The Summa for Confessors as a Genre and Its Religious Intent." In *The Pursuit of Holiness in Late Medieval and Renaissance Religion,* edited by Charles Trinkhaus with Heiko A. Oberman, 126–30. Leiden, Netherlands: E. J. Brill, 1979.

———. "Summae Confessorum." In *Les Genres littéraires dans les sources théologiques et philosophiques médiévales: Définition, critique, et exploitation,* 227–37. Actes du Colloque international de Louvain-la-Neuve, 25–27 May 1981. Louvain-la-Neuve, Belgium: Publications de l'Institut d'Etudes Médiévales de l'Université Catholique de Louvain, 1984.

Bühler-Reimann, Theodor. "Enquête—Inquesta—Inquisitio." *Zeitschrift der Savigny-Stiftung für Rechtsgeschichte,* Kanonische Abteilung 92 (1975): 53–62.

Bynum, Caroline Walker. ". . . and Woman His Humanity: Female Imagery in the Religious Writing of the Later Middle Ages." In *Gender and Religion: On the Complexity of Symbols,* edited by Caroline Walker Bynum, Steven Harrell, and Paula Richman, 257–88. Boston: Beacon Press, 1986. Reprint in *Fragmentation and Redemption: Essays on Gender and the Human Body in Medieval Religion,* 151–79. New York: Zone Books, 1991.

———. *Holy Feast and Holy Fast: The Religious Significance of Food to Medieval Women.* Berkeley: University of California Press, 1987.

———. "Religious Women in the Later Middle Ages." In *Christian Spirituality: High Middle Ages and Reformation,* edited by Jill Raitt, 121–39. New York: Crossroad, 1985.

———. "Women's Stories, Women's Symbols: A Critique of Victor Turner's Theory of Liminality." In *Anthropology and the Study of Religion,* edited by Frank Reynolds and Robert Moore, 105–25. Chicago: Center for the Scientific Study of Religion, 1984. Reprinted in *Fragmentation and Redemption: Essays on Gender and the Human Body in Medieval Religion,* 27–51. New York: Zone Books, 1991.

Carolus-Barré, Louis. "'Jeanne, êtes-vous en état de grâce?' et les prières du prône au XVᵉ siècle." *Bulletin de la Société des Antiquaires de France,* 1958: 204–8.

Cazenave, Annie. "Aveu et Contrition: Manuels de confession et interrogatoires d'Inquisition en Languedoc et en Catalogne (XIIIe–XIVe siècles)." In *La Piété populaire au Moyen Age,* vol. 1, 333–53. Actes du 99e Congrès National des Sociétés Savantes, Besançon, 1974. Paris: Bibliothèque Nationale, 1977.

Champion, Pierre. "Les Juges de Jeanne d'Arc." *Revue universelle* 1 (1920): 301–12.

———. Introduction to volume 2 of *Procès de condamnation.* Translated by Coley Taylor and Ruth R. Kerr as "On the Trial of Jeanne d'Arc." In *The Trial of Joan of Arc: Translated into English from the Original Latin and French Documents,* edited by Wilfred Phillip Barrett, 477–539. London: Routledge, 1931. Reprint, New York, 1932.

Charpentier, Jacques. "A propos du procès de Jeanne d'Arc." *Revue de Paris* 70 (1963): 48–52.

Chenu, Marie-Dominique. *Introduction à l'étude de Saint Thomas d'Aquin.* Montreal: Institut d'Etudes Médiévales, 1950. Translated by A. M. Landry and D. Hughes as *Toward Understanding Saint Thomas.* Chicago: Henry Regnery Company, 1964.

Chevalier, Ulysse. "L'Abjuration de Jeanne d'Arc au cimetière de St-Ouen et l'authenticité de sa formule: Etude critique." *Mémoires de l'Académie des sciences de Lyon* 7 (1903): 87–170.

Chiffoleau, Jacques. "Sur la practique et la conjoncture de l'aveu judiciaire en France du XIIIe au XVe siècle." In *L'Aveu: Antiquité et Moyen Age,* 341–80. Actes de la Table Ronde organisée par l'Ecole Française de Rome avec le concours du Centre National de la Recherche Scientifique et l'Université de Trieste, Rome, 28–30 March 1984. Rome: Ecole Française de Rome, 1986.

Christian, William A. *Apparitions in Late Medieval and Renaissance Spain.* Princeton: Princeton University Press, 1981.

Cohn, Norman. *Europe's Inner Demons: An Enquiry Inspired by the Great Witch-Hunt.* New York: Basic Books, 1975.

Contamine, Philippe. *De Jeanne d'Arc aux Guerres d'Italie: Figures, images, et problèmes du XVe siècle.* Orléans: Paradigme, 1994.

Copeland, Rita. "Why Women Can't Read: Medieval Hermeneutics, Statutory Law, and the Lollard Heresy Trials." In *Representing Women: Law, Literature, and Feminism,* edited by Susan Sage Heinzelman and Zipporah Batshaw Wiseman, 253–386. Durham, N.C.: Duke University Press, 1994.

Crane, Susan. "Clothing and Gender Definition: Joan of Arc." *Journal of Medieval and Early Modern Studies* 26, no. 2 (Spring 1996): 297–320.

David, Jean-Michel. "La Faute et l'abandon: Théories et practiques judicaires à Rome à la fin de la république." In *L'Aveu: Antiquité et Moyen Age,* 69–87. Actes de la Table Ronde organisée par l'Ecole Française de Rome avec le concours du Centre National de la Recherche Scientifique et l'Université de Trieste, Rome, 28–30 March 1984. Rome: Ecole Française de Rome, 1986.

Davis, Natalie Zemon. *Fiction in the Archives: Pardon Tales and Their Tellers in Sixteenth-Century France.* Stanford, Calif.: Stanford University Press, 1987.

———. *The Return of Martin Guerre.* Cambridge: Harvard University Press, 1983.

———. *Society and Culture in Early Modern France.* Stanford, Calif.: Stanford University Press, 1965. Reprint, 1975.

Defourneaux, Marcelin. *La Vie quotidienne au temps de Jeanne d'Arc.* Paris: Hachette, 1952.

Delaruelle, Etienne. *La Piété populaire au Moyen Age.* Turin: Bottega d'Erasmo, 1975.

Delaruelle, Etienne, Edmond René Labande, and Paul Ourliac. *L'Eglise au temps du Grand Schisme et de la crise conciliaire (1378–1449).* Paris: Bloud and Gay, 1962–64.

Delcourt, Marie. "Le complexe de Diane dans l'hagiographie chrétienne." *Revue de l'Histoire des Religions* 153 (1958): 1–33.

Denifle, Heinrich, and Emile Châtelain. *Le Procès de Jeanne d'Arc et l'Université de Paris.* Nogent-le-Rotrou, France: Imprimerie Daupeley-Gouverneur, 1897.

Desama, Claude. "La Première Entrevue de Jeanne d'Arc et de Charles VII à Chinon (mars 1429)." *Analecta Bollandiana* 84, nos. 1, 2 (1966): 113–26.

De Vries, Kelly. "A Woman As Leader of Men: Joan of Arc's Military Career." In *Fresh Verdicts on Joan of Arc,* edited by Bonnie Wheeler and Charles T. Wood, 3–18. New York: Garland, 1996.

Dinzelbacher, Peter. *Vision und Visionliteratur im Mittelalter.* Stuttgart: Anton Hiersemank, 1981.

Dinzelbacher, Peter, and Dieter R. Bauer, eds. *Frauenmystik im Mittelalter.* Ostfildern bei Stuttgart: Schwabenverlag, 1983.

Dondoine, Antoine. "Le Manuel de l'inquisiteur (1230–1330)." *Archivum Fratrum Praedicatorum* 17 (1947): 85–194. Reprint in *Les Hérésies et l'Inquisition, XIIe-XIIIe siècles: Documents et études,* edited by Yves Dossat, 84–194. Aldershot, England: Variorum, 1990.

Dubois, Page. *Torture and Truth.* London: Routledge, 1991.

Dumas, Georges. "Letter from Doctor G. Dumas." In Anatole France, *The Life of Joan of Arc,* translated by Winifred Stephens, 2:401–6. New York: John Lane, 1908. Revised 1909.

Dunand, Philippe-Hector. *Etude historique sur les voix et visions de Jeanne d'Arc.* 2 vols. Paris: Charles Poussielgue, 1903.

Duparc, Pierre. "La Délivrance d'Orléans et la mission de Jeanne d'Arc." In *Jeanne d'Arc: Une Epoque, un rayonnement*, 153–54. Colloque d'Histoire Médiévale, Orléans, 1979. Paris: Editions du Centre National de la Recherche Scientifique, 1982.

Dworkin, Andrea. "Virginity." In *Intercourse*, chap. 6. New York: Free Press, 1987.

Enders, Jody. *Rhetoric and the Origins of Medieval Drama*. Ithaca, N.Y.: Cornell University Press, 1992.

Esmein, Adémar. *Histoire de la procédure criminelle en France et spécialement de la procédure inquisitoire depuis le XIIIe siècle jusqu'à nos jours*. Paris: I. Larose et Forcel, 1882. Translated by John Simpson as *A History of Continental Criminal Procedure with Special Reference to France*. Boston: Little, Brown, 1914. Reprint, South Hackensack, N.J.: Rothman Reprints, 1968.

Faire Croire: Modalités de la diffusion et de la réception des messages réligieux du XIIe au XVe siècles. Actes de la Table Ronde, Rome, 1979. Rome: Ecole Française de Rome, 1981.

Favier, Jean. *Paris au XVe siècle, 1380–1500*. Paris: Association d'une Histoire de Paris, 1974.

Feret, Pierre. *La Faculté de Théologie de Paris et ses docteurs les plus célèbres*. Vol. 4: *Moyen Age*. Paris: Alphone Picard et Fils, 1897.

Foucault, Michel. *Surveiller et Punir: Naissance de la Prison*. Paris: Gallimard, 1975. Reprint, 1993. Translated by Alan Sheridan as *Discipline and Punish: The Birth of the Prison*. New York: Vintage Books, 1979.

———. *L'Histoire de la sexualité*. Paris: Gallimard, 1976. Reprint, 1997. Translated by Robert Hurley as *The History of Sexuality*, vol. 1: *An Introduction*. New York: Vintage Books, 1990.

Fournier, Paul. *Les Officialités au Moyen Age: Etude sur l'organisation, la compétence, et la procédure des tribunaux ecclésiastiques ordinaires en France de 1180 à 1328*. Paris: Plon, 1880.

Fraikin, Jean. "Notices des sources du procès de Jeanne d'Arc." In *Jeanne d'Arc: Une Epoque, un rayonnement*, 227–36. Colloque d'Histoire Médiévale, Orléans, 1979. Paris: Editions du Centre National de la Recherche Scientifique, 1982.

———. "Regard sur l'au-delà de Jeanne d'Arc." *Tradition wallonne* 10 (1993): 50–51.

———. "Was Joan of Arc a 'Sign' of Charles VII's Innocence?" In *Fresh Verdicts on Joan of Arc*, edited by Bonnie Wheeler and Charles T. Wood, 61–72. New York: Garland, 1996.

Fraioli, Deborah. "L'Image de Jeanne d'Arc: Que doit-elle au milieu littéraire et religieux de son temps?" In *Jeanne d'Arc: Une Epoque, un rayonnement*, 191–96.

Colloque d'Histoire Médiévale, Orléans, 1979. Paris: Editions du Centre National de la Recherche Scientifique, 1982.

————. "The Literary Image of Joan of Arc: Prior Influences." *Speculum* 56 (1981): 811–30.

France, Anatole. *Vie de Jeanne d'Arc*. 2 vols. Paris: Calmann-Lévy, 1908. Revised, 1909. Translated by Winifred Stephens as *The Life of Joan of Arc*. 2 vols. New York: John Lane, 1908. Revised, 1909.

Francq, H. G. "Jean Gerson's Theological Treatise and Other Memoirs in Defence of Joan of Arc." *Revue de l'Université d'Ottowa* 41, no. 1. (January–March 1971): 58–80.

Garçon, Maurice. "Les Procès de Jeanne d'Arc. Portrait de juges." *Les Annales* 64 (1967): 5–19.

Les Genres littéraires dans les sources théologiques et philosophiques médiévales: Définition, critique, et exploitation. Actes du Colloque International de Louvain-la-Neuve, 25–27 May 1981. Louvain-la-Neuve, Belgium: Publications de l'Institut d'Etudes Médiévales de l'Université Catholique de Louvain, 1984.

Ginzburg, Carlo. *I Benandanti: Richerche sulle stregoneria e sui culti agrari tra cinquecento e seicento*. Turin: Guilio Einaudi, 1966. Translated by John and Anne C. Tedeschi as *Night Battles: Witchcraft and Agrarian Cults in the Sixteenth and Seventeenth Centuries*. Harmondsworth, England: Penguin Books, 1985.

————. "Checking the Evidence: The Judge and the Historian." *Critical Inquiry* 18, no. 1 (Autumn 1991): 79–92.

————. *Il Formaggio e i vermi: Il cosmo di un mugnario del'500*. Torino: Giulio Einaudi, 1976. Translated by John and Anne C. Tedeschi as *The Cheese and the Worms: The Cosmos of a Sixteenth-Century Miller*. Baltimore, Md.: Johns Hopkins University Press, 1980.

————. *Miti, emblemi, spie: morfologia e storia*. Turin: Giulio Einaudi, 1986. Translated by John and Anne C. Tedeschi as *Clues, Myths, and the Historical Method*, 156–69. Baltimore, Md.: Johns Hopkins University Press, 1984.

————. *Storia notturna: una decifrazione del Sabba*. Turin: Giulio Einaudi, 1989. Translated by Raymond Rosenthal as *Ecstasies: Deciphering the Witches' Sabbath*. Harmondsworth, England: Penguin, 1992.

Glénisson, Jean, and Victor Deodato da Silva. "La Practique et le rituel de la reddition aux XIVe et XVe siècles." In *Jeanne d'Arc: Une Epoque, un rayonnement*, 113–22. Colloque d'Histoire Médiévale, Orléans, 1979. Paris: Editions du Centre National de la Recherche Scientifique, 1982.

Glorieux, Palémon. *La Littérature quodlibétique de 1260 à 1320*. 2 vols. Brussels: Le Salchoir Kain, 1925.

Grabmann, Martin. *Die Geschichte der scholastischen Methode*. 2 vols. Berlin: Akademie Verlag, 1985–88.

Gravdal, Kathryn. *Ravishing Maidens: Sexual Violence in Medieval French Literature and Law*. Philadelphia: University of Pennsylvania Press, 1980.

Guenée, Simonne. *Bibliogaphie de l'histoire des universités français des origines à nos jours*. Vol. 1: *Généralités: Université de Paris*. Paris: A. et J. Picard, 1981.

Guillemain, Bernard. "Une Carrière: Pierre Cauchon." In *Jeanne d'Arc: Une Epoque, un rayonnement*, 217–27. Colloque d'Histoire Médiévale, Orléans, 1979. Paris: Editions du Centre National de la Recherche Scientifique, 1982.

Gy, Pierre-Marie. "Le Précepte de la confession annuelle et la détection des hérétiques." *Revue des sciences philosophiques et théologiques* 58 (1974): 444–50.

———. "Les Bases de la pénitence moderne." *La Maison-Dieu* 117 (1974): 63–85.

———. "Les Définitions de la confession après le quatrième concile du Latran." In *L'Aveu: Antiquité et Moyen Age*, 283–96. Actes de la Table Ronde organisée par l'Ecole Française de Rome avec le concours du Centre National de la Recherche Scientifique et l'Université de Trieste, Rome, 28–30 March 1984. Rome: Ecole Française de Rome, 1986.

Hadot, Pierre. "La Préhistoire des genres littéraires philosophiques médiévales dans l'Antiquité." In *Les Genres littéraires dans les sources théologiques et philosophiques médiévales: Définition, critique, et exploitation*, 1–9. Actes du Colloque international de Louvain-la-Neuve, 25–27 May 1981. Louvain-la-Neuve, Belgium: Publications de l'Institut d'Etudes Médiévales de l'Université Catholique de Louvain, 1984.

Hanawalt, Barbara A., and Susan Noakes. "Trial Transcript, Romance, Propaganda: Joan of Arc and the French Body Politic." *Modern Language Quarterly* 57, no. 4 (December 1996): 605–31.

Harf-Lancner, Laurence. *Les Fées au Moyen Age: Morgane et Mélusine. La naissances des fées*. Geneva: Editions Slatkine, 1984.

Harmand, Adrien. *Jeanne d'Arc: Ses costumes, son armure. Essai de reconstitution*. Paris: Librairie Ernest Leroux, 1929.

Hotchkiss, Valerie R. *Clothes Make the Man: Female Cross Dressing in Medieval Europe*. New York: Garland, 1996.

Huizinga, Johan. *Herfsttij der Middeleeuwen: Studie over levens- en gedachtenvormen der veertiende en vijftiende eeuw in Frankrijk en de Nederlanden*. Haarlem, Netherlands: H. D. Tjeenk, Willink, 1919. Translated by Rodney J. Payton and Lurich Mammitzsch as *The Autumn of the Middle Ages*. Chicago: University of Chicago Press, 1996.

Jantzen, Grace M. *Power, Gender, and Christian Mysticism*. Cambridge: Cambridge University Press, 1995.

Jeanne d'Arc: Une Epoque, un rayonnement. Colloque d'Histoire Médiévale, Orléans, October 1979. Paris: Editions du Centre National de la Recherche Scientifique, 1982.

Jeay, Madeleine. "Clercs et paysans au XVe siècle: Une relecture de l'épisode de l'arbre aux fées dans le procès de Jeanne d'Arc." In *Normes et pouvour à la fin du Moyen Age,* 145–63. Actes du colloque La Recherche en Études Médiévales au Québec et en Ontario, 16–17 May 1989, Montreal. Edited by Marie-Claude Déprez-Masson. Montreal: Editions CERES, 1989.

Justice, Steven. "Inquisition, Speech, and Writing: A Case from Late-Medieval Norwich." In *Criticism and Dissent in the Middle Ages,* edited by Rita Copeland, 289–322. Cambridge: Cambridge University Press, 1996.

Kelly, H. Ansgar. "The Right to Remain Silent: Before and after Joan of Arc." *Speculum* 68, no. 4 (October 1993): 992–1026.

Kieckhefer, Richard. *Unquiet Souls: Fourteenth-Century Saints and Their Religious Milieu.* Chicago: University of Chicago Press, 1984.

———. *European Witch Trials: Their Foundation in Popular and Learned Culture, 1300–1500.* Berkeley: University of California Press, 1976.

Kleinberg, Aviad M. *Prophets in Their Own Country: Living Saints and the Making of Sainthood in the Later Middle Ages.* Chicago: University of Chicago Press, 1992.

Krumeich, Gerd. *Jeanne d'Arc in der Geschichte: Historiographie, Politik, Kultur.* Sigmaringen, Germany: J. Thorbecke, 1989.

La Capra, Dominick. *History and Criticism.* Ithaca, N.Y.: Cornell University Press, 1985.

———. *Rethinking Intellectual History: Texts, Contexts, Language.* Ithaca, N.Y.: Cornell University Press, 1983.

Lagorio, Valerie M. "The Medieval Continental Women Mystics: An Introduction." In *An Introduction to the Medieval Mystics of Europe,* edited by Paul E. Szarmach, 161–93. Albany: SUNY Press, 1984.

Lang, Andrew. *La "Jeanne d'Arc" de M. Anatole France.* Paris: Perrin, 1909.

———. *The Maid of France: Being the Story of the Life and Death of Jeanne d'Arc.* London: Longmans, Green, 1908. Revised, 1909.

———. "The Voices of Jeanne d'Arc." In *The Valet's Tragedy and Other Studies,* 193–227. London: Longmans, Green, 1903.

Langbein, John H. *Torture and the Law of Proof: Europe and England in the Ancien Régime.* Chicago: University of Chicago Press, 1977.

Lea, Henry Charles. *A History of Auricular Confession and Indulgences in the Latin Church.* 3 vols. Philadelphia: Lea Brothers, 1896. Reprint, New York: Greenwood Press, 1968.

———. *A History of the Inquisition of the Middle Ages.* 3 vols. New York: Harper and Bros., 1887. Reprint, New York: Macmillan Company, 1922.

———. *Superstition and Force: Essays on the Wager of Law, the Wager of Battle, the Ordeal, Torture.* 3 vols. Philadephia: Lea Brothers, 1866.

Le Cacheux, Paul. *Rouen au temps de Jeanne d'Arc et pendant l'occupation anglaise (1419–1449).* Paris: Auguste Picard, 1931.

Leff, Gordon. *Paris and Oxford Universities in the Thirteenth and Fourteenth Centuries: An Institutional and Intellectual History.* New York: John Wiley and Sons, 1968.

Legendre, Pierre. "Aux Sources de la culture occidentale: L'Ancien droit de la pénitence." In *Ecrits juridiques du Moyen Age occidental,* 575–95. London: Variorum Reprints, 1988.

Le Goff, Jacques, ed. *Hérésies et sociétés dans l'Europe pre-industrielle, 11ᵉ–18ᵉ siècles.* Paris: Mouton, 1968.

———. *L'Imaginaire médiéval.* Paris: Gallimard, 1985. Translated by Arthur Goldhammer as *The Medieval Imagination.* Chicago: University of Chicago Press, 1988.

———. *Les Intellectuels au Moyen Age.* Paris: Editions du Seuil, 1957. Reprint, 1985. Translated by Teresa Lavender Fagan as *Intellectuals in the Middle Ages.* Cambridge: Basil Blackwell, 1993.

Lerner, Robert E. *The Heresy of the Free Spirit in the Later Middle Ages.* Berkeley: University of California Press, 1972.

Le Roy Ladurie, Emmanuel. *Montaillou, village occitan de 1294 à 1324.* Paris: Editions Gallimard, 1975. Translated and abridged by Barbara Bray as *Montaillou: The Promised Land of Error.* New York: Vintage Books, 1979.

Lethel, François-Marie. "Jeanne d'Arc et l'ange." In *Colloque sur l'ange,* 55–70. Centre européen d'art sacré. Pont-à-Mousson, Meurthe-et-Moselle, 26–28 June 1981. Abbaye des Prémontrés, Pont-à-Mousson, France: Imprimerie du Centre Culturel des Prémontrés, 1982.

———. "La Soumission à l'Eglise militante: Un Aspect théologique de la condamnation de Jeanne d'Arc." In *Jeanne d'Arc: Une Epoque, un rayonnement,* 181–91. Colloque d'Histoire Médiévale, Orléans, 1979. Paris: Editions du Centre National de la Recherche Scientifique, 1982.

Lévy, Jean-Philippe. *La Hiérarchie des preuves dans le droit savant du Moyen Age depuis la Renaissance du droit romain jusqu'à la fin du XIVᵉ siècle.* Paris: Librarie de Recueils Sirey, 1939.

—————. "Le Problème de la preuve dans les droits savants du Moyen Age." In *La Preuve: Recueils de la Société Jean Bodin pour l'Histoire Comparative des Institutions*. Vol. 2: *Moyen Age et temps modernes*, 137–67. Brussels: Editions de la Librarie Encyclopédique, 1965.

Lightbody, Charles Wayland. *The Judgments of Joan: Joan of Arc, a Study in Cultural History*. Cambridge: Harvard University Press, 1961.

Little, Lester. "Les Techniques de la confession et la confession comme technique." In *Faire Croire: Modalités de la diffusion et de la réception des messages réligieux du XIIe au XVe siècles*, 87–99. Actes de la Table Ronde, Rome, 1979. Rome: Ecole Française de Rome, 1981.

Luce, Siméon. *Jeanne d'Arc à Domremy: Recherches critiques sur les origines de la mission de la Pucelle*. Paris: Champion, 1886.

Makdis, George. "The Scholastic Method in Medieval Education: An Inquiry into Its Origin in Law and Theology." *Speculum* 49 (1974): 640–61.

Manselli, Raoul. "De la *persuasio* à la *coercitio*." Le *Crédo, la morale, et l'Inquisition*. *Cahiers de Fanjeaux* 6 (1971): 175–97.

Merkle, Gertrude H. "Martin Le Franc's Commentary on Jean Gerson's Treatise on Joan of Arc. In *Fresh Verdicts on Joan of Arc*, edited by Bonnie Wheeler and Charles T. Wood, 177–88. New York: Garland, 1996.

Merlo, Grado Giovanni. "Coercition et orthodoxie: Modalités de la communication et d'imposition d'un message religieux hégémonique." In *Faire Croire: Modalités de la diffusion et de la réception des messages réligieux du XIIe au XVe siècles*, 101–18. Actes de la Table Ronde, Rome, 1979. Rome: Ecole Française de Rome, 1981.

Michaud-Quantin, Pierre. *Sommes de casuistique et manuels de confession au Moyen Age du XIIe au XVIe siècles*. Louvain, Belgium: Lauwelaerts, 1962.

Michelet, Jules. "Jeanne d'Arc." In *Histoire de France*, vol. 5. Paris: Lacroix, 1841. In *Oeuvres complètes*, vol. 6, edited by Paul Viallaneix. Paris: Flammarion, 1978. In *Jeanne d'Arc et autres textes*, edited by Paul Viallaneix. Paris: Gallimard, 1974. Translated by Albert Guérard as *Joan of Arc*. Ann Arbor: University of Michigan Press, 1957. Reprint, 1967.

Monnayeur, Jean-Baptiste. *Traité de Jean Gerson sur la Pucelle*. Paris: Champion, 1910.

Moore, R. I. *The Formation of a Persecuting Society*. Oxford: Basil Blackwell, 1977.

Murray, Margaret Alice. *The Witch-Cult in Western Europe*. Oxford: Clarendon Press, 1921. Reprint, 1962.

Neveux, François. *L'Evêque Pierre Cauchon*. Paris: Denoël, 1987.

Ong, Walter J. *Orality and Literacy: The Technologization of the Word.* London: Metheun, 1982. Reprint, London: Routledge, 1995.

Paré, Gérard Marie, Adrien Marie Brunet, Pierre Tremblay, and Gabriel Robert. *La Renaissance du XIIe siècle: Les Ecoles et l'enseignement.* Paris: Vrin, 1933; Ottowa: Publications de l'Institut d'Etudes Médiévales d'Ottowa, 1933.

Patlagean, Evelyne. "L'Histoire de la femme déguisée en moine et l'évolution de la sainteté féminine à Byzance." *Studi Medievali,* 3rd series, 17 (1976): 597–623.

Pernoud, Régine. *Jeanne devant les Cauchons.* Paris: Editions du Seuil, 1970.

Pernoud, Régine, and Marie-Véronique Clin. *Jeanne d'Arc.* Paris: Fayard, 1986.

Perroy, Edouard. *La Guerre de cent ans.* Paris: Gallimard, 1945. Translated by W. B. Wells as *The Hundred Years War.* London: Eyre and Spottiswoode, 1951. Reprint, New York: Capricorn, 1965.

Peters, Edward. *Inquisition.* New York: Free Press, 1988. Reprint, Berkeley: University of California Press, 1989.

———. *Torture.* New York: Basil Blackwell, 1985. Revised, 1996.

Peters, Edward, ed. *Heresy and Authority in Medieval Europe: Documents in Translation.* Philadelphia: University of Pennsylvania Press, 1980.

Petroff, Elizabeth Alvida. *Body and Soul: Essays on Medieval Women and Mysticism.* Oxford: Oxford University Press, 1994.

Peyronnet, Georges. "Gerson, Charles VII, et Jeanne d'Arc." *Revue d'Histoire Ecclésiastique* 84, no. 2 (March–June 1989): 334–70.

Piltz, Anders. *Medeltidens lärda vörla.* Stockholm: Bokförlaget, 1978. Translated by David Jones as *The World of Medieval Learning.* Oxford: Basil Blackwell, 1981.

Poulet, Charles. "Jeanne d'Arc à Chinon: Les Causes naturelles et surnaturelles de l'acceptation royale." *Historisch Tijdschrift* 1 (1922): 13–22.

La Preuve: Recueils de la Société Jean Bodin pour l'histoire comparative des Institutions. Vol. 2: *Moyen Age et temps modernes.* Brussels: Editions de la Librarie Encyclopédique, 1965.

Quicherat, Jules-Etienne-Joseph. *Aperçus nouveaux sur l'histoire de Jeanne d'Arc.* Paris: Jules Renouard, 1850. Translated by H. G. Francq as *New Aspects of the Case History of Jeanne d'Arc.* Brandon, Manitoba: Brandon University Press, 1971.

Rapp, Francis. "Jeanne d'Arc, témoin de la vie religieuse en France au XVe siècle." In *Jeanne d'Arc: Une Epoque, un rayonnement,* 169–79. Colloque d'Histoire Médiévale, Orléans, 1979. Paris: Editions du Centre National de la Recherche Scientifique, 1982.

Rashdall, Hastings. *The Universities of Europe in the Middle Ages.* Edited by F. M. Powicke and A. B. Emden. Vol. 1: *Salerno-Bologna-Paris.* Oxford: Oxford University Press, 1895; reprint, 1936.

Reinach, Salomon. "Observations sur le texte du procès de condamnation de Jeanne d'Arc." *Revue historique* 148 (March/April 1925): 200–223.

Robertson, D. W. Jr. "A Note on the Classical Origins of 'Circumstances' in the Medieval Confessional." *Studies in Philology* 43 (1946): 6–14.

Rocolle, Pierre. "Images de la captivité." In *Jeanne d'Arc: Une Epoque, un rayonnement,* 243–44. Colloque d'Histoire Médiévale, Orléans, 1979. Paris: Editions du Centre National de la Recherche Scientifique, 1982.

————. *Un Prisonniere de guerre nommé Jeanne d'Arc.* Paris: S. O. S., 1982.

Rusconi, Roberto. "De la prédication à la confession: Transmission et contrôle de modèles de comportement au XIII⁰ siècle." In *Faire Croire: Modalités de la diffusion et de la réception des messages réligieux du XII⁰ au XV⁰ siècles,* 67–85. Actes de la Table Ronde, Rome, 1979. Rome: Ecole Française de Rome, 1981.

Russell, Jeffrey Burton. *Dissent and Order in the Middle Ages: The Search for Legitimate Authority.* New York: Twayne Publishers, 1993.

————. *Witchcraft in the Middle Ages.* Ithaca, N.Y.: Cornell University Press, 1972.

Sackville-West, Vita. *Saint Joan of Arc.* New York: Literary Guild, 1936.

Scarry, Elaine. *The Body in Pain.* Oxford: Oxford University Press, 1985.

Schibanoff, Susan. "True Lies: Transvestism and Idolatry in the Trial of Joan of Arc." In *Fresh Verdicts on Joan of Arc,* edited by Bonnie Wheeler and Charles T. Wood, 31–60. New York: Garland, 1996.

Schmitt, Jean-Claude. "Religion populaire et culture folklorique." *Annales* 5 (September/October 1976): 941–53.

Schneiderman, Stuart. *An Angel Passes: How the Sexes Became Undivided.* New York: New York University Press, 1988.

Seward, Desmond. *The Hundred Years' War: The English in France 1337–1453.* New York: Atheneum, 1978.

Solterer, Helen. *The Master and Minerva: Disputing Women in French Medieval Culture.* Berkeley: University of California Press, 1995.

Stock, Brian. *The Implications of Literacy: Written Language and Models of Interpretation in the Eleventh and Twelfth Centuries.* Princeton: Princeton University Press, 1983.

Swanson, R. N. *Religion and Devotion in Europe, c. 1215–1515.* Cambridge: Cambridge University Press, 1995.

Tanon, Célestin Louis. *Histoire de tribunaux de l'inquisition en France.* Paris: Larose, 1893.

Tanz, Sabine. *Jeanne d'Arc: Spätmittelalterliche Mentalität im Spiegel eines Weltbildes.* Weimar: Verlag Hermann Böhlaus Nachfolger, 1991.

Tardif, Adolphe. *La Procédure civile et criminelle au XIII–XVᵉ siècles.* Paris: Picard, 1885.

Tentler, Thomas N. *Sin and Confession on the Eve of the Reformation.* Princeton: Princeton University Press, 1977.

Thomas, Antoine. "Le 'Signe Royal' et le secret de Jeanne d'Arc." *Revue historique* 103 (1910): 278–82.

Trinkhaus, Charles, with Heiko A. Oberman, eds. *The Pursuit of Holiness in Late Medieval and Renaissance Religion.* Leiden, Netherlands: E. J. Brill, 1979.

Les Universités européenes du XIVᵉ au XVIIIᵉ siècle: Aspects et problèmes. Actes du colloque international à l'occasion du VI centenaire de l'Université Jagellonne de Cracovie, 6–8 May 1964. Geneva: Slatkine, 1967.

Vauchez, André. "L'Aveu entre le langage et l'histoire: Tentatives de bilan." In *L'Aveu: Antiquité et Moyen Age,* 409–17. Actes de la Table Ronde organisée par l'Ecole Française de Rome avec le concours du Centre National de la Recherche Scientifique et l'Université de Trieste, Rome, 28–30 March 1984. Rome: Ecole Française de Rome, 1986.

———. "Jeanne d'Arc et le prophétisme féminin des XIVᵉ et XVᵉ siècles." In *Jeanne d'Arc: Une Epoque, un rayonnement,* 159–68. Colloque d'Histoire Médiévale, Orléans, 1979. Paris: Editions du Centre National de la Recherche Scientifique, 1982. Translated by Margery J. Schneider as "Joan of Arc and Female Prophecy in the Fourteenth and Fifteenth Centuries." In *The Laity in the Middle Ages,* edited by Daniel E. Bornstein, 255–64. Notre Dame, Ind.: University of Notre Dame Press, 1993.

———. *The Laity in the Middle Ages: Religious Beliefs and Devotional Practices.* Edited by Daniel E. Bornstein. Translated by Margery J. Schneider. Notre Dame, Ind.: University of Notre Dame Press, 1993.

———. *La Sainteté en occident aux derniers siècles du Moyen Age d'après les procès de canonisation et les documents hagiographiques.* Rome: Ecole Française de Rome, 1981.

Verger, Jacques. "Les Universités françaises au XVᵉ siècle: Crise et tentatives de réforme." *Cahiers d'histoire* 21 (1976): 43–66.

———. "The University of Paris at the End of the Hundred Years War." In *Universities in Politics: Case Studies from the Late Middle Ages and the Early Modern Period,* edited by John W. Baldwin and Richard Goldthwaithe, 47–78. Baltimore, Md.: Johns Hopkins University Press, 1972.

Vincent-Cassy, Mireille. "Comment obtenir un aveu? Etude des confessions des auteurs d'un meurtre commis à Paris en 1332." In *L'Aveu: Antiquité et Moyen Age*, 381–400. Actes de la Table Ronde organisée par l'Ecole Française de Rome avec le concours du Centre National de la Recherche Scientifique et l'Université de Trieste, Rome, 28–30 March 1984. Rome: Ecole Française de Rome, 1986.

Viola, Coloman. "Manières personnelles et impersonnelles d'aborder un problème: Saint Augustin et le XIIe siècle. Contribution à l'histoire de la *quaestio*." In *Les Genres littéraires dans les sources théologiques et philosophiques médiévales: Définition, critique, et exploitation*, 11–30. Actes du Colloque international de Louvain-la-Neuve, 25–27 May 1981. Louvain-la-Neuve, Belgium: Publications de l'Institut d'Etudes Médiévales de l'Université Catholique de Louvain, 1984.

Wallon, Henri. *Jeanne d'Arc*. 2 vols. Paris: Firmin-Didot, 1860. Reprint, 1876.

Warner, Marina. *Joan of Arc: The Image of Female Heroism*. London: Weidenfeld and Nicolson, 1981.

Watkins, Oscar D. *A History of Penance, Being a Study of the Authorities*. 2 vols. London: Longmans, Green, 1920.

Wayman, Dorothy G. "The Chancellor and Jeanne d'Arc, February–July, A.D. 1429." *Franciscan Studies* 17, nos. 2–3 (June–September 1957): 273–305.

Weinstein, Donald, and Rudolph M. Bell. *Saints and Society: The Two Worlds of Western Christendom, 1000–1700*. Chicago: University of Chicago Press, 1982.

Weiskopf, Steven. "Readers of the Lost Arc: Secrecy, Specularity, and Speculation in the Trial of Joan of Arc." In *Fresh Verdicts on Joan of Arc*, edited by Bonnie Wheeler and Charles T. Wood, 113–32. New York: Garland, 1996.

Wheeler, Bonnie, and Charles T. Wood, eds. *Fresh Verdicts on Joan of Arc*. New York: Garland, 1996.

White, Hayden. *The Content of the Form: Narrative Discourse and Historical Representation*. Baltimore, Md.: Johns Hopkins University Press, 1987.

Wippel, John F. "The Quodlibetal Question As a Distinctive Literary Genre." In *Les Genres littéraires dans les sources théologiques et philosophiques médiévales: Définition, critique, et exploitation*, 67–84. Actes du Colloque international de Louvain-la-Neuve, 25–27 May 1981. Louvain-la-Neuve, Belgium: Publications de l'Institut d'Etudes Médiévales de l'Université Catholique de Louvain, 1984.

Wirth, John. "Théorie et practique de l'image sainte à la veille de la réforme." *Bibliothèque d'humanisme et Renaissance* 48 (1986): 319–58.

Wood, Charles T. *Joan of Arc and Richard III: Sex, Saints, and Government in the Middle Ages.* New York: Oxford University Press, 1988.

————. "Joan of Arc's Mission and the Lost Record of Her Interrogations at Poitiers." In *Fresh Verdicts on Joan of Arc,* edited by Bonnie Wheeler and Charles T. Wood, 19–29. New York: Garland, 1996.

Index

Karen Sullivan is associate professor of literature at Bard College, where she teaches medieval continental literature in translation. She has published numerous articles on Joan of Arc and Christine de Pizan and is currently writing a book on heresy and literature in the Middle Ages.